'Sitwell writes with wit . . . Woolton's tasks covered everything from the logistics of moving fresh food around the country so that discontent could be kept to a minimum and doing dodgy deals in the back streets of Alexandria to access fresh supply routes, to advising housewives on how to make the best of the meagre rations . . . It is story that deserves to be more widely known.'

Scotland on Sunday

'*Eggs or Anarchy* is more than politics or nutrition, it is a human story . . . excellent.'

Waitrose Weekend

'A riveting read full of delicious historical details about how one unassuming man battled against all odds to keep bellies full and morale high despite the dreaded food rationing. Excuse the pun, but I could have eaten this book up with a spoon.'

Red Magazine

EGGS OR ANARCHY

THE REMARKABLE STORY OF THE MAN
TASKED WITH THE IMPOSSIBLE:
TO FEED A NATION AT WAR

WILLIAM SITWELL

**SIMON &
SCHUSTER**

London · New York · Sydney · Toronto · New Delhi

A CBS COMPANY

First published in Great Britain by Simon & Schuster UK Ltd, 2016
This paperback edition published by Simon & Schuster UK Ltd, 2017
A CBS COMPANY

1 3 5 7 9 10 8 6 4 2

Simon & Schuster UK Ltd
1st Floor
222 Gray's Inn Road
London WC1X 8HB

www.simonandschuster.co.uk

Simon & Schuster Australia, Sydney
Simon & Schuster India, New Delhi

The author and publishers have made all reasonable efforts
to contact copyright-holders for permission, and apologise
for any omissions or errors in the form of credits given.
Corrections may be made to future printings.

A CIP catalogue record for this book
is available from the British Library

Paperback ISBN: 978-1-4711-5107-1
Ebook ISBN: 978-1-4711-5108-8

Typeset in the UK by M Rules
Printed and bound by CPI Group (UK) Ltd, Croydon, CR0 4YY

Simon & Schuster UK Ltd are committed to sourcing paper
that is made from wood grown in sustainable forests and support the Forest
Stewardship Council, the leading international forest certification organisation.
Our books displaying the FSC logo are printed on FSC certified paper

For Alice and Albert

CONTENTS

AUTHOR'S NOTE

The quotes from Lord Woolton – and other main protagonists such as his wife Maud Woolton or Winston Churchill – are mainly based on Woolton's own writings, from his memoirs, diaries, a long tribute he wrote to his late wife, from his letters and other personal writings and also the diaries of his wife Maud. While his memoirs are more tempered, his private writings are quite extraordinary in both style, tone, temper and sound. So most quotes, dialogue and speech come from those writings – often using multiple sources for individual scenes – which would make the constant referencing of them tiresome. If I have ever paraphrased, elongated or massaged a quote, it is done faithfully and with respect for both the original source material and the reader.

1

A NEW MAN AT THE MINISTRY

Late afternoon, Thursday 3 April 1940. Seven months into the Second World War and, in an office in London's Tothill Street in Westminster, a grey-haired man in his late fifties, dressed in a three-piece pin-striped suit, with a watch chain, was placing the few remaining items left on his desk – a small framed picture and an ink pot – into a box. In an ashtray a pipe smouldered.

Fred Marquis, latterly ennobled as Lord Woolton, was leaving his post, an advisory position with the less-than-exciting title of Director General of Equipment and Stores. His new role had a simpler name and was a touch more glamorous: in a matter of hours he would be Minister of Food.

The previous day, Woolton had received a telephone call from the Prime Minister's office, asking if he would visit Neville Chamberlain at seven o'clock that evening.

'I understand that your department is running so smoothly that you are now unnecessary,' were Chamberlain's opening words when they met.

Woolton, in his memoirs, wrote that it was 'said without a smile, in his rather cold manner, and I realized that for some reason or other he proposed to remove me'.

Woolton assumed that he would then be released to return to his actual day job, as head of the Manchester-based (and country's biggest) department store chain, Lewis's.

'Am I now free to go and look after my own business affairs?' asked Woolton.

Chamberlain replied that this was not his intention, instead he was making some changes in his Cabinet and he wanted Woolton to join the government as Minister of Food.

The task would see Woolton heading a ministry whose job was, in simple terms, to feed Britain and her colonies during the straitened times of the Second World War.

That meant 41 million men, women and children in Britain and Northern Ireland, with an oversight of the 532 million people of the British Empire. He would have to manage the purchase and importation of food, ensure its fair distribution across the country, tackle the very low productivity of home-grown sustenance, and, with the system of rationing that had begun on 8 January of that year, ensure that abuses of the system were kept to a minimum – and a black market thwarted.

Woolton left Downing Street, discussed the proposal with his wife Maud and then accepted the job the following day. At which point he immediately began to feel apprehensive.

'I was embarking on a new life,' he later reflected, 'at the age of fifty-eight, with many fears about my own capacity to succeed in these new and unaccustomed fields of parliamentary responsibility, and with a profound sense of the dire consequences to the country if I failed.'

As he cleared his office he considered the challenges of the coming days. His new offices were just north of Oxford Street, physically some two miles away from the political machine of government in Whitehall.

He would get his feet under the desk and spend the days and nights reading to get on top of the subject. There was a large bureaucracy that supported the ministry and he wondered how immovable a beast it would be.

He pondered on the day he would be presented to the press as the new minister and vowed to be ready for the difficult questions that would be thrown his way.

Those first few days of reading and research would be invaluable; he was a stickler for detail and accuracy. He was also a man of firm mind and steely determination, and remained resolute that no decision, no public comment should ever be made without a very clear understanding of the facts.

There was a knock at the door and the secretary – who had served him well since he had taken up his post at the Ministry of Supply just days after war had been declared – announced a visitor.

'Sir Henry French is here for you, Lord Woolton,' the secretary said.

Woolton looked startled. He had heard about this man; a career civil servant, Sir Henry French was the Ministry of Food's Permanent Secretary, classically implacable and solemn. Sir Henry had joined the Civil Service in 1901 at the age of eighteen as a second-division clerk to the Board of Agriculture; moving slowly but steadily up the ranks, he had built a reputation as a sound, if inflexible, administrator until joining the Ministry of Food at the start of the war. Fifty-six when war broke out, Sir Henry had spent thirty-eight of those years in the same department. He was, according to the *Oxford Dictionary of National Biography*, 'unapproachable and vain. He made up his mind about people and rarely changed it.' He was known to wear the responsibilities of his job in the lines on his face, and there was no known evidence that he had a sense of humour.

Woolton wondered how they would get on. He was a man who liked to get things done, who would often circumvent the traditional channels to implement decisions. Since starting work for the government some six months previously, his battles with the Civil Service had already landed him in hot water. He was keen to start this new job on the front foot. He would be ready for Sir Henry French.

He would settle into his new office, take a puff on his pipe, having spent time studying the machinations of his new ministry. Then he would call upon his Permanent Secretary.

But, it seemed, Sir Henry was already a step ahead of him and had come to stalk Woolton before he had even left his old job.

Sir Henry entered the room, the two men shook hands and, before any platitudes were offered, the civil servant informed Woolton that he had come simply to inform him that the following day he was to address a meeting at the Queen's Hall.

'I was horrified,' Woolton reflected.

This grand building, on Langham Place, was, before the war, a concert hall, but it now served as an ideal place for important political speeches, where the press and public could attend in large numbers (the building would later be destroyed by an incendiary bomb in the blitz of May 1941).

The speech, explained Sir Henry, would bring the press up to date with the Ministry of Food's plans, schemes and tactics.

'But I can't make a speech about something about which I know nothing,' Woolton exclaimed to Sir Henry. The Permanent Secretary looked surprised at this answer and Woolton quickly understood that this was exactly what one did in the upper echelons of politics.

'There was no escape,' he mused in his diary at the prospect of the following day's event, 'The meeting was widely advertised and a wide range of important people had been invited – from press to the Prime Minister's wife, Mrs Chamberlain.'

The occasion had originally been arranged for his predecessor, William Morrison.

'This meeting will be an excellent opportunity for you to make your mark with the public,' said Sir Henry, who then handed him a few sheets of paper, adding 'And here, Minister, is your speech.'

'My trouble was that I had not formulated any policy,' wrote Woolton, 'but Sir Henry told me that there was no difficulty about that, because he had the whole statement most clearly laid out for me.'

It was, explained Sir Henry, officials who decided the

policy and Woolton's job 'to expound the policy, to explain it to the public.' Woolton did not like this. 'That was not my conception of the function of a minister. There was a further difficulty in that I am incapable of making a speech that I have not prepared myself.'

It was now the early evening and, reflected Woolton, 'there was no escape from this meeting. The Press indicated that they were anxious to hear my policy.'

There was nothing he could do. So he cancelled his evening plans, left his old ministry and resolved to work at home until the small hours.

'I sat up all that night studying the papers and getting myself acquainted with the current position of food supplies,' he recalled. 'I felt like a barrister briefed to appear in Court. But what a Court!'

The following day, after just a few hours sleep, he found himself in the Queen's Hall, on a platform alongside Sir Henry French and another ministry official, looking out at a full auditorium and a pack of pressmen flashing their cameras. Questions were shouted, he was asked to pose this way, then that, he felt almost blinded by the ceaseless flashing lights. Then, as the cacophony turned to a murmur and the room began to hush, he heard the whirr of the BBC news cameras, he saw the recording equipment of the radio teams.

As an official introduced the Ministry of Food's new boss to the hall, Woolton considered his resolve that previous night. He would look out at the audience, but in his mind would see far beyond. 'My audience is not the aggregate of the public who are listening but the detail of the individual in front of the domestic receiving set,' he thought to himself, as he recalled in his memoirs. 'In the front of my mind I keep a picture of a man in his cottage, sitting without a collar, with slippers on, at the end of the day's work, with children playing on the rug, with his wife washing up in an adjoining room with the door open.'

If his talk was successful, Woolton allowed himself to imagine an additional moment in that scene. As his voice would come over the radio, 'a visitor arrives in the middle of my broadcast. The man says: "Sit down and shut up; we are listening to Woolton."'

On a table in front of Woolton was the stack of papers that contained the new minister's speech, dutifully presented the previous day. To the right of that were some smaller sheets of writing paper, with notes scrawled across them.

Just before Woolton stood to command the microphone, he conspicuously moved the stack of papers to the left, effectively discarding them, and instead picked up his own notes. He nodded with a faint look of amusement in his eyes to Sir Henry, who could not conceal a look of intense alarm. And then Lord Woolton rose to his feet and uttered the first words of his new career.

2

INTRODUCING FRED

Frederick James Marquis was a particularly treasured child to his parents Thomas and Margaret. He was born on 23 August 1883. Fifteen months earlier, his parents' first born, Ernest, had lived for only eleven days.

His mother Margaret thus cherished this baby, who remained the couple's only child. As she cradled Fred gently as a new-born, so she held him tightly while he grew. She dreaded the day she would have to relinquish him to the care of teachers as school. Then would come the tortuous prospect of his teenage years, giving way to his early twenties, when he might spend nights and even weeks away if he was to satisfy her almost impossible dream that he could attain a university education.

And so as Fred grew up and did escape the nest, Margaret

formed a metaphorical leash, as secure and strong as the force she used to hold him as a baby, except it now came in the form of a constant cavalcade of letters.

Her missives were as frequent as today a worried mother might send an email. The letters came daily – sometimes there were two a day. More often than not, her main subject was laundry. She would sit at home fussing about exactly which clothes he had, which socks he might have on his feet, which shirt on his back. She felt she knew for sure every item of clothing he had in his drawers; each pair of shoes on the floor of his wardrobe, the suit hanging up, the pyjamas under his pillow.

Invariably, the direction of traffic with the letters was one way. It meant Margaret would have to imagine her son's response and so follow it up with another missive that scolded him.

'My Dear Boy,' she started one morning, when Fred was in his late teens, her fraying nerves rendering her just a little cross: 'I told you [sic] would require a clean shirt before the end of the week but you thought not.' Washing had become an obsession. 'I wonder if you have a shirt ready,' she continued, 'you said you are going out to dinner on Thursday.'

Knowing exactly the number of shirts he had, her calculations had raised the dreadful possibility that his evening shirt, if not dirty, was certainly not pressed.

There was further horror in her mind about those items resting under his pillow.

'Bring your pyjamas with you, really they must be awfully dirty, it is ages since you had clean ones,' she implores of him, wondering when his next trip home would be. Indeed, it was vital he bring back home a large bundle of laundry. 'If I were you,' she writes, 'I would put all of them in a bag and then once carrying would get all the dirty things home so that I can see to them and have them ready by the time they are wanted.' Now, anyone casually browsing through the life of Frederick Marquis, first Earl of Woolton, might have been surprised to learn that his mother Margaret didn't just fret about her son's laundry, she actually did it herself.

For when Woolton died at the age of eighty, in 1964, his home was a large pile in Sussex, he had been chairman of the Conservative Party, his son had been at the leading English public school Rugby, and one of his grandsons was down to attend Eton College with two others destined for Harrow School. He spoke with the clipped tones of the elite aristocracy and, as he recorded privately himself, Walberton House, where he lived near Arundel, had 'an adequate staff and a lift'.

Yet Woolton's origins were not just humble, they were emphatically working class. Whereas today the modern politician would barely let an interview pass without eulogising on their near poverty-stricken roots, Woolton never mentioned his very real unassuming origins, indeed he rather buried them.

The house where he was born was on a terrace, long since demolished, in Salford, Manchester. While his mother's letters betray a well-educated woman, his father, Thomas, was an itinerant saddler; his only two surviving letters are written in pencil and reveal just the bare bones of literacy. A note to young Fred (thanking him for a gift of some kind of personal item with his name embossed upon it), reads, free of grammar: 'I am so pleased with it I would not have wished for anything else it is fine and fancy the initials are great.' In another letter, penned on Fred's eighteenth birthday in 1901, his father says: 'it does not seem long since you were only quite a little kid but we must not look back in what you are now one of the rising lights and I hope you may have health to continue to rise with love from Pa.'

Thomas's family had been smallholders, farming in Lancashire. Their small acreage was on the Fylde plain, a flat piece of ground jutting out to the Irish Sea. His father, James, was the second son and had been given none of that modest patch of land to manage; so he found a job as landlord of a pub called the Black Bull Inn in nearby Kirkham. The town was familiar territory for the family, and among the stone tomb chests and monuments in the graveyard of St Michael's Church are several gravestones that bear the family name of Marquis.

James married his barmaid Harriet, apparently to save having to pay her a wage, and, so goes the family story, he threw his newly-wed's bonnet into the fire on returning from their wedding, saying: 'You won't need that for working.'

His son Thomas received the same scant generosity and found a role as a saddler to service the horses and coaches used by those staying at the inn. On his father's death in 1879, the inn fell into new hands and Thomas found himself unemployed. He moved to Liverpool, the big city that was then a magnet for the rural dispossessed; but presumably he was unsuccessful in his quest to find work as, by 1883, he had moved again to Salford, although he had at least found a wife in Margaret Ormerod.

In fact he never did seem to find a constant occupation,

his early skills as a saddler finding diminishing custom as the motorcar began to outsell the horse-driven coach. The impression is of a man more often morose and inactive. 'Our Da is not much better but no worse,' writes Margaret on several occasions. News of him in her letters includes his fixing a wardrobe, visiting the bank and putting down rat poison.

Margaret, meanwhile, clings to Fred. It appears she doesn't enjoy good health, is generally lonely and has few, if any, friends. Any family back in Kirkham are never mentioned with any warmth, and if anyone calls on her they come at the wrong time and then stay too long.

The thrust of her days revolves around Fred and whatever he is doing, and while she keeps a constant watch on him, desperate not to let him go, she also relies on him completely. Once he hits his late teens he looks after all of her finances and he buys her everything, from envelopes to fruit. All the while she continues to scold him; he doesn't write to her often enough – one suspects he couldn't have matched her record even if he'd had the spirit or time for it – he doesn't keep himself out of the rain, his friends are suspect and he works too hard. She dotes on him, desperate that, as she writes to him, he will 'do something proper', imagining fancifully that he could one day attain such status as to be knighted. 'Wouldn't it be great?' she writes, but adds: 'It won't happen if you sit up working until two in the morning. For you will wear all your strength out whilst you are only a young man.' In fact Woolton would spend much of his life working until two in the morning. But at the time his mother was fussing about this particular aspect of his life he was studying at Manchester's College of Technology.

His education had begun in 1897 at Ardwick Higher Grade School. He was there until fourteen when, having won a County Council Exhibition, he went to Manchester Grammar School.

Already he had attained more than any of his family forebears. Then came a moment when he achieved something his grandfather, pouring a jug of ale at the Black Bull Inn, would have scoffed at as fantasy. Fred was offered a place at Cambridge.

But he turned it down. Many years later he claimed the reason for this was that his father had told him, on the day he received the telegram with the news from Cambridge, that doctors had recently given him just six months to live. Fred's response was to tear up the telegram and pledge to stay at or near home to help look after his father.

As it transpired, the doctors were a little off the mark. Thomas Marquis lived for a further forty-eight years. Perhaps it was an act of extraordinary selfishness, or maybe it was fear; knowing his wife's possessive obsession with their son, perhaps Thomas dreaded the consequences if Fred moved away to Cambridge.

But there was another reason. Much as Fred would have loved to have gone up to Cambridge, to study and live with the country's best-educated sophisticates, he would not have been able to afford the living costs. He would have struggled to pay for accommodation, let alone the high living; the eating, the drinking, the vacations in Europe with new-found friends. His wife Maud would later write in her diary that he wanted to go to Cambridge 'very badly, but he couldn't afford it'.

Frederick Marquis may have been destined to progress

through the class system, but a move to Cambridge aged twenty was a leap far too early.

So he stayed in Manchester, a city that he never ceased to romanticise about. He said of it later that it was 'not so much a city as a state of mind ... Manchester's straight talk, her ferocious contempt for appearances, her unconcealed uninhibited friendliness for people she liked, her gentle cherishing of certain cultural values.' It was a place where the local sport was, he said, 'bubble pricking', a sport that he was to indulge in, although mostly privately in the pages of his diary, many years later when he joined the Second World War government.

The city also had an undercurrent of socialism which Fred actively engaged in, joining the Fabian Society, an organisation that worked to promote such things as equality in life, power, wealth and opportunity. It was an activity that those very government colleagues he would later disparage would cite as evidence that Woolton was a 'pinko'; a not-quite-red but communist sympathiser in the midst of establishment Conservatives. Woolton's early life did indeed see him on the left of the political spectrum; but as he progressed through life he would come to view capitalism as the key solution to poverty. Socialism for him would become a dirty word, an ideology that would not achieve anything. And this man, who at one time worshipped the thinking of Scottish socialist Keir Hardie, would eventually become a passionate Conservative and finally chairman of the establishment Tory party (in 1946, although he would not actually become a paid-up member of the Conservatives until Churchill's party was defeated in the General Election of 1945). Woolton would make a journey from intellectual socialist, to practical businessman to right-of-centre politician.

While the Manchester of the early 1900s certainly had prosperity – it was a town that had grown rich on the cotton trade, had access to the coalfields of the north and had been the beating heart of the Industrial Revolution – it also had its bleak side.

Just half of the homes in the late Victorian era, whose male inhabitants were the cogs of the great revolution from agrarian to machine economy, had running water. Up to thirty families would share the same outdoor privy, rubbish was collected infrequently, and many houses became brick warrens whose dank passages led to tiny rooms devoid of natural light or ventilation.

Fred was more than aware of this standard of living as his parents' home was not exactly on the smart side of town. And he stayed here – to study a mix of chemistry and psychology, followed by an MA in economics – until 1906. The subjects came easily to him.

'I had a natural aptitude for the sciences,' he wrote later in life. He also expressed considerable pride that one teacher was a Professor Samuel Alexander. He was, wrote Woolton, 'One of the greatest of the living philosophers of the time.' Three times a week he would lecture to a select group of just three students. To be chosen for this group was no mean achievement. Woolton delighted in recording the professor's view that 'there was only one person in ten thousand who had the mental capacity to understand what he was talking about.' Their tutorials would start at 4.15 p.m. in Professor Alexander's rooms; the philosopher would usher in his students, pour himself a cup of tea, feed his dog and then talk until eight o'clock. 'He poured out to us his wisdom that was so profound and knowledgeable, that was so exciting, and often disturbing, as to leave us in a state of wonderment as to what we were going to do with it all,' wrote Woolton. But it was this teaching that convinced 20-something Fred that he should become a sociologist; that he should analyse how human society organises itself.

As part of his postgraduate studies, in 1908, he moved for a time to Liverpool, finding lodgings with fellow graduates at 129 Park Street. This was a slum district, near the dock road, in the south of the city, where poverty was even more acute than in his native Manchester. The activities of these graduates were part of what was known as the 'settlement movement', a late nineteenth-century idea which countenanced that poverty could be alleviated by the creation of communities where rich and poor would live close together and share their knowledge and skills. A forerunner of this was Toynbee Hall in the East End of London. Created by a Church of England curate Samuel Barnett, the vision was that future leaders would live and work in such areas and – having been face-to-face with poverty – would later, with their understanding of the real issues involved, be able to enact radical change. Clement Attlee, the Labour Prime Minister between 1945 and 1951, was one such individual who, in 1910, spent a year at Toynbee Hall.

Woolton once reflected on this period of his own life, writing that he was living there, 'in the same spirit as the medical students of the time who were inquiring into the causes of TB'. This was a scientific investigation into the causes and problems of poverty, 'on our very doorstep', he wrote. Yet in spite of the serious subject matter, he was later keen to make it clear that it was not a life of drudgery. He spent a great deal of time, he wrote, 'frankly enjoying myself' and with 'no clear idea of how I proposed to earn a living'.

Fred recalled neighbours whose houses were 'generally vermin-ridden', and with 'human inhabitants [who] were mostly the poverty-ridden victims of sweated labour and casual employment'. These were streets of brick-built houses from the early 1820s, terrace upon terrace of densely packed buildings, the exteriors black from soot, the insides damp and dirty. The streets were filled with raggedy children. On warmer days women sat outside stitching or selling clothes, old shoes or boots, while the men sat on the steps of pubs dressed in thick jackets, worn trousers and rounded felt hats.

Fred and his student pals would not have been the only visitors to this part of Liverpool. The slums drew all kinds of people wishing to study – or correct – its inhabitants. There were housing reformers and temperance advocates, the latter arguing that it was alcohol that created so much of the poverty. Child protectists came, as did photographers hoping to win competitions with their images of people living amid dirt and grime. It wasn't until the late 1950s that the slums were cleared. Almost half of the housing stock was deemed unfit for human habitation, and thousands of homes were then demolished. Families were moved away to towns like Skelmersdale, Kirkby or Widnes.

But with all this evidence laid out before him, right outside his door, student Fred was able to garner data during the day and debate the subject around the coal-fired stove at night.

Fred was made a warden of the settlement and Philip, later Lord, Rea, who became a Liberal politician and merchant banker, recalled meeting him then. 'He had at that time, as I think he always had, a slightly chilling aspect when one first met him, but as soon as he spoke – as soon as his eyes twinkled – one knew that he had a warm heart.'

The consequences of poverty never left Fred. Neither did he ever forget the shock of hearing one day in 1908 that a female neighbour had died, her body lying undiscovered for days. The woman had died of starvation. She had neither asked for help, nor had anyone ever come to her aid.

Those two years on Park Street shaped the mind of Fred Marquis. 'It was an experience that was to fashion much of my thought and actions for the rest of my life,' he recalled.

He had also been joined in what became a passion for social work by Maud Smith, the woman who would become his wife.

Maud was the daughter of a stern man called Thomas Smith. A mechanical engineer, specialising in the construction of boilers and locomotives, he had been married three times and had, Woolton once noted, older brothers the same age as Fred's own father. He was a passionate believer in education and was thus gratified that Maud and her sister would take advantage of it, but he was very wary of young men and had an almost violent dislike of the idea of his daughters becoming romantically attached. Maud never forgot a piece of advice her father once gave her on noting, in her late teens, that she was dressed up and going out to a party. 'Remember this,' he said, 'I would rather see my daughters lying in their coffins than married to any man.'

However independent she might have been, she could not totally cast off her father's views and it made her wary of members of the opposite sex. 'The truth was she was frightened of men,' Woolton later wrote, adding: 'She was always somewhat critical of them and greatly preferred the company of women.'

As students of the same university, their paths crossed occasionally but these were days when women students did not speak to male students in college grounds. It was, wrote Woolton, 'considered very forward, and of course we never used Christian names in speaking to one another either in college or outside'.

Yet one day, for some reason and at a time when Fred and Maud barely knew each other, Maud broke with convention. It was a day of examinations and groups of men and women were nervously anticipating a few hours of intense thinking and writing.

'We both entered the examination hall for the same examination at the same time,' Woolton recalled. 'To my intense surprise, as we entered the hall, Maud stepped out from a group of girls and wished me luck. It was all on the impulse of the moment – we had scarcely met before – and I don't know and I've never known which of us were more surprised.'

The pair got to know each other better eighteen months later in 1906, when, by chance, they found themselves joint secretaries of the University Sociological Society. Woolton recalled that Maud had 'a challenging determination to resist any effort of men to come within any approach to dominating her. At the first it made our relationship a little difficult.'

They had a shared interest in social conditions, political philosophy and current politics and worked together successfully in the society. But, wrote Woolton, 'it was made abundantly clear to me that our relationship was of a strictly unemotional variety.'

And thus their friendship continued for sometime on a purely platonic basis, even though Thomas Smith died, removing one obstacle to marriage. However, Fred was reluctant to move things forward at the time, because he had so little money, later admitting, 'I was frightened of the responsibility of marriage. Not only was I quite unable to see a future for myself which could financially sustain matrimony, but I had the gravest doubts about whether I had the qualities which could make for happiness in my wife.'

Maud meanwhile gave him no encouraging signals. One day a chemist Fred knew approached him, saying that he wanted to propose to Miss Smith. 'I'd like to be sure of your own intentions, Fred,' he said, 'so that I know, so to speak, that she has not already been promised to you.'

This was very noble, thought Fred, and knowing Maud well enough he decided to speak to her about it. 'He has many virtues,' he told her, 'and I advise you to go and see him.'

'But he's so dull,' replied Maud.

'The sky was getting clearer,' Woolton reflected. By this time he had also left university and was earning money as a senior mathematics master at Burnley College. He had also been appointed Warden of the David Lewis Hotel and Club Association in Liverpool – which provided cheap beds in the city's docklands and was promoted by the successful store,

Lewis's – and the University Settlement. He had a salary, a flat, an income of £400 a year, two maids and subsidised food, fire and light.

The pair had another conversation and, in his words, 'we decided we would both like to take the risk.'

Fred proposed properly and, he wrote, 'as soon as we became publicly engaged she changed in her attitude to me and all the defences were withdrawn.' And the tone of her letters to him changed dramatically. Any formality was gone and, like so many engaged couples, she expressed her anxiety at waiting for the wedding day to arrive. 'I do wish we were married,' she wrote in March 1912. She also sent him constant missives urging him to 'rest', joining his mother in telling the workaholic Fred to slow down occasionally – 'gracious you don't seem to know what it means . . . do mind what you are doing.' She was also relieved Thomas Smith hadn't lived to evaluate her beloved: 'I'm glad that you never met my father,' Maud once told Fred, 'I'm sure that if you had you would have been sent summarily on your way.' Her letters were always full of affection ending with the likes of 'Goodbye beloved . . . Here's a kiss . . . I shall miss you . . . I wish you were here . . . Always your sweetheart . . . Please don't overwork . . .'

Finally, on 10 October 1912, in a Unitarian ceremony in Liverpool, the couple were married. Fred's mother Margaret, who approved of Maud, could not resist revealing her fear at the prospect of her son making a final wrench from the nest. The day before their wedding Margaret wrote Maud an emotional letter in which she made no attempt to hide her feelings. 'We don't want you to take our boy away from us,' she pleaded desperately. 'You come to us and we shall be happy and contented seeing you two living for each other.'

Maud possibly did not have in mind that she would spend her married days living with Fred and his parents, but for the time being, that's what happened. In her letter Margaret said she was finding it hard to express herself: 'Excuse this letter for I can't write. If you could read inside me you would be able to understand.' Having finished the missive and signed it 'Mammie' – as she always would to her son – she returned to it later and wrote more on the blank back page, worried, perhaps, that Maud might have got the wrong idea about her.

'I feel sure we shall get on all right why shouldn't we. You are going to make Fred happy which is all I want and of course you to be happy in doing it.' And a last sentence suggests that Maud wasn't altogether comfortable with how her new mother-in-law clung to her son: 'Perhaps as you know me more you will find out all that I would be to you if only you will let me.'

Margaret then wrote a letter to Fred a few days later while the newly-weds were on honeymoon. 'Surely you will not look so tired and worried when you come back,' she clucked and then started panicking about his suitcases, which were, apparently, delayed. 'It is strange that your luggage is so long in getting to you, I hope you have got it by now.' She added that Fred's father had taken a gas stove away to be fixed, that a friend had brought her some rabbits to eat and she asked him if he'd pay the bill for a delivery of tea.

Meanwhile Fred devoted himself to his work and studies. There were the many hours he spent considering the links between ill health and physical incapacity. He learned the importance of providing pregnant women with rounded nutrition, and became almost obsessed with the importance of having good teeth. He grew to understand more than many the importance of nutrition in enabling a fulfilling life.

Thirty years later Lord Woolton found himself running the ration and feeding Britain during a world war. 'It was this experience, in a poverty-ridden district of Liverpool, that gave me the stimulus to use the powers of a war-time Minister of Food,' he wrote.

In preparing for his role as the nation's feeder, Lord Woolton had started far earlier than anyone could have possibly imagined.

3

STEPPING STONES TO GOVERNMENT

Woolton's route to the Ministry of Food took in spells of teaching, lecturing, social work, school management and journalism until, in the 1920s, he found his metier in the retail business.

To his huge frustration, but doubtless his mother's great relief, he had been rejected from military service during the First World War. Exactly why is a slight mystery, but, having been medically examined, he was deemed C3. There is no record of him having 'badly deformed toes or flat feet' (common ailments among those listed as C3s). But in later years, during the subsequent war, he occasionally admits in his diaries to feeling ill and having colitis, a long term inflammatory bowel disease. Indeed in August 1942 he gave an interview with the author J. B. Priestley. Priestley asked him why he had been rejected seven times as an army recruit. 'His reply,' wrote Priestley with delicate diplomacy, 'is indicated by my punctuation:'

(Priestley, incidentally, was at first a little suspicious of Woolton and wrote: 'When I first met him I thought him too urbane to be genuine, that smooth clean shaven face under the grey hair, that perfect careful dress, that precise and cautious speech, that refusal to be hurried about anything, it was all too suave for words.' Yet he ended up being a great admirer.)

So it's likely that throughout his life Woolton suffered from intermittent abdominal pain. Typically, though, he used this to his advantage, taking a constant principled stance against rich, and thus in his view unnecessary, food. In June 1942, for example, he recorded a meal he had with some people who represented the cereals business. 'They gave me lobster for lunch,' he wrote in his diary. 'My constitution wasn't built for dealing with high living, and I was sick at night and have felt queer ever since.'

According to his cook, Mrs Pomford, Woolton had unfussy tastes. 'He is the easiest man in the world to please about his meals,' she told the *Daily Express* in April 1940.

But thus prevented by a delicate constitution from joining many of his friends who had gone to war, aged thirty-one in 1914, he became an economist in the War Office. There he had a range of roles, including managing the provision of blankets for the French and Belgian armies, and providing soap for the Russians.

After the First World War, he dabbled in journalism. In this domain he didn't bring his fevered intellectual brain to the subject of employment for the low-skilled poor or the construction of affordable homes. No, the subject he alighted on was the boot trade, and he wrote articles on the subject for the *Times Trade Supplement*. Spotting a post-war gap in the market, he tried a career in the boot-making world – he had dipped a toe in this field in the War Office, having had some dealings with supplying Russian soldiers with footwear. Of course, Woolton's style of toe-dipping saw him becoming secretary to the Leather Control Board and then being appointed to the role of Civilian Boot Controller.

He had noticed how smart men always stopped to put on galoshes – those rubber over-shoes – before they stepped out in inclement weather, and pondered on there being an opportunity for him: 'I thought that there ought to be in America a market for men's high class shoes that would make it unnecessary for them to wear galoshes whenever they went out in the rain,' he recollected later. So, having first set up a federation to maintain and build on the reputation of Britain's bootmakers, liaising and making allies with the bootmakers' union, he made a business trip to the United States.

It was during that trip he renewed his acquaintance with another passenger, Sir Rex Cohen, managing director of the Lewis's department store. Sir Rex had come across Fred while the younger man was working as a warden of one of the store's social experiments: providing accommodation at the local docks. Sir Rex had offered Fred a job but he refused. Now on the boat, accompanied by their wives, the Cohens and Wooltons became good friends. So impressed was Sir Rex by this assured thirty-something entrepreneur, he decided to accompany Fred as he went on his boot mission around America.

Before leaving England, Fred had been challenged about his boot idea by a cynical colleague he had known from his time in the War Office. 'I am going into business,' he told the man, Harry Bostock. 'I swear to you that I will make a business so successful and profits so large that tears of envy will roll down your cheeks.'

Fred didn't manage to sell his newfangled, high quality boots to the Americans, but his travels with Sir Rex Cohen across the States led the boss of Lewis's to one firm conclusion. Cohen could see a remarkable determination in this young man and renewed his determination to employ him.

The two finally came to an agreement and Woolton joined the firm. 'To go into retail business in 1920 was more of an adventure than I knew,' he wrote. One of his personal challenges was to see if he could merge his business aspirations with his social conscience. Was it possible to make money *and* look after people? He dreamed of social harmony but also had an instinctive knack for business. As he wrote: 'Could the "dream" and the "business" become a work-a-day reality?'

He was joining a sixty-four-year-old family business and he was an outsider. As Rex Cohen himself put it: 'This is the first time that I have ever invited anybody who was not of my family, and not of my [Jewish] faith, to join me.'

The store had been founded in Liverpool in 1856 by David Lewis and had humble beginnings as a small shop selling men's and boys' clothing. It steadily grew in size and merchandising scope, branching into being a 'Universal Provider' and spreading along Ranelagh Street before acquiring a second premises on Bold Street. By the early 1880s it had become a successful department store with branches in Manchester, Birmingham and Sheffield. In 1886, after the founder's death, the store was bought out by Louis Cohen, a senior partner in the firm. It was his son Rex, who ran the business with his brother Harold, who had hired the young man he'd met on the boat to America.

Fred was to experience all aspects of the business – a rollercoaster ride of retail – and it wasn't long before, aged thirty-seven, he was made joint managing director of Lewis's at a time when it was growing to become the biggest retail operator in the UK. Fred, during his forties and fifties – between 1920 and 1939 – was pivotal in growing the business.

By the outbreak of the Second World War there would be Lewis's department stores in Liverpool, Manchester, Glasgow, Leeds, Stoke-on-Trent and Leicester. The company would later open in Oxford, Blackpool, Bristol, Newcastle as well as buying and running Selfridges in London.

His mother Margaret died in 1923, but not before seeing her son's burgeoning career. 'You know it was my one and sole ambition for you to be a parson, never thought of anything higher, did we?' she wrote to him in her old age. 'But fancy what a height you have got to. We often talk about it.'

By the mid 1930s, Frederick Marquis was a successful businessman, a man in a trade that had become respectable, a chap who dressed impeccably, owned a substantial home (Hillfoot House in Liverpool, along with a cook, Elizabeth Pomford and her husband Albert, the butler), as well as a flat in London – and membership of the exclusive gentlemen's club Brooks's on St James's Street – and a holiday home by

Lake Windermere (Fallbarrow, bought in 1931). He had a small family, a daughter Peggy, born in 1917, and a son Roger, born in 1922, and a social life that first dallied on the edge of and then became intrinsic to fashionable London society.

In recognition of his services to the British retail industry, he was knighted in July 1935. F. J. Marquis Esq. was written to from 10 Downing Street and told that the Prime Minister intended to submit his name to the King to confer a knighthood. The letter was stuck proudly into a private album at home, along with a picture of the new knight in top hat and tails on his way to Buckingham Palace for the investiture.

The newly ennobled Sir Frederick then filled the entire album with the hundreds of telegrams and letters he received from everyone, from friends in London to merchandising managers in Manchester. Although he wasn't political, he had already made his concerns about the rising power of Nazism plain by ending Lewis's trade with Germany after its invasion of Austria in 1938, urging other companies to do the same. But poor health, which had dogged him in private for some time, suddenly interrupted his working life. In the summer of 1938, Maud recorded in her diary that: 'He was in bed for most of August and it left him very depressed. He had got a streptococcal infection and in spite of not making a full recovery he had gone back to work.'

The following January Stanley Cohen, vice chairman of Lewis's, asked to come and meet the couple together. 'Fred has been ill,' he stated frankly to Maud in front of her husband, 'he doesn't seem to be getting better properly and he needs a long holiday. Take him away for three months.'

Both Maud and Cohen ignored Woolton's protestations that he couldn't possibly take that sort of time out and the business needed him. And so for three months in early 1939, the couple went to South Africa, accompanied by Peggy.

'The result was that Fred got renewed health, which was providential,' Maud wrote in her diary. She then added: 'As a matter of fact I want to state here now that during both our lives there is marked evidence that a higher power than us has seeded us in most of our actions. All fits in. If Fred hadn't had this holiday, he couldn't have carried on.' And without that return to health and the protection of that higher power Woolton would have been unable to accept a role that would eventually lead him to the Ministry of Food.

The moment they got back a letter arrived from the War Office. On 18 April 1939, Sir Harold Brown, director of munitions production at the War Office, wrote asking Woolton if he would take a position as 'a distinguished industrialist who has a full knowledge of the various branches of the clothing trade, to advise the Department in regard to our plans and problems'.

It was the spring of 1939 and, as the storm clouds of war gathered, the country was reluctantly preparing for the cataclysm to come. Woolton, for whom the army was not an option, believed he should serve his country in another way. He was given the mundane title of Technical Advisor on Textiles in the War Office. As the army quickly expanded in anticipation of war, which would be declared on 3 September of that year, Woolton's job was an ill-defined position between the War Office and the Ministry of Supply.

It transpired that those 'problems' referred to by the

War Office included a lack of communication between the departments, and a wall of bureaucracy which made the actual buying and supplying of clothes for the army almost impossible.

Woolton regretted accepting the job almost immediately. 'In all my life I had never found myself in such a position,' he wrote. 'I saw clearly that war was coming. I had undertaken responsibility. I found nowhere a sense of urgency and I foresaw war breaking out with the army completely unprepared.'

Maud also reflected on the chaos, writing, 'The army clothing was still on a peace time basis. It brought in conscription and it had no uniforms.' She also thought this step of her husband's, into the world of government, was not a good one. 'The whole idea seems the height of folly,' she wrote.

After his first day in the job Woolton reported back to Maud. 'Do you know there are only five firms in this country making uniforms? And no one else seems to want to make them,' he told her.

'For the first month,' wrote Maud, 'he had a very sticky time.'

There was, for example, the issue of trousers and trouser buttons (this being the pre-zip era for flies). Orders had been placed for trousers for soldiers, but because of the system in place, the department that placed the trouser orders was unable to place orders for buttons as these were not deemed actual clothing material. They had to be purchased by another department with a separate budget. But which department and which budget, no one was able to fathom. While the War Office held a budget for trousers, it didn't have one for buttons.

'I asked [the Contracts department of the War Office] what orders had been placed for trouser buttons – and the answer was none,' Woolton wrote. 'Trouser buttons were supplied by the contractors, not by the War Office. I enquired whether the contractors had placed orders for trouser buttons; no one knew. So I pointed out to them the essential nature of the trouser button . . . how the whole morale of any army in the long run might depend upon its trouser buttons.'

Woolton went to see one of Prime Minister Neville Chamberlain's top officials at 10 Downing Street, Sir Horace Wilson, to voice his frustrations about the shambolic system. Whether he voiced his concern that the British army might go to war with its flies undone or, worse, its trousers down is not recorded.

'You are up against the machine of the Civil Service,' Sir Horace told his flustered guest. 'I have myself often been up against it in my forty years of experience. It has beaten me on many occasions, just as it is now beating you.'

This was a red rag to a bull. Woolton was not accustomed to being beaten by faceless institutions or the implacable logic of Whitehall mandarins. He jumped up out of his chair furiously.

'You have landed me in an impossible job,' he bellowed. 'If all you can tell me is that I am being beaten by a machine, I'll go and break its neck!'

Sir Horace replied: 'Well, you'll have to make a success of this as your commercial reputation depends on it.' That remark, noted Maud in her diary, 'made F [Fred] see red.'

'By God,' he stormed, 'my commercial reputation doesn't depend on this. But I'll tell you one thing, your political reputation does, so you'd better see to it that you give me all the help you can.'

Woolton left Downing Street, slamming the famous door as he stepped out. 'I'm not sure whether [I did it] with shame or with gratification,' he later reflected, hinting at a note of embarrassment for having lost his temper in the smart confines of the Prime Minister's office. 'I'm afraid I used some language that was unsuitable for Number Ten Downing Street.'

Galvanised by his anger, Woolton started firing off memos and knocking heads together. He realised that if he approached the various problems as a businessman rather than a politician he might have more luck.

He put a call into Sir Warren Fisher, the head of the Civil Service machine, insisting on a meeting which was granted and during which he outlined the gravity of the situation. 'The army will not be clothed in time unless I am allowed to put aside the peace-time system of contracting and am given a completely free hand to run the clothing of the army as a business organisation,' he told him.

Fisher nodded sagely and indicated that the Treasury would concur. 'You have complete authority,' he said. 'I will give instructions in the Treasury in accordance with this interview.'

Woolton recorded, triumphantly, that 'the way was all clear'. His own civil servants were flabbergasted. 'You know, Sir, it isn't fair,' one told him. 'We have been labouring for months, and you come in, pick up a telephone, and get an interview that none of us could have got, and then get financial authority for which there is no parallel.'

Within four months Woolton had increased the number of firms making uniforms from five to 500. By the summer he had clothed the army and felt his job was done. He had battled against the Civil Service and won, and, as a non-military man, he had served his country at a crucial time. Soldiers were clothed and as they marched to war their trousers would stay up.

'Well, there you are,' he told Maud. 'I've done what they asked me, in fact a great deal more. Now I'll go back to my job.'

But before he had a chance do so much as gather a board meeting of Lewis's, he received a rather pleasant notice from Downing Street. In King George VI's birthday honours list of June 1939 Sir Frederick Marquis was elevated to the peerage 'for public services'. He received the news one May morning while shaving.

Maud was, as was her habit, opening his letters while he got washed and dressed at their London apartment, Whitehall Court. 'Maud was always almost childishly interested in receiving letters,' Woolton reflected years later, when he wrote a long tribute to her for the benefit of his family after she had died.

'Oh, here's a letter from the Prime Minister marked secret,' Maud said from the bedroom as she worked through his usual pile of letters. Woolton professed that he had no curiosity about it so told his wife to go ahead. The last time he had been honoured, he had managed to get to the letter first and had kept his knighthood a secret from her until the announcement was made.

'You can't leave me out this time,' she said. 'The PM wants

to send you to the Lords.' Maud came into the bathroom, found a bit of her husband's cheek that was free of soap, and kissed him. 'I'm glad your services are being recognised in this rather startling way,' she said.

Before agreeing to accept the peerage, Woolton decided to make a journey north from London to Rugby, where the couple's son Roger was studying at the Warwickshire public school. It had been founded in 1567 by a purveyor of spices to Queen Elizabeth I as a free grammar school for the boys of local towns Rugby and Brownsover.

The title being offered was hereditary, so if Fred was to be ennobled he wanted to make sure his son was aware of his future responsibilities. Roger was a shy boy with a stammer that would never leave him. Later in life he would wear his father's celebrity and success heavily. Where his father was self-assured and pragmatic, Roger always lacked confidence and was vulnerable. It was to his boarding school that Woolton made a special journey. While he was to be ennobled for his diligent good works, Roger would be simply saddled with the hereditary title. For a man with a distinctly working-class background, Woolton was very aware of what wearing the ermine meant. He was closing in on a very elite part of society, and Roger needed to be properly informed and have the seriousness of this honour made clear to him. Woolton was becoming increasingly aware of his legacy. There was already a financial one – having made a considerable amount of money at Lewis's – and in due course he would set up a web of trusts for his offspring and their descendants. Now a peerage was being added to the mix.

The conversation with Roger would be formal, not that

this was out of the ordinary. Woolton was not the type to kick a football around with his son. In later life he was known to dutifully pat his grandchildren on the head but it didn't occur to him that he should be anything but stern and forthright with his son. An only child who had long escaped his own semi-literate father, he did not do touchy-feely emotion.

Having fetched Roger from his boarding house, perhaps father and son took a walk and then sat down on a bench that overlooked the school's famous playing fields. According to Maud's diary, Woolton told his seventeen-year-old son the news, and 'pointed out that Roger would inherit'.

'If you don't want the title and the responsibilities that go with it then I will tell the Prime Minister that I do not wish to accept this honour,' Woolton said to his teenage son.

'Roger was very sensible about it,' wrote Maud who believed that 'he realised he was being seriously consulted, and decided that he was willing to shoulder the responsibilities when they arrived.'

Of course the idea that Roger would have suggested otherwise, and then that his father would have told the Prime Minister that his son's ambivalence to the honour meant that he would decline it, is ludicrous.

Roger was then given special permission by his school to attend a dinner in London thrown by Maud to celebrate her husband's elevation to the peerage. Doubtless, seated around the table with Woolton's various business colleagues and friends, the teenage Roger would have again had it impressed upon him what responsibilities lay in the years ahead.

As a result, another private family album was stuffed with newspaper cuttings and messages of congratulations. With

Maud, Fred, in his words, 'had fun choosing a title', finally picking the name of Woolton (the district of his childhood in Liverpool). Using his own name was ruled out at the start, having been informed that to be called Baron Marquis might confuse people that he'd been made a marquess; he wasn't quite ready to make that final leap to aristocracy (he'd need to wait another sixteen years before he would be made an earl). Maud had counselled against one idea that he become Lord Windermere, in honour of the beloved stretch of water where they had a holiday home. She was happy to be Fred's wife, but thought the joke that she was his permanent fan (in reference to Oscar Wilde's play *Lady Windermere's Fan*) would wear thin fairly quickly.

Woolton noted that Maud would enjoy her title of Lady Woolton. 'She was now more than one up on those snobs in Mossley Hill,' he wrote referring to the stuck-up ladies of that district of Liverpool where she had once worked.

Freshly ennobled and just five days after war was declared, on 8 September 1939 Woolton was asked to take on another government job – this time as Director General of Equipment and Stores, working in the newly formed Ministry of Supply. This added the job of equipment to that of clothing – with which he was now familiar – and there were some 16,000 different articles to manage. 'But,' noted Maud, 'having already got the clothing into ship-shape, the task wasn't so difficult.'

Fred and Maud, as Lord and Lady Woolton, now realised that a return to normal life was becoming ever more distant. Maud noted in her diary that the reason for his barony was more than a recognition of his retail work and any other public service. The government 'realising the country was coming to a crisis needed men like F. They knew he wouldn't go in to the House of Commons so this was the best way to use him.'

But these jobs managing supplies seemed almost petty for a man who had run the huge and logistically complicated business of Lewis's. It was therefore of no great surprise when, in April 1940, Neville Chamberlain, casting around to find someone who might be able to run a ministry whose job it was to nourish Britain in time of crisis, landed upon Woolton. The first incumbent, William Morrison, had not been an unqualified success.

Given that Lord Woolton by now had been responsible for clothing much of the nation, it wasn't impossible that he might make a reasonable fist of feeding it, reckoned Chamberlain, so he invited Woolton to Downing Street for a meeting. 'The Prime Minister obviously had not sent for me to give him advice,' he said. 'He told me that I had clearly demonstrated a capacity for organisation on a large scale in an emergency, that he wanted me to do it again on what he regarded as a more important front than clothing the army, now that these supplies were secure.'

Chamberlain asked him to be Minister of Food. Woolton's first reaction was to claim ignorance of the subject: 'I know nothing about food except as a consumer,' he protested. He also insisted that he would only accept the role if he could operate as a businessman would in charge of a critical department. 'I am anxious not to get mixed up in politics,' he told the PM.

Chamberlain attempted to reassure him on this point. But there was another concern. While Woolton could function as a businessman in government, he would have to cease his real business ventures. 'Do you have any idea of the amount of financial sacrifice that would be involved in my giving up my several and very lucrative business appointments?' he demanded to Chamberlain, a little taken aback. Woolton added that he'd also have to ask his wife what she thought. This rather irritated Chamberlain, who had expected an immediate answer: 'Why do you need to ask your wife?' he said.

Woolton left considering the financial downsides and assuming that Maud would not welcome it. They had, after all, become rather used to the trappings of considerable wealth by now. 'To accept government office meant a complete severance of all business connections and a very heavy loss of income,' he mused privately. His two previous jobs had not been of ministerial level. 'I'll have to give up all of my directorships,' he told Maud. 'There's a financial downside to that, you know.'

'What does it matter?' she replied. 'When you are asked to do something in war time, unless it's peculiarly distasteful or against one's principles, there is only one answer.'

Woolton returned to Downing Street the following day to accept the role. Chamberlain produced a smile more warmly than Woolton had ever thought possible from this dour and serious man. His previous and usual demeanour, according to Woolton, being always 'conducted in a formal and almost frigid manner'.

'They always told me you would make any sacrifice for your country,' the PM told him, 'and they were right.'

So Woolton became a member of the government, and

Chamberlain proposed to ask the King that he be further made a member of the Privy Council, an indication that Woolton would become one of the most senior players and advisors in government.

'He accepted on the Wednesday and it was made public on Thursday,' wrote Maud.

Woolton was taking on the biggest task of his life. Approaching the age of fifty-seven, he was no spring chicken in the vanguard of entrepreneurial youth. This grey-haired, patrician-looking gent who might, in normal circumstances, have been looking forward to a graceful retirement from the rigours of business, was going to be more active than he could ever have imagined. He would need every ounce of energy and acumen in the tough days and months that lay ahead. As he went home that evening, armed with Sir Henry's draft speech, he steeled himself for the task in front of him, not a little nervous at what might happen.

4

THE MINISTRY OF FOOD

Day One

The Ministry of Food was situated in a corner building that overlooked Portman Square. Rented by the government, Portman Court had been chosen to locate the ministry away from Whitehall. His office was an unexciting spacious room with a large estate desk covered with neat stacks of papers. A rust-coloured material covered various chairs and there was a large mahogany conference table.

Woolton would sit at his desk or wander about the room thinking, dressed smartly and formally in one of his three-piece suits. His favourite was charcoal-dark double-breasted and striped, and he was never more comfortable than when clad in its thick and heavy material. Out of the office he wore a trilby and at weekends, a warm day in the country perhaps, he might dress down in a lighter suit or wear tweed and knee-length plus-fours. As a man who had risen from a family where there was never any spare money, this formality was important to him. Although he was known, if out walking in his beloved Lake District, to swap his suit and tie for a hearty costume of longish red shorts, long socks and walking shoes.

In evenings at home with Maud he might remove his jacket as he and his wife sat by the fire and read poetry by the nineteenth-century American writer Henry Longfellow, or the works of the seventeenth-century Baptist preacher John Bunyan. Longfellow's anti-materialistic moral and cultural values appealed to the god-fearing Woolton; likewise the sermons of Bunyan appealed to his Unitarian beliefs, which Maud shared with considerable fervour.

Woolton had no time for lighter pursuits so it suited him to be a workaholic. Once he had finished relishing the contents of his red ministerial box, he could stir his heart with the reading of a religious tract or two. There is little evidence that he enjoyed music, he needed to be dragged to the theatre and his way of letting off steam was to pen his diary in which, so often, he described his acute judgements and analysis of others – and their many weaknesses.

After Woolton's debut at the Queen's Hall, having gone off script and – further against the will of Sir Henry French – given several additional interviews to the large number of pressmen assembled, he headed for the novelty of a ministerial car and went straight to his new offices. As he sat that day at his desk and straightened the pictures that had been moved from his Tothill Street office, he was about to light his pipe when Sir

Henry French knocked and entered. Woolton stood, proffering a hand, and knowing that his off-script speech would not have made Sir Henry a happy man. But he hoped the following day's newspaper coverage might exonerate him.

Sir Henry muttered a greeting without any hint of a smile for his new minister. 'Of course, I must tell you that we are very sorry to lose Mr Morrison,' he said abruptly of Woolton's predecessor.

'Yes I'm sure you must be,' replied Woolton. 'But not as sorry as I am to come.' Sir Henry looked vexed but settled into a chair and then, referring to a typed page on his lap, spoke.

'You will be able to rely on the department to do everything in its power to protect you, Minister,' Sir Henry told him. Woolton looked surprised, partly given that 'this remark to me,' he later wrote, 'was in the nature of an official statement. I did not remember anyone wanting to "protect" me since I was a child.' Yet it was clear that this statement was not made out of some warm benevolence, with one man privately sympathising with a new minister.

'And, Sir Henry,' said Woolton, 'what is it that you are so kindly offering to protect me from? Do tell me what it is that makes you feel that it is necessary to make these pleasant, but I do hope superfluous, remarks?'

Sir Henry breathed deeply, looked down at his papers, then back at Woolton. He may not have actually sighed and may have done everything in his steely civil servant's power not to, but that's exactly what it looked like to the minister. It irritated Woolton considerably to be thought of as a new boy, out of his depth.

'We in the department, Minister,' said Sir Henry, 'are very

conscious of the fact that you have had no parliamentary experience, and that you might not realise that if you make mistakes the House of Commons will blow you out of the water.'

These were dramatic words. Woolton's staff thought he needed protection – 'the protection of the professional for the amateur,' as Sir Henry saw it. 'It revealed the same feeling,' reflected Woolton, 'that I had [later] sensed in Mr Churchill, namely that I was not going to last long in office.'

The officials clearly thought little of Woolton. They would have preferred him not to have been given such an exalted position. Woolton recalled another job offer that had come his way a few months before war had broken out. It had not been a flattering invitation. Woolton thought of it as he listened to Sir Henry. 'It was these officials,' he said angrily in his diary, 'who had thought that my rank should be of an area livestock officer.'

Woolton, ever the optimist, considered that he should show appreciation for this pledge of protection. And so he paused before delivering his response to French.

'Sir Henry, I will never cease to be grateful to you. What you have said will no doubt affect the way I practise my job throughout the whole of the time that I am lucky enough and have the honour to serve in government.' It was a magnanimous and charming Woolton, and for a brief moment French must have thought that he had cowed his man with remarkable speed. But Woolton looked at this long-serving civil servant and decided that he really ought to start as he meant to go on. So he resolved to give the man a small lecture. Woolton was reacting in exactly the opposite way French had hoped.

'Don't you worry about the House of Commons, let's just feed the people,' said Woolton blithely. 'Most businessmen will tell you that if they are right more than six times out of every ten in the judgements they make, they have found the way to commercial success. I shall make plenty of mistakes, and give the House of Commons plenty of targets. When you find I have made mistakes, only be alarmed if you find me sticking to the wrong judgement: that's where the danger lies, and I promise you that when I am wrong I will change direction with a speed that will also alarm you.

'But I do want you to do one thing for me. Whenever I suggest any plan, I want you to oppose it, tell me all the objections to it, all the snags etc. I'm quite strong-minded to stick to my plan if I think it will work. I can then argue my case with others, with peers and with members of Parliament.'

It was, felt Woolton, fear of what the House of Commons would do that was, he later wrote, 'the most dangerously inhibiting force on the creative capacity of ministers'. Yet Woolton would not go blindly into battle. He understood that Sir Henry French was a very experienced civil servant who had seen many talented ministers fall because they had not won over the House of Commons. So he vowed to meet and charm members of both the House of Commons and House of Lords.

In the papers for the first time as Minister of Food

Woolton used his debut at the Queen's Hall to set the tone for his time in office. The subject, avoidance of waste, was one close to his heart; he chose homely phrases to chime with his audience, calling on women to 'mobilise themselves on the Kitchen Front'. He told them that if everybody wasted one slice of bread a day it would take thirty shiploads of wheat a year to make it up.

He asked the nation's cooks to use their skill to make the best use of what was available and to avoid the comfortable habits of peacetime. Addressing the issue of tea rationing he asked that everyone use 'one spoonful for each person and none for the pot'.

Instead of delivering Sir Henry's policy statement of ministry objectives and strategy, he had launched a campaign, likening the nation's housewives to soldiers. 'I want them to go into training for the days which may come when the whole staying power of the nation will depend on their being able to keep up the energy of the industrial workers of this country by feeding them sufficiently when supplies are difficult, when things they have become accustomed to eat and to use are no longer available,' he was reported as saying in the *Liverpool Daily Post* on 6 April 1940. 'The food is stored, enough of it to make Hitler – if he were a sensible and level-headed man – begin to wonder.'

A first thrill at hearing the generous reception of him given by the press was quickly followed by what he described as 'a sense of danger'; the danger to 'either praise or blame to men in public life and I made up my mind that, whilst I remained in office, I would not read what the press said about me unless it was constructive and involved action – and I kept to that.' When his relationship with the press went through stormy waters, as it must for any minister at some point, this adopted wisdom provided a modicum of solace.

But for now the man who soon coined the slogan 'we not only cope, we care' for his ministry was being lauded for his easy style.

The *Evening Express* reported that Woolton 'saw the press for the first time as Minister of Food,' the paper quoting him as saying: 'I suppose I am really going to run the biggest shop in the world.'

He had asked the journalists present at the press conference to treat him gently, 'I have had no experience of ministerial office before,' the *Evening Express* reported. 'I beg of you, as the "new boy", not to be too critical of those people who are now learning this new and difficult job.' He spoke of the 15,000 people who were carrying out the work of the ministry. 'I am responsible for their actions, but how can they all be perfect, when they are just like you and me. They will make mistakes, but don't criticise them too heavily. They are in new jobs. They are learning the ropes.'

Most newspapers reported on the meeting as part of the news of the reshuffle, so fast had the appointment occurred. 'Lord Woolton For Food', heralded *The Times* on 4 April 1940.

The *Manchester Evening News* on the same day wrote, 'Having clothed the army Lord Woolton, now Minister of Food, starts tomorrow to feed the nation.' The headline read: 'Food Hoarders – You Are Warned.' The paper had managed a brief interview with the new minister after his Queen's Hall speech in which Woolton delivered a warning: 'I appeal to housewives not to hoard anything that is in daily use. It is selfish to hoard. I have no doubt about the way to treat hoarders.'

Woolton had also mentioned, rather grandiosely, the business interests he was sacrificing for the role. He said he was 'giving up about ten directorships besides the chairmanship of Lewis's,' adding, somewhat hopefully with regard to his bank balance, 'As soon as the war is over and I am released from office I hope to resume my commercial life.'

The *Liverpool Daily Post* wrote warmly that one of their own had taken up a senior post in government. His appointment was, they wrote, 'peculiarly interesting to Liverpool, and apart from that is a strikingly good one. Hitherto the Food Ministry has been fumbling along in a way that seems inexcusable seeing that there was the experience of the last war to draw upon.' Woolton 'is just the man to do it', the paper continued, adding, 'His experience in business as well as his sociological interests have made him specially sensitive to the feeling of the people, while his gift for organisation should enable him to get the best out of his department.'

The *Daily Mail* also carried an interview with Woolton in which he spoke of his credentials for the post. 'For many years, as managing director of one of the largest chain stores in the country, it was part of my job to feed 40,000 families every day,' he said. 'I know the problems and I understand the difficulties of food distribution. I can assure the housewife that, in my new post, I will have their interests at heart.'

There were frowns, meanwhile, at Woolton's appointment from some of the Tory establishment. 'An obscure business peer, Lord Woolton, has been made Minister of Food,' sniffed the Tory MP Henry 'Chips' Channon in his diary on 3 April.

Even his own wife told the *Daily Mail* on 5 April of his lack of food expertise, stating: 'I would never call him an expert on food' – and then saying of herself: 'I've never cooked anything in my whole life.' (Lady Woolton was soon altering this tune, telling the *Scottish Daily Express* a fortnight later that she liked potatoes ... 'sliced and cooked underneath the joint ... you put an onion in each corner – or a little grated onion – and the potatoes get all the juice from the meat and a little touch of the onion and they're delicious.' She added that: 'My husband is a very easy man to cook for ...')

'Kitchen food, served straight from the pan or the dish is the tastiest you can get,' Woolton said (on day one of his job he was also giving the women of Britain detailed cooking instructions) and the *Express* reported. 'Don't throw away the best part of the potato – the part under the skin. Cook your potatoes in their jackets. Try out unusual dishes. Don't say you can't be bothered with new-fangled ideas.'

It appears to have been the last time that Woolton offered his own cooking tips. Fifteen months later he would give an interview in the *Daily Sketch* – on 22 January 1942. This time he was honest about his own inability to cook. 'There was once a sausage shop at the back of the Bank of England,' he told the paper. 'A man asked the owner to lend him £5. "I'm sorry," answered the sausage maker. "The Bank of England and I have an understanding. I agree not to lend money and the bank agrees not to make sausages." That, says Lord Woolton, is my position. I leave the cooking to the experts – the British housewives.'

But in those early days as Minister of Food Woolton did something that his predecessor and his other government colleagues could not. He brandished his earthy credentials: 'I have lived in working-class houses and have eaten this [simple] sort of food, and enjoyed it much better than most of the elaborate stuff, we, many of us, have to live on in hotels.'

That paper was one of many newspapers that quickly warmed to this side of Woolton; 'this Lancashire business-man,' as it described him, was someone in 'an entirely new line of ministers – "one of us" rather than "one of them"'. In a story run on 1 May, the *Express* reported that Woolton's ministerial car was a twelve horsepower Austin saloon, 'like the one in your garage at home,' the paper commented. It contrasted Oliver Stanley, the War Minister, who drove a 27 horsepower car and Sir Kingsley Wood, at that moment the Lord Privy Seal, who used 28 horsepower: 'more than twice as much as the Food Minister,' said the paper. 'I find it perfectly satisfactory and perfectly comfortable,' Woolton was reported as saying, doubtless to the huge irritation of his gas-guzzling colleagues. The 'Food Minister saves petrol,' said the *Daily Express*. (Family legend, incidentally, has it that Woolton never learned to drive, an early experiment resulting in a collision with a stall of oranges, after which it was chauffeurs all the way.)

Another journalist once noted that Woolton would take the priority label off the windscreen on his car after office hours, so that, unlike most senior government members, he didn't then take advantage of its associated traffic and parking perks.

Meanwhile the unnamed 'agricultural' reporter from the *Daily Express* on 4 April was yet another journalist granted an interview on Woolton's first day in the job. He was impressed with how the minister told his secretary to ignore the telephone when it rang: 'Just take off the receiver and leave it off,' he demanded. Woolton added that this would annoy the exchange but 'it will ensure the comfort of this conference.' The reporter noted how 'a permanent civil servant near him squirmed in horror [presumably Sir Henry French], but the new minister just smiled.'

The journalist went on to describe Woolton as 'brimful of ideas, this good looking man with a broad forehead from which the greyish hair has started to recede. The bushy, sandy eyebrows seem immobile, but there are lines in his fresh face that suggest a smile that's always ready. His voice is soft, tuneful, distinct: his speech is slow and deliberate; Lord Woolton stresses his points by tapping his pencil or waving his spectacles.'

This new minister 'knows the slums', he continued. 'I am going to run the biggest shop the world has ever seen,' Woolton said. 'To supply the nation's food is a stimulating thought: it strikes the imagination. But there are so many places where it could so easily go wrong.'

The *Sheffield Star* reported that Woolton seemed to speak with a refreshing honesty. 'If anything goes wrong,' it reported him as saying on 8 April 1940, 'if the meat is fat or the bacon stringy, or the butter too salty, or the cheese too "asty" – I know for a certainty that the natural instincts of the people will say that if that fellow Woolton conducted his own business like he conducts the nation's, he would be closed down in a week. I won't complain.'

A. J. Cummings in the *News Chronicle* on the same day noted that 'the appointment of Lord Woolton has been received with so remarkable a chorus of public approval that, if he were at all superstitious, the new minister might remember uneasily the warning to beware when men speak well of you.'

While Woolton was pleased at the coverage he was getting during these first few days, Sir Henry did not remark on it. Indeed his office seemed distinctly uninterested. So Woolton, proud at how it was going thus far, sent a message to his office at Lewis's asking that all the press cuttings be saved for his own private collection. If the Ministry of Food didn't wish to collect his press notices for posterity, he certainly would.

Woolton's challenge

Woolton's early press coverage may have been good but it didn't lessen the scale of the task ahead of him. The papers that he'd studied late into the night before his appearance at the Queen's Hall set out the number of mouths that needed feeding; the exact state of Britain's food security; the amount of food grown in the country; and how much it relied on imports.

When the Second World War started, the UK had a population of around 46.5 million. But the British government needed to know exactly how many mouths there were to feed, given how many people were serving overseas or who had emigrated without the knowledge of the authorities. It was also vital to know where they were living, to enable the ministry to distribute food effectively.

It was therefore decided that an identity card system should be imposed which would assist both in food control, and offer a boost to domestic security. So on 29 September

1939 – declared as National Registration Day – everyone in the UK, save servicemen and women, was asked to fill in a form that would reveal their name, address, sex, date of birth, marital status and occupation, at precisely 6.30 p.m. that day.

Some 65,000 enumerators had been employed to distribute forms and help people fill them in. Public service announcements echoed out of wireless sets across the country, during which the broadcaster explained that the forms were 'very simple', adding that servicemen and women on the home front need not be included as they would be fed by their employers.

'I hope nobody will be coy about their date of birth,' said the voice on the radio. But some were coy. A number of women, at first, decided not to admit the existence of their sons, fearful that they would be called up into the armed forces. But many soon relented when they realised that the form would mean the issue of a ration book and access to their share of food.

By nightfall on 29 September, 41 million people had registered, incidentally showing that 9.3 million women said they carried out 'unpaid domestic duties' with 581,000 claiming they worked as live-in, paid servants or cleaners. And of the 6 million children noted in the registration, just 2 per cent lived in London, showing how effective evacuation had been.

Of the servicemen and women who were excused from the register, there were 230,000 men in the regular Army, which with Reservists and Territorials amounted to 684,000 in total. Woolton was not responsible for feeding them. But he did need to ensure that food was secured for the 532 million souls in the British Empire.

Fortunately it was the Empire that fed Britain, rather then the other way around. Yet this was only good fortune in peacetime. Britain was a net importer of food, and when war broke out less than a third of the food on British tables was produced at home. Half of all meat, three-quarters of all cheese, cereals, fats and sugars and four-fifths of fruit came from overseas, forming the 55 million tons of food shipped to Britain each year. It was a major challenge for Woolton. The threat of enemy attacks on shipping, and the inevitable cuts to supply lines would mean that Britain would need to start – and begin in haste – to increase the amount of food it produced at home. Indeed, the German U-boats that prowled the oceans around the UK quickly saw that 55 million ton figure plummet to just 12 million. By 1940, 728,000 tons of food destined for British home ports would be lost to the bottom of the sea.

Having studied the numbers of people that needed feeding, Woolton looked at how they should be fed. The League of Nations – the intergovernmental organisation founded in 1920 as a result of the peace conference that had ended the First World War – had decreed that working men needed 3,000 calories per day.

Woolton's ministry had decided to use this figure for its wartime calculations.

Fortunately the health of the nation seemed rather more robust at the start of the Second World War than some forty years previously, when the army had struggled to recruit healthy men to serve in the Boer War, with service doctors rejecting 60 per cent of those who came forward. Whereas between 8 and 12 of June 1939, when of 17,856 men aged twenty to twenty-one examined for the military, 15,081 were passed as Grade 1 (fit) (84.5 per cent), with 1,583 – or 8.8 per cent – being deemed Grade 2 (fit except for minor disabilities). This figure was encouraging, but it made it even more important that the impending ration did not have a detrimental effect on health.

Moreover a study of working-class families conducted in the London boroughs of Fulham, Bethnal Green and Canning Town reported that in wartime, 'the possibility may arise that some foods normally consumed will no longer be available, and that the diet, although physiologically adequate, may become monotonous to the extent of being a danger to public morale.'

At the time, as the report also revealed, breakfast consisted of 'bread and spread' for most – be they children or adults – and the most widely used drink at that time of day was tea. 96 per cent of those surveyed drank tea, the remainder consuming either 'cocoa or coffee'.

There was then a cooked meal – known to the people of those boroughs as 'dinner' – in the middle of the day, with 'bread and spread' creeping onto many tables. There was little evidence of any pudding being eaten, although many ate a piece of fruit. If there was a pudding, it was a 'milk pudding'; and the richer working-class families might eat a pie or a tart. The only drink that featured at dinner was tea. The obsession with drinking water would not appear for a good fifty years hence.

'Bread and spread' cropped up again at tea, with the wealthier having something cooked; and if 'supper' was served later in those communities, it seemed to comprise of simply bread and cheese – and not a cheese board, a piece of cheddar was quite exuberant enough.

Woolton considered how plain the items were that adorned the tables of the British people, and how it tallied pleasantly with his own dislike for rich food. But it would still be a challenge to fulfil. He made some notes for the Cabinet, writing, quite plainly, that his policy would be 'to feed the people of this country, taking into account their varied requirements and their capacity to pay; and to feed them in such a manner that they can get on with their job of national service'.

It was a simple statement. But delivering it would be an extraordinary challenge.

The Lords and Commons

Three weeks into Woolton's new role, and Sir Henry French informed him that a meeting had been facilitated with key members of Parliament – from both Lords and Commons – in one of the committee rooms. It was surely a daunting prospect, addressing a gathering of people from both the elected house and a chamber of inherited power and influence. The value of the cloth alone that was stitched around the limbs and girths of those men – not to mention the gold signet rings, the heirloom watches and chains, and the silver cigarette cases – could have been exchanged for enough grain to feed a large proportion of the population.

'If you feel I have failed, you must not hesitate to say so,' he told them. 'All I care about is trying to help with the conduct of the war, and if somebody else could be a more effective

Minister of Food than I, then you should know that it is not a position I have sought and I would be willing to give way.' This seemed to go down well with those present. He added: 'But I must warn you that I will not be inhibited in my efforts. I will sometimes fail and you will criticise that. Sir Henry French has already warned me that if I fail, individuals in this room will, to quote him: "blow me out of the water". But I will not let fear of failure prevent me from my job's aim: to feed the people of Britain.'

This gathering of MPs and peers was, Lord Woolton considered later, 'Probably one of the most useful meetings that I ever had.' Members of both houses warmed to him and it would help shield him from some parliamentary criticism, especially while he had battles on his hands within government. But there were men in that room – particularly from the House of Lords – who were not won over, and would remain his nemeses throughout his term in office.

Woolton also had a job to do within his own ministry, and the team of men and women around him. 'The whole place was rather unhappy,' his wife Maud wrote, 'there was resentment about.' Sir Henry, unfortunately, did not add to the gaiety of the place. 'He's an odd man,' she noted. 'He's frustrated, I think I'm right in saying, feeling that everybody is against him [he had been passed over twice for promotion] and not knowing how to manage people.' One person he was having trouble managing was Woolton. The morning after Woolton's meeting with peers, the minister assumed that his Permanent Secretary might cut him some slack, given how well received he appeared to have been by both houses.

But at their morning conference Sir Henry didn't even refer to the meeting the previous day. Instead he sat down in Woolton's office and gave the new minister a lesson in protocol. Woolton recorded his words in his diary that night.

'The way it works, Minister, is thus: If a section head has an issue which they wish to raise with you, then they will report to one of three senior members of the department, those individuals, and myself of course, being the only ones who have access to you. Between us we will then present the problems together with the relevant papers.'

Woolton listened to this protocol and promptly decided to completely ignore it. Maud wrote that he 'began to see all sorts of people, much to Sir H's alarm ... it was against precedent.'

Even the way in which these meetings took place was also irregular. Woolton didn't summon them to his office, he just turned up at their desks. 'Since every man is more natural when sitting in his own chair, I would like to go round and sit down for a while and hear what problems faced the many heads of sections in the ministry,' he wrote.

Woolton described this informality as 'a new form of shock treatment'. There was a rigidity to the way things happened and, he wrote, 'This was the sort of organisation I wanted to break down.' He was convinced it would improve morale: 'I surmised that they were not a very happy crowd – and certainly they were depressed.'

A few weeks in to his new job Maud wrote: 'Sir Henry French is a bit of a thorn in the flesh to F. He is an odd man and seems to make many enemies. He is on the look out for insults I think, and on the other hand very self-opinionated. He puts his foot in it very easily.'

To improve morale in the ministry, Woolton arranged a visit by King George VI, and wrote afterwards that the event 'did more for the internal morale of the Ministry of Food than anybody else would have done in a year'.

And Woolton soldiered on with Sir Henry, feeling that he had managed tougher assignments than engaging with his senior civil servant. He invited him for dinner on several occasions, and within a matter of months something quite extraordinary happened. In the summer of 1940, Maud wrote of a conversation she had had with a senior official from the Ministry of Food. 'Do you know,' the official told her, 'I actually heard French laugh in the corridor today.'

5

SPRING–SUMMER 1940

On 10 May 1940, Neville Chamberlain resigned as Prime Minister, to be replaced by Winston Churchill. Lord Woolton reckoned his days as Minister of Food were over.

He would look back on his unfeasibly short political tenure with a shrug of the shoulders and get back to his retail business. He had been in the job for only a month, and within that short period felt he had made some headway. But as Woolton was aware of the fragility of political careers, there would be no loss of pride for him. He had been away from Lewis's for over a year and the board would welcome him back.

So he was unique among senior government colleagues in not fearing the chop as Churchill went to Buckingham Palace to seek the commission from the King to form a government. There was, he remembered, 'an atmosphere of intense excitement'. Rather than wait to be summoned and told he would not be needed in the reformed administration, Woolton decided to send a letter to Churchill.

'I have only been in office a few weeks,' he wrote from his study in Flat 110, 4 Whitehall Court, the family's small London apartment. Woolton would write his diary there in the evenings at a desk in the sitting room, with its view out to Horse Guards Parade.

'I have no claims on your consideration and if it is more convenient for you not to include me in government, I shall not only understand but would be glad to return to my business.' To show some well-meaning intention he added that he'd be equally glad, 'to serve the country in any other capacity as I have no desire for ministerial office'.

In fact, he privately rather hoped that Churchill would indeed let go of him, and not just because he didn't relish the politics. He wanted to get back to what he was really good at; running big business, making money. He did not profess to know Churchill personally – the two of them had spoken only a couple of times at political events – but the pair had actually met before, although it was a long time ago. Woolton would recall it, but it would not figure in Churchill's memory.

In 1904, Winston Churchill had ventured upon Fred Marquis's student turf up in Manchester where he had been selected as a prospective parliamentary candidate for Manchester North West, an area known as the Exchange Division. Churchill was fighting to win the seat for the Liberal Party, after he had quit the Conservatives during a row about trading tariffs in the British Empire. He would go on to win the seat and have a short tenure from 1906 to 1908.

The invitation was to address a group of local businessmen in the Memorial Hall, a Venetian Gothic building – all arches and red brick – on Albert Square. Already Mr Churchill had a reputation as a considerable debater, so Fred, then chairman of the university debating society, decided to go along, uninvited, and see what the fuss was about. He arrived early, tucked himself into a seat behind the hall's grand piano and watched the room fill up. Soon the hubbub faded away as Churchill arrived and walked to the stage. Applause spread across the room as he came into view. The speech he made was rousing, of course. Then there were questions.

It just so happened that the first raised hand came from a young man sitting behind a piano. 'What will you, Mr Churchill, or the Liberal government of which doubtless you will be a member, do about unemployment in this country if your new party is returned to power?' asked Fred.

While the businessmen in the room had cheered Churchill's rousing speech, this dose of reality in the room stirred them for different reasons.

'To my great surprise I heard loud cheers and applause,' recalled Woolton. When the noise faded Churchill gave his reply. But whatever he said did not impress twenty-one-year-old Fred Marquis. 'I got a very unsatisfactory answer,' he recalled. His words were 'exasperatingly indefinite, if not evasive.' And while Fred just sat back in his chair disappointed, a contingent of students at the back whose views were, in Woolton's words, 'more violent than mine', started shouting and then moving forwards through the hall. They looked menacing enough for Churchill to be ushered off the stage and out of the hall through a back exit; Fred's question had been the first and last of the evening.

Churchill never recalled the undergraduate who started this minor incident and, despite some brief political dealings, when Woolton was sent for by Churchill as he planned his first government, 'it was quite obvious,' he wrote after the pair finally met at the new bomb-proof Admiralty, off the Mall in London, 'that he did not know me.'

Maud wrote of the feverish atmosphere that abounded around Whitehall after Churchill took office on Friday 10 May. 'Speculation was rife,' she wrote. It wasn't until the Monday that her husband was sent for. 'We had no idea whether he would be asked to stay on,' she continued. 'We thought that Churchill, who had to give office to a lot of his supporters, and also to include several Labour men, and Liberals, would want the MoF for a politician.'

Over the weekend, recorded Maud, there were meetings and lunches and dinners at which MPs and others speculated about who would get jobs in the new Cabinet. She wrote of one MP saying, 'Woolton will have rung up the PM and said, "Do you want me or don't you – because it's all the same to me, only I'd like to know." This finally went round as having happened.'

When they finally met on Monday the two discussed his position, as Woolton recorded in his diary. 'Do you want to stay on?' asked Churchill gravely.

'That is for you to decide, Prime Minister,' he replied, reminding him of the letter he had written to him. 'But I am at your disposal.'

'Do you think you can manage all these civil servants?' the new Prime Minister asked. 'It is a very large staff.'

'I have been accustomed to controlling a staff of 13,500 and don't anticipate any difficulty on that score,' Woolton replied. He added that his only fear was being 'completely ignorant' of parliamentary procedure. Churchill paused and then said that he should continue in the role, but it wasn't exactly a ringing endorsement.

'Well you'd better try for a bit,' was how he put it. Woolton reflected many years later that Churchill 'had very little confidence in me and I heard some time afterwards that he had said to some of his friends, "We shall have to be ready with a rescue squad for Woolton."'

Initially a working relationship looked promising. When Woolton presented his food policy to the new-look government that summer, he knew that Europe would soon be facing food shortages and he thought it would be a wise move if the Chancellor of the Exchequer translated part of the nation's gold reserves into non-perishable food goods to help guard against the nation's hunger.

It was a suggestion that ultimately won the backing of Winston Churchill, who responded: 'The natural Treasury preference for gold or foreign exchange over wheat and whale oil as a capital asset may not be entirely justified in the present exceptional circumstances. Non-perishable foodstuffs will certainly be consumed sooner or later; their possession will set free shipping to bring in munitions should an emergency arise. Gold, on the other hand, and foreign securities, may well prove of perishable quality in the economic world in store.'

But the pair had an early conflict, and it was on a matter than neither could have anticipated.

On Woolton's staff, as parliamentary secretary, was Robert Boothby MP. Elevated to the peerage in the 1950s, Boothby would later gain notoriety for the company he kept with East End gangsters and his affairs with the likes of cat burglar Leslie Holt, whom he met in a gambling club. A few months into Woolton's tenure as Food Minister under Churchill, he discovered that the forty-year-old Member of Parliament for Aberdeen and Kincardine East had received a gift of shares from a company of which he was chairman; one that supplied the vitamins which were being added to the bread available as part of the ration.

This conflict of interest didn't impress the straight businessman in Woolton and he complained about it to civil servants and senior colleagues. Boothby was forced to sell the 5,000 shares he had been given but netted over £8,000 in the process. Woolton then had a meeting – in October of that year – with Churchill in which the matter was discussed.

'I think the Prime Minister was very annoyed with me for having made a fuss about it,' he wrote, 'and we had a rather unpleasant interview.'

'I will enquire into it and see what I think,' Churchill told him, irritated at what he saw as a distraction. Woolton would not let him leave it like that. 'When I know what your opinion is I will be glad if you would consider whether I should remain as minister,' he said. 'I have no intention of having a Marconi scandal association with a department of which I am head.' This was an inflammatory remark; the scandal he referenced took place in 1912, when senior members of

Asquith's Liberal administration had bought shares in the US wireless firm in the knowledge that the British government was about to issue the company with a lucrative contract.

'Unless it is made abundantly clear that Boothby has no sort of financial interest in anything that is being done by the Ministry of Food, then I shall not remain minister,' continued Woolton. Churchill was cross and asked his then Chancellor of the Exchequer, Kingsley Wood, also in the meeting, to deal with it. 'I don't understand these things,' Churchill said, attempting to brush the issue aside.

But Woolton continued to press his point. 'There are standards in good class business and they are very high ones,' he said referring to his life outside of politics, which was bound to infuriate Churchill further. 'Those standards do not include giving the chairman shares in a company instead of an increase in salary,' he said. The matter should not, he thought, be dealt with by the Chancellor but instead by legal minds. 'I insisted on it being handled by Law Officers of the Crown,' he recorded in his diary.

But he left the meeting feeling aggrieved. 'I came out of the whole thing with a sort of conviction that it was I who had the shares and done something wrong,' he wrote. And in the margin of Maud's diary – where she recounts the affair – Woolton added some comments (something he did throughout the diary, on reading it later in life) saying, 'I began to feel in the dock myself.'

While Boothby was made to sell the shares, Woolton was astonished that he was allowed to keep the money: 'whether they decided then to tax him on the proceeds, I don't know,' he wrote, adding a little mournfully, 'I came away with the feeling that my colleagues regarded me as a difficult and angular person.' Word also reached Woolton that Kingsley Wood had been disparaging about him to others, saying, apparently, that at the meeting 'Woolton had been very Wooltonish.'

It later transpired that Churchill did reprimand Boothby on this issue; and over another matter. A select committee was appointed to investigate allegations concerning Boothby's chairmanship of a committee lobbying to get government funds in 1939 over losses they had incurred relating to the Munich agreement, which permitted Nazi Germany to annex parts of Czechoslovakia along its border. Woolton wrote in his diary that the British Secret Service reported that they had found a letter which claimed Boothby had made several hundred thousand pounds from the deal.

Boothby protested his innocence and the claims went away, but not without Churchill giving him a severe dressing down, not that he chose to share this with Woolton. Churchill, he raged in his diary, 'didn't have the grace to tell me anything about it'. Unable to get rid of Boothby he declared simply that he was a 'man with no virtue'.

Woolton bumped into Boothby, socially, one lunchtime in April 1941. He was at L'Escargot, the restaurant in London's Soho. Woolton's lunch companion was his Director of Flour Milling, Norman Vernon; Boothby's lunch companion was Noël Coward.

After lunch, Boothby approached Woolton saying that he was hoping to join the Air Force. 'They're very anxious to have me,' he said. 'I had a commission in the last war, so it looks like I'll be able to get another in this one.'

Woolton wondered why Boothby was telling him this.

Then the MP added, discreetly, 'I'm anxious, of course, that I'm able to defend myself against any unpleasant charges. Anything that might suggest I was ever dishonest . . .'

Woolton looked at the man squarely and said, 'No one thinks that you are dishonest.' This pleased and reassured Boothby. Then Woolton added: 'But many people think you are very foolish.'

It was clear that Churchill had a poor view generally of business people in government; they may have had organisational capacities and some foresight but they always failed to impress the public through the process of parliament. (Woolton had himself some sympathy for this view; 'the training and the atmosphere of doing business in both spheres is widely different,' he commented.) It was not an opinion Churchill only voiced in private. He openly mocked the idea of business people in politics during meetings. 'Whenever men trained in business have come into government it has been disastrous,' he once barked. Woolton recalled challenging the PM on his view, what he called Churchill's 'provoking accusation'. Unfazed, Churchill proceeded to write off a number of senior politicians, but he omitted mentioning his Minister of Food, so the then Secretary of State for the Colonies, Oliver Stanley, piped up. 'Well Winston, how are you going to explain Woolton?'

Churchill replied not to Stanley but looked at his Food Minister – every bit the buffed, polished and confident businessman-cum-politician – with a beaming smile. 'But, my dear Fred, surely you are not suffering from the delusion that the public regard you as a businessman – they think of you as a philanthropist.'

The nation, felt Churchill, saw Woolton as a benevolent figure, a kindly grocer, a Father Christmas for times
of austerity, doling out small gifts from his big red sack
with even-handed wisdom. He hadn't come into politics
the hard way, suffering unpopularity, fighting tough seats
in elections, dealing with the chicanery of party politics,
coping with vituperative journalists. No greasy pole for
Woolton, he had simply been appointed to a senior position in government. But this confident 'Uncle Fred', as he
had been nicknamed in the press, would soon find himself
coming unstuck, with civil servants, Cabinet colleagues and
the press, thought the PM. And then he would be proved
right. Woolton would have to be rescued, or, more probably, ditched.

So, just weeks into the job, Woolton realised that he didn't
just have an enemy in Hitler and his German machine, calcu-
latingly trying to starve Britain; he didn't just have the brick
wall of an insurmountable Civil Service; there wasn't simply
the mere problem of food distribution, the extraordinarily
complicated procedure of food imports and the effects on
public morale if things went wrong – Woolton had a foe right
there in government, a battle on his hands with his boss, the
most powerful politician in Britain.

But this unexpected new front didn't put him off. Indeed
it further steeled him for the fight. 'I was determined not to
fail in my part of the war effort,' he wrote. 'And I got a certain amusing stimulation out of the idea that I would show
this astute parliamentarian that a businessman also could
do a government job and manage both his department and
Parliament.'

Rationing

Despite vociferous newspaper campaigns against it run by, among others, Lord Beaverbrook's *Daily Express*, rationing had finally been introduced on 8 January 1940, preceding Woolton's arrival.

It had been branded an attack on civil liberties by many, a view with which Lord Woolton for one had some sympathy. But shortages meant that without rationing there would not be sufficient food to go around.

The *Daily Express* wasn't alone in its condemnation. *Picture Post* magazine described the introduction of rationing as 'the most unpopular Government decision since the war began'. Meanwhile, the *Daily Mail* insisted it was a 'stupid' decision for a country with an extensive empire and said: 'It would be scarcely possible – even if Dr Goebbels were asked to help – to devise a more harmful piece of propaganda for Great Britain.'

However, people who suspected they were always at the back of the queue and wondered if friends, neighbours and local shopkeepers were profiteering, were generally happy to see the introduction of rationing. In a poll, 60 per cent said they thought rationing was necessary. They knew, even if it lacked variety, they would get a square meal.

The government's Ministry of Information was quick to compare the good fortune of the British public with that of Germany, where rationing had begun with hostilities. The British were told they could expect better butter rations and more eggs, bread and meat. 'It would hardly be an exaggeration to say that every other obtainable foodstuff is rationed in Germany while in Great Britain it is officially stated that initially all other foodstuffs may be freely purchased,' the ministry declared.

For the British the first supplies to be restricted that January were those of butter and bacon – both limited to 4oz – and sugar, capped at 12oz per person, per week. That was followed in March by the rationing of meat, dealt with by price rather than weight.

In July, when Woolton was in charge, tea was rationed and that was followed in March 1941 with restrictions on jam, marmalade, syrup and treacle. Two months after that, albeit reluctantly by Lord Woolton (aware of its importance to many manual workers who relied on it in packed lunches), cheese was rationed. Eggs were rationed that year too.

In 1942 rice, dried fruit, condensed milk, breakfast cereals, tinned tomatoes, tinned peas, soap, sweets and chocolates, biscuits and oats were all added to the list. Sausages were the final wartime addition, being rationed during 1943.

Allowances for each food fluctuated during the conflict. For example, the sugar ration tended to increase in the summer months to encourage people to harvest fruits and make jam. After butter was rationed the greatest amount available to adults per week was 8oz, the least amount being 2oz. Sweets that children could look forward to were kept to 16oz a month, an amount that was at times halved.

Rations books were buff-coloured for adults, and green for children. They weren't a replacement for cash, which still had to change hands over the counter. It was a control on the amounts that could be bought each week or month, marked off by the shopkeeper so they could not be used twice. Vegetables and fruit weren't rationed, nor was fish; but they were often in short supply as cargo ships and the fishing fleet were hounded by U-boats. Even before rationing was introduced there were voluntary controls imposed on the purchase of sugar, to prevent people stockpiling.

Rationing was administered by Woolton's ministry where on file, as far as the civil servants could tell as a result of National Registration Day, was the name and address of every citizen of the United Kingdom. With each National Registration Number would come a ration book.

As Katherine Knight commented in her book *Spuds, Spam and Eating for Victory*, 'the ration book was our passport to getting enough to eat.' Ration books, with that individual serial number, were posted out to everyone entitled to receive rations – including members of the Royal Family. While different types of book were sent to those with different needs, such as those with babies or infants, and pregnant mothers, or with extra rations for items such as cheese for registered vegetarians, and with temporary documents for service personnel on leave, the ration was otherwise universal.

By January 1940 everyone should have received their ration book. One's ration book became a very precious commodity. It was a sensible precaution to leave it in a safe and accessible place, so when the siren sounded in the event of an air raid, as you took your gas mask and your identity card, in the words of Katherine Knight, 'you were wise to grab your ration book.' Each individual would then have to register at a chosen shop. On each page of coupons the retailer's name and address would need to be entered.

So one needs to imagine a life in which movement was

pretty limited. No nipping into a store you happened to be passing by to purchase something just because you were hungry, no passing by a butcher and walking in to buy a couple of steaks because they looked nice in the window, no random trips to a store you liked the look of, no weekend supermarket trips grabbing anything you might want or need or indeed filling 'til overspill – in fact, no freedoms whatsoever when it came to food. Today it is almost impossible to conceive of these privations. The only choice that was possible was the freedom to register with a different shop for different items, assuming there was one local to you. So, for example, you could choose to buy sugar in one store and bacon in another.

In the early stages of the war the coupons in the ration book were valid for only one week, but this was soon relaxed so that, for example, you could forgo buying butter one week and then purchase twice as much the next – assuming the store would let you.

Meat, however, had to be bought during the designated week. If you missed the chance, that meant no meat. But you could buy a whole month's worth of tea at one time. Alcohol was also scarce, which made drowning one's sorrows at the lack of gastronomic indulgence rather difficult.

Shopkeepers would keep your coupons and then send them to the local Food Office, who would then allocate them with a buying permit, enabling the shop to buy new stock from regulated wholesalers.

While the food supply to the country's larders stalled, so did the prospect of new kitchen equipment. You could forget the idea of upgrading any of your cooking tools. No new cookers or kitchen appliances were made during the war, as factories were turned over to everything and anything demanded by the war effort.

The administration of the ration was a feat of considerably complicated proportions; all done, of course, without a single computer, just people and paper. At a local level there were Food Offices – some 1,200 of them – whose job it was to administer rationing in towns and villages. It would be to a member of the Food Office that you would report, if, for example, you had lost your ration book in that air raid or you were a pregnant woman seeking a certificate that might entitle you to orange juice. Those Food Offices reported to a Food Control Committee – 1,520 across the country – whose job it was to deal with retailers, hospitals or caterers. The committees in turn took orders from nineteen Divisional Food Offices – in England, Scotland, Wales and Northern Ireland – who reported directly to the Ministry of Food.

The ministry was itself a complex bureaucracy, with its divisions, departments, scientific experts and administrative staff, its buildings managers, as well as code-breakers and other security-related workers. At the top were senior civil servants and leading them, of course, was Lord Woolton, 'the minister for girth control', as someone once joked at a public lunch during the war.

His ministry was not an organisation hastily cobbled together at the outbreak of war. Months before, civil servants had planned and built the department; much of that planning had been done after careful study of the work of the Ministry of Food during the First World War, and the system of rationing that had been put in place then. But, wrote Woolton, 'there was this difference. Rationing and restriction were introduced in the First World War to meet emergencies that had arisen. The planners – wisely with the "Black Book" of the history of the first Ministry of Food ever before them – had built up the conditions for a new ministry to operate at once should war break out.'

So this time the government would not wait until the nation was half-starved before it did something about food; except that what was created was a giant bureaucracy run by civil servants whose instincts, according to Woolton, were to curb enterprise and commercial practice, the exact facets that were needed in order to buy food.

Woolton, free of the political pressures that the elected politicians he sat alongside in the Cabinet faced, was less concerned with the internal machinations of the ministry than the reason it actually existed: to stop Britain from starving. 'The machine, if the bald truth be told,' he commented, 'was unduly concerned with its own meticulous organisation, whilst the major task before it was not to satisfy Parliament that it had made no mistakes, but the more difficult task of feeding over 40 million people,' adding, 'the machine had no common touch with the people.' As he cast his eye around his ministry he pondered on the struggles he had had to clothe the army during his time at the War Office. 'I found myself once again faced with the same circumstances,' he later wrote, 'only now I had learned my lesson.'

It was all very well having a huge and complex food ministry but Woolton felt that it would not achieve its aims, would not deliver actual food to people when they needed it in ongoing times of crisis, unless he could rule it with an iron rod.

Woolton felt he needed to run his ministry in the way he ran department stores. 'The man who is head of a business and succeeds – making success and failures – must not be inhibited by the fear of failure,' he wrote. 'The government machinery is completely different from this. I knew that the machinery of government is not there to serve Parliament but to serve the public,' he went on, reflecting that he 'had better waste very little time in applying business methods'.

One radical move Woolton made was to replace some civil servants with businessmen, not unlike himself. For example, Sir John Bodinnar, who came from a Wiltshire sausage-making firm, was made head of one of the supply departments; while John Cadbury, from the famous chocolate-making dynasty, was, of course, put in charge of cocoa. Woolton later reflected that he was lucky to have been able to secure the services of such people, who 'undertook more arduous, and often more dangerous, missions than they were ever called to face in their ordinary business lives'.

However bullish he was at how the department needed to be run he was worried that it would be, in his words, 'onerous'. He would, at the very least, have a battle on his hands with his civil servants. But, he confessed, the feeling was probably mutual. 'Whatever fears I may have had,' he confided, 'they were at least equalled by those that my civil servants had of my methods.' He knew that Sir Henry French was strongly opposed to the beckoning in of businessmen, believing the detailed organisation of the department was the job of civil servants like himself; indeed, so unhappy was Sir Henry about Woolton's changes and methods that he consulted a civil servant higher up the chain of command.

Woolton himself feared one of them would have to resign if their disagreement became further inflated.

However, Sir Henry decided to back down – although he made his reservations known to Woolton in no uncertain terms. Yet a powerful relationship developed between the two and continued to flourish. Only a year after the incident, Sir Henry admitted to Woolton: 'Last Christmas I told you that I had never been – officially – more miserable in my life. This Christmas I would like to tell you that in forty-odd years of Civil Service life I have never been so happy.'

But whatever misgivings Woolton had of the Civil service machine, he was forever grateful for the preliminary work that had been done on rationing. As war broke out, ration books had already been printed, along with a mass of forms. Local Food Offices and committees stuffed with members of civic society had been set up. The machine was ready. So by the time Lord Woolton arrived, 'the problem was not to create machinery,' he wrote, 'but how and when to use it.'

So he took an early and tough decision. He wanted to implement rationing before it was actually needed. 'I planned not to be driven to rationing by realised shortages,' he wrote; instead he would 'put something in the cupboard'. There would be days when supplies would fail, but he wanted to be ready for that. The nation's cartoonists picked up on this and gave him the nickname of 'Squirrel'.

Thus he aimed to get through the hardest part of rationing by the summer of 1940. It would hurt, but it would be essential. So by July, when tea, cooking fats and margarine were officially limited, he commented, 'we had broken the back of rationing'. Of course it had not been popular. The public, for example, 'did not want meat to be rationed – and who can blame them?'.

Then that month he went a step further and banned the making and selling of ice cakes. It meant that even on one's wedding day you couldn't have a traditional cake.

And while the British public disliked such limitations, there was no one more disdainful of it than the Prime Minister. Churchill, Woolton commented, was 'benevolently hostile to anything that involved people not being fed like fighting cocks.' He felt that Woolton relished restricting food. The minister, of course, believed he was simply being pragmatic.

Woolton also saw rationing as an opportunity to improve the country's nutrition. He gathered together a professor of biochemistry, the President of the Royal Society, the Minister of Agriculture, among others and, as he commented, 'with this highly skilled advice of widely different approach, we worked out a diet for the nation that would supply all the calories and all the vitamins that were needed for different age groups, for the fighting services, for the heavy manual workers, for the ordinary housewife, for the babies and children, and for the pregnant and nursing mothers.'

The zeal with which he administered the ration, and for which Churchill would relentlessly mock him, came from his earlier life spent working in social service. Having seen the effects of malnutrition, having witnessed the deaths of elderly people from nothing less than starvation, now a unique situation presented itself. It had never happened before and would be unlikely to happen again, as the island nation of Britain became a closed shop. Lord Woolton could pretty much control exactly what and how much every individual in Britain could eat, making him the envy of nutritionists, dieticians, and indeed anyone interested in the health of the nation, before or since. The war presented him an extraordinary opportunity, and he wrote of his 'all-embracing planning ... I determined to use the powers I possessed to stamp out the diseases that arose from malnutrition,' he wrote, 'especially those among children such as rickets.'

Attached to his diaries were newspaper clippings, touching on the subject of health and body weight; some of those cuttings dated back decades, indicating a lifelong interest in the subject. One such cutting, from Weldon's *Illustrated Dressmaker* from 1900, read: 'There is no doubt that excessive corpulency is a disease, requiring as much careful diagnosis, treatment and attention as any other malady.'

The article went on to talk of a Mr F. C. Russell of London WC1 who was described as 'a most experienced and capable authority as to the best means of reducing superfluous flesh'. The gentleman recommended vegetable-based tonics that had 'most marvellous results in the reduction of fat'.

Another clipping, whose origins are unknown, suggested a form of exercise: 'Going up and down stairs slowly, holding the body erect while doing so is beneficial.'

A clipping from the *Manchester Guardian* of 24 March 1905 was of a letter from T. C. Horsfall. He wrote that the 'physical condition of German is far superior to that of English urban population'. Apparently one reason for this is that 'German people are much under the control of officials.' Perhaps Woolton bore this in mind for the coming days when, rarely in the life of a nation, the English people would be under the control of one official, namely him.

In the late 1950s, five years after the final end of rationing and almost twenty years after he had taken the reins as Britain's food provider, he reflected somewhat gloriously on his achievement. 'The health of the children today is the reward of that policy.'

6

THE SECRET LIFE OF COLWYN BAY

While Lord Woolton had a good number of staff at his Ministry of Food offices in Portman Square, a canny observer would have noticed that for such an important department it seemed to be a remarkably slim organisation. Indeed civil servants from other ministries communicating between departments began to wonder where exactly the vast number of staff that were surely needed to run the Ministry of Food actually were. In early July 1940 a letter was dispatched from the Burma Office in Whitehall by a civil servant called Johnston writing to a Mr Hutton at the Ministry of Food. He wished to discuss liaison arrangements but was having a problem: 'I am afraid that I find some difficulty in replying to your letter of the 5th of July regarding the liaison between our two departments,' he wrote. 'My difficulty arises partly from the fact that we have no information as to what has happened to the Ministry of Food.'

While there was the office at Portman Court, as far as he was concerned the ministry had all but disappeared. And in fact, this is exactly what had happened. In haste, and in the greatest secrecy, 5,000 civil servants and their accompanying paraphernalia to operate – from pencils to cars – had departed with speed and in such a way that no one seemed to notice and fewer knew.

Orders had gone out as part of an operation called Yellow Move. Under this edict, the most important ministries were to relocate so that their operations could continue free of bombs or sabotage. Lord Woolton's ministry was considered one of those vital to war victory.

So the reality was that Woolton in Portman Square had just a skeleton staff. The rest had moved to a sleepy North Wales seaside town called Colwyn Bay, partway between Anglesey and Liverpool.

During the early stages of the war, the King had sent a telegram to the Ministry of Food. 'The security of the home front is as vital as that of the Fighting Front and I appreciate to the full the work of the ministry staff, both in London and throughout the country, in safeguarding the supply and distribution of the people's food.'

Those words 'throughout the country' disguised the extraordinary secret that the department responsible for the feeding of Britain and her colonies was now in the nicely vulnerable and easy-to-bomb confines of Colwyn Bay. Secrecy was paramount because, had Hitler known, he would have taken great satisfaction in smashing every limb and tentacle, heart and head of this vital asset. Yet even both civil servants and spies in London appeared thwarted.

But as vital as it was for Britain to be fed, it was as inconvenient for the people of Colwyn Bay, as their lives were to be turned upside down.

Miss Constance Smith, for example, was the headmistress of Penrhos College, by Rhos-On-Sea. The school, built in the Victorian era with views out over the Irish sea, was just up the road from Colwyn Bay.

It was a warm summer morning in early July of 1940 and she had, doubtless, sat down and breathed a sigh of relief as the last of her pupils had been waved off as they left for the summer holidays. Miss Smith presided over this all-girls boarding school and after trunks, files of school work, hockey sticks, games kit and toys had been bundled into cars and buses, what seemed to be a perpetual noise of chatter and laughter would finally have ebbed to silence.

The teachers would have been quick to get away and the remaining school staff – cooks and porters – would have cleaned and sorted the kitchens, housemaids would have mopped and polished the floors and emptied bins, the beds and furniture would have been covered with dust sheets, before Miss Smith would do a final walk around the school, locking doors and checking windows.

Life at the school seemed pretty normal. The end of term was just like any other end of term. While there was of course a war on, the population of Penrhos College, indeed most of the people of Colwyn Bay, were living almost blissfully unaware of it. The only chilling reminders – aside from the typical privations of rations and the ever-present worry of loved ones away on war duties – being the low hum of German bombers as they flew home, high over the shores of the Welsh coast, having done their worst to the unfortunate towns and cities of Coventry or Liverpool.

But there was never a bomb dropped near Miss Smith's school, nor over the town. The Germans had bigger fish to fry; Goering had ordered German planes, co-ordinated from occupied Paris, to destroy Liverpool. Miss Smith would have counted her lucky stars that her metier had led her to a life of running Penrhos, with its rambling buildings, large school hall, chapel and hockey fields.

Perhaps with the summer holidays ahead of her, with school reports written by the end of the week and the checking of a few maintenance jobs done – some painting, a few rattling windows replaced – she would retreat to her own family home. Then, ten days before the start of the Michaelmas term, she and key staff would return to the empty school. They would plan for the coming months, everything from organising accommodation for new girls, revisiting dormitory lists, sorting classes, liaising with other schools on sports fixtures and planning menus.

If she was sitting contemplating a relaxing summer, her attention might have been taken by the sight of a Model Y Ford chugging up the drive towards the school. Was this a girl returning – her parents beetling back because something had been left behind? It certainly wasn't a delivery van or the postman.

As the car drew closer, she would have seen two men dressed in identical dark grey suits and looking horribly formal. One can imagine the pang of nerves that could have jangled in the pit of her stomach.

At exactly the same time, a couple of miles away, at the Meadowcroft Hotel on Llannerch Road East, owners Stan and Hester Barlow nervously greeted a man carrying a clipboard who had pinged the bell at the reception desk in the hall. The couple would have come out of the sitting room where they attended to their guests. Their hotel had forty-two rooms; among the guests were several men and women of advanced years who, old and infirm, were permanent residents.

The man with the clipboard would have spoken firmly and without emotion: 'I am requested to requisition this building on behalf of His Majesty's Government,' went the formal announcement. 'I shall hereby serve you formal notice of requisition in order to obtain vacant possession. I, or one of my colleagues, shall then take a schedule of condition of this building and make an inventory of any residual contents – fixtures or fittings.' Perhaps he stopped and went off script at this point. 'So that's things like wall lights, curtains, fitting cupboards and wardrobes.' Then it would have been back to his notes as the ashen-faced Barlows could do nothing but stand there and listen. 'I must inform you that all persons in this building are to vacate in six hours, taking with them all their personal possessions. Actual possession of this building will not be taken until all the visitors have vacated the premises, or at the expiration of six hours. The occupier may remove all perishable food, or other valuables, articles etc which he wishes, providing this is done within the space of a few hours.'

While the Barlows were receiving the news at how their lives were to change within hours, from relative quiet to an uncertain future, the same was happening at Penrhos College. Miss Smith would have been relieved that there were no children in residence. Her job would be to coerce her colleagues into vacating the school before setting about the task of finding and then moving to new premises. She would not let the school simply shut.

Miss Smith would have been informed of the following, according to contemporary notices: 'a schedule of condition will be made of the building as well as an inventory of contents. Before the inventory and schedule of condition is commenced, the occupier, or the manager, shall be requested to see that his staff before they leave, and under their supervision, remove all wines, spirits and imperishable food, linen, silver, crockery, valuables etc, into a room for temporary storage. This room must be locked and sealed in the presence of the manager. Rooms suitable for this purpose, e.g. pantries, linen rooms, cupboards etc, must be selected on account of dryness, etc, but as far as possible, rooms suitable for office accommodation shall not be used. As soon as this is done the staff must vacate the building, and if discharged by the management can seek re-employment by HM Office of Works, in accordance with the notice affixed in the entrance hall.'

Miss Smith was given ten days for herself and her staff to pack their things and go. The situation was rather different at the Meadowcroft Hotel. The establishment, which advertised itself as 'ideally suited in quiet surroundings' could not, surely, be vacated in six hours, as the elderly residents would not have coped. So on this occasion the man from the ministry relented. He gave them forty-eight rather than six hours to leave and find new accommodation.

Across town similar events unfurled. Hotels, hostels, schools and several private residences had visits. Orders were given, lives duly turned upside down. Within days, Colwyn Bay was transformed; the Ministry of Food was coming to town.

But while Woolton's ministry was moving there, he seems to have gone to great pains to spend as little time as possible in the town, preferring to base himself in London and only visit for brief periods. It appears that he tried very hard to ensure that no meetings went on for so long that he needed to spend the night. And this was no doubt fortuitous, because if he had ever needed to stay the night, as his officials had requisitioned all the hotels in the town as offices, finding him a last-minute bed would be difficult.

The closest Woolton stayed to Colwyn Bay was at the Station Hotel at Llandudno Junction, some five miles away. And so that he could avoid the inconvenience of having to take a car from the station, or even walk the short distance, to the ministry's headquarters at the Colwyn Bay Hotel, he organised for a special railway halt to be constructed where the line passed the hotel. It meant that he could alight like the king of some not too insignificantly minor African republic.

As Colwyn Bay-based historian Graham Roberts commented, when Woolton visited the town on official business he would arrive at the hotel and be able to 'alight with great pomp'.

Meanwhile, the ministry's move was as intricately planned as it was brutally implemented. Just a few weeks before those visits to Miss Smith and the Barlows, two civil servants, Bert Fillmore, a senior executive officer, and Tim Deeves, head of branch, came to Colwyn Bay to drive around the town and double-check on the arrangements they had cooked up at their offices of the Ministry of Food in Portman Square.

The Colwyn Bay Information Bureau, in peacetime a useful place for tourists seeking the likes of bed and breakfast accommodation or local insight on the best beaches, had been asked to provide a venue for their meeting. One employee was asked to attend the encounter as a witness. He was wide-eyed as the pair discussed dispersal plans and, referencing maps of the town, identified and then ticked off a list of every hotel and boarding house in Colwyn Bay and the surrounding area. Naturally he was sworn to secrecy, as were local policemen who were required to share the workload of informing individuals about the impending requisitions.

Thus it was a Colwyn Bay copper who arrived at the Edelweiss Hotel on Lawson Road, which advertised itself as an 'AA Approved' guesthouse and 'The most pleasantly situated hotel in Colwyn Bay', to inform the owner that its premises were required by the government. The hotel was to be given a vital role in the coming years as it was used as the Bread Division, the headquarters for the distribution of loaves across the country.

Meanwhile Miss Smith's Penrhos College would house departments for strategy, planning, and a 'Margins Committee', which policed the strict rationing rules.

It was the ingenuity of Constance Smith that saw the Duke of Devonshire agreeing to let the school use his ancestral pile, Chatsworth House in Derbyshire, for the rest of the war. Over the summer months, convoys of lorries ferried beds, blackboards and desks from Wales to Derbyshire. Senior pupils were asked to come back to school a few days early and Michaelmas term, 1940, for Penrhos College began on time and in the particularly refined quarters of one of Britain's finest stately homes. The house librarian gave lessons on subjects such as snuffboxes and miniature portraiture; the girls swam and splashed about in the Sea Horse Fountain in summer and, later, in the early months of 1942, they skated down the iced-over long water at the front of the house.

Back in Colwyn Bay, the Mount Stewart Hotel became the Bacon and Ham Division, Rydal School housed the Meat and Livestock Department, or 'the Black Pudding Department' as it was known, and a detached private house on Pwllycrochan Avenue, Merton Place, became the headquarters for food propaganda. Under Lord Woolton's instruction, the people who worked in this somewhat gloomy and innocuous three-storey house were tasked with selling the message to the British people (via any media possible, from posters to radio) that not only was abiding by the ration one's patriotic duty, but it was in fact good for them. The nation's sparse diet would actually make them feel better and be better. They also let it be known that fighting troops would receive a richer mix of food, which, in turn, was healthier for them.

It was, wrote local historian Graham Roberts, 'a balancing act between maintaining the morale at home and maintaining the strength and morale of the army'.

And so the town, in its schools, private houses, hotels and hostels, housed all the key departments of the Ministry of Food. There were scientific advisors, food experts of every conceivable field, as well as secretaries galore.

Schoolchildren and locals could only gawp opened-mouthed when the train from London began to spill out what a local newspaper at the time described as 'aliens in an alien land of churches, chapels and pubs, [carrying] their brief cases and rolled umbrellas'. They arrived, said a resident, 'wearing their city suits, starched shirts, ties and Anthony Eden hats, with Brylcreemed hair'. Along with them came the fur-nishings that would be required to convert boarding-house sitting-rooms into offices, and school halls into secretarial hothouses. Trainloads of thick brown linoleum arrived at the station; so much of it, historian Graham Roberts reports that 'some of this stuff still remains to this day'.

Across the town of Colwyn Bay, and stretching out to sur-rounding villages like Rhos-On-Sea, the Ministry of Food's departments were rehoused from the Edwardian baroque splendour of Whitehall to the rather more quaint, hum-drum, and drab semis of this North Wales seaside town. From departments analysing numbers of ships needed to bring food across the Atlantic, to vast pools of typists, from cereal prod-uct divisions to animal feed logistics and personnel offices, the town was transformed almost overnight. There was the accommodation too, with men and woman separated, natu-rally, and offices and spaces set aside for eating and socialising.

Yet in spite of all this activity and disruption, these strangers with their social lives and their actual work, remained dis-creet, excepting the odd local newspaper report. As Roberts writes: 'Had Hitler bombed Colwyn Bay as comprehensively as he did Coventry, he would have created far more havoc. The British people could have faced starvation.'

The secrecy occurred by no mere chance. Orders were

given to civil servants, logistical staff and many others not to speak about the operation. And once settled in North Wales, information regarding the ministry and its efforts was strictly controlled.

It was a plan effected by the men and women stationed at the Colwyn Bay Hotel. This gothic, turreted building, designed by John Douglas, the Victorian architect of everything from churches to shops, housed the Ministry of Food's headquarters. The hotel, which overlooked the bay itself, contained not just senior ministry officials but officers of the Communication Division. Run by two men, John Jenner and Vic Groves, this department's job was to oversee the coding and decoding of every cable that arrived or left the ministry.

One room in the hotel was known as The Desk. Here, overseen by Jenner and Groves, six executive officers – who resided at St Enoch's Hotel, also on the sea front – sat poring over documents and referring to their government department code books. Every cable that arrived, from any corner of the world, be it about food purchases or shipping, would arrive coded. It would then be decoded and passed to the relevant department. Dispatching clerks ferried these messages around the town, from building to building, careering along the streets and avenues on bicycles. The telephone was not considered secure, nor was it reliable, so uniformed messengers, with small crowns on their lapels, were charged with ferrying round communications. This was disturbing enough during the day for the genteel residents of the town, but the messengers were also busy at night, as cables arrived from Canada and the United States. These needed dispatching and officers would often have to work until the early hours decoding the long messages, some up to 20,000 words in length, so they could be distributed by the morning.

The cyclists were organised into groups led by a 'Supervisory Messenger', one of them a local, John Hughes, who, too old to join the army, was provided with a uniform, a group of young men and some motorbikes. While less urgent missives could be carried on a bicycle, the motorbikes were for messages that needed transferring with speed.

The other communications hub was on the second floor of 5 Penrhyn Buildings, above Bruce's Fruit and Veg shop. Behind the gracefully curved façade of the neo-Georgian block, built in the thirties, was stationed a sound-proofed room, a clandestine news centre; this was a secret BBC studio, linked to transmitters across Britain, which could be operated with others across the country in the event of a German invasion successfully taking over the BBC's London HQ.

But while great efforts were made to maintain operational secrecy of all the communication hubs, there was another government machine whose very *raison d'être* was conceal-ment and security. For also in the town – on the corner of Kenelm Road and Llanerch Road East to be precise – was MI5. The North Wales branch of the British Secret Service was housed in the modestly rambling confines of the Melfort Hotel, its postal address being 'Post Office Box 55, Colwyn Bay'.

The office was run by a Captain Finney, who lodged at a house nearby. The property was requisitioned from owners Mr and Mrs J. M. Clay-Beckitt, who were given just twenty-four hours to vacate. Captain Finney had little sympathy for anyone who got in the way of his plans to find office or living space for his colleagues. 'If I cannot get accommodation for the agents by fair means I shall use foul methods,' he was reported as saying.

As well as responsibilities to the Ministry of Food, they needed to ensure there were no spies in their midst. But MI5 was also there as part of Plan Hegira. This was a top-secret scheme in which double agents would be quickly evacuated from London in the event of an impending German invasion and successful capture of the city. These agents could not be allowed to fall into enemy hands, so rather than shoot them – and their families – they would be given sanctuary in Colwyn Bay. Lists were drawn up of the key agents and Captain Finney earmarked where he could accommodate them. The National Archives records the names of these double agents: there was Snow and Celery, Dragonfly, Gander and Summer, along with Careless, Rainbow and Gelatine. And in 1941, under real threat of invasion, Captain Finney had them all whisked out of London.

Doubtless as Gander and his German wife and children stood at the bar of the White Lion Pub, just outside Colwyn Bay in the village of Llanelian yn Rhos, they might have been joined by a besuited civil servant, a girl from the typing pool, a motorcycle messenger and, perhaps, a sixty-something expert in livestock shipping. None of them would have been able to discuss what it was they were actually doing there, and this mismatch of people – this bizarre immigra-tion – with their cheerily inane remarks about the weather, must have struck any remaining locals of North Wales as extremely curious.

7

Autumn 1940

After a summer of acclimatising to Winston Churchill's style of government, Woolton concluded in his diary – in September 1940, at the height of the Battle of Britain, the air war against the German Luftwaffe raging in the skies above southern England – that the Prime Minister's 'whole interest is in war organisation – hence his lack of interest in the Ministry of Food. Churchill is not really interested, in spite of his long experience, in any of the civil or social problems.'

He also opined generally on politicians, writing: 'I don't think there's much room in the political world for a person who just takes pleasure in getting a job done. That's why so many of them make speeches about things they are going to do, and the press encourages them, because it's news.'

On 13 November 1940, he had lunch with Lord Kemsley – owner of a newspaper empire that included the *Sunday Times* and the *Daily Sketch*. The pair were chatting about Woolton's senior government colleagues. 'How many members of the Cabinet would you employ at your firm, Lewis's?' asked Kemsley. 'At the most two,' Woolton replied, 'and one for only a short time.'

Woolton appeared to fight a constant battle to get his patch of homeland sustenance onto the agenda; so often, in particular, having to make his case to get his hands on ships to import food – because too often they were commandeered by his colleagues to use as transport for troops.

Woolton also wrote, on 30 September, that 'the PM and senior politicians aren't thinking seriously about post-war problems.' Given the precariousness of Britain's fate at that time, alone in the world against a Nazi-controlled Europe, perhaps that's not surprising.

Meanwhile his relationship with Sir Henry French continued to improve. What was once consternation at how Woolton conducted himself in taxing meetings was turned into admiration. On 8 October Woolton met a Canadian delegation to discuss, as he put it, 'how best they could help us by producing food that we could import from them'.

Prior to the meeting he had met Canadian Major-General Andrew McNaughton, at lunch, during which the soldier had outlined his post-war scenario. 'The German nation must be severely punished,' he told Woolton. 'His "peace" proposal,' wrote Woolton, 'was the decimation of the German population.'

His afternoon meeting was with James Gardiner, the Canadian Minister for Agriculture and Defence; a man, apparently – wrote Woolton – regarded as the future Prime

Minister of Canada. 'He's an entirely undistinguished-looking little man,' he mused. Woolton was a little cross to discover that 'the object of his coming was to enable him to sell so much wheat forward for years to Great Britain that he would be able to increase the amount of money that the Canadians were paying to farmers.'

'Canadian farmers did so well in the last war,' said Gardiner. 'Prices rose so high that they are now becoming a little concerned at the fact that prices are not rising now.'

This, wrote Woolton, was a rather 'naïve' remark. 'Achieving price rises for Canadian farmers is not the object of the war,' barked Woolton witheringly. 'But we will do what we can to help in getting bacon from them.'

However the subject on the table was not bacon but wheat and there was, wrote Woolton, 'a great flurry going on among the civil servants who were sitting behind me'.

Woolton then explained that not only was he not interested in propping up the price of Canadian wheat, but that the price was too high. If Canada could not sell it at the price he was prepared to offer, then he wouldn't buy their bacon either. Of course he needed the bacon, but decided that a little brinkmanship with this 'undistinguished-looking little man' wouldn't do any harm.

The discussion was, he later thought, 'amusing' because he could sense the officials going 'hot and cold'. 'It is customary for ministers to read carefully prepared briefs: I had read the briefs, but had not brought them with me and was conducting the negotiations in my own way.'

'I was told afterwards that the Treasury officials could scarcely contain their horror,' wrote Woolton; one official passed a note to Sir Henry French that simply read: 'Pull your man up.'

Sir Henry scribbled a note back which read, 'Don't worry. It will come out all right.'

Woolton added: 'Apparently I caused some disturbance to the Colonial Office, the Board of Trade and the Treasury, and it speaks well for French when he said afterwards that he thought I had dropped a number of bricks, and was glad of it.'

Twelve days later Woolton met with Gardiner again and he offered to buy all of their surplus production of bacon – 190,000 tons a year at a price of £80 a ton.

'I was almost ashamed of offering the price – it was so low,' he wrote in his diary, 'but we were very short of dollars.' Woolton also offered to buy 124 million bushels of wheat at $85 dollars. Gardiner said he wanted $90, 'to keep his farmers happy,' wrote Woolton, adding: 'I am getting tired of trying to make farmers happy: it seems to me that the higher the price the more they grumble – a bit like spoiled children.' Then he added with a snigger, 'Anyhow, if they accept the bacon price they will really have something to grumble about.'

A few days later a message came back from the Canadians. They agreed to Woolton's price for their wheat and he, happily, bought their bacon.

Sir Henry was impressed. The ministry lifer appeared to be getting the hang of his maverick minister. But Woolton's antics continued to astonish others. The following morning, 9 October, he was running late for a Cabinet meeting and, as he wrote, 'caused a minor sensation'. His chauffeur was nowhere to be found but Woolton decided to go down to the front door and wait for him there. As he stepped out onto the street, a mail van drew up. 'I immediately hopped in,' he wrote, 'told the driver who I was, and asked him to take me to Downing Street.'

Arriving at the Prime Minister's front door he thanked the driver, noticing 'an expression of amazement on the face of the policeman at No 10 at the sight of a Minister of the Crown descending from a mail van'.

While Woolton was able to swat tiresome Canadians or civil servants, there was nothing he could do about Nazi Germany's campaign of bombing London. It started in earnest on 7 September 1940, and a month later the bombs came very close to Lord Woolton's home in Whitehall Court.

On 13 October, just a few days after a bomb had been dropped on the War Office, right in front of Whitehall Court, he recorded 'the worst night of bombing that we have experienced'. The following evening, incendiary bombs had dropped on the actual building and several fires had started; the night after a huge bomb on the War Office shook Whitehall Court 'and us', wrote Woolton, 'and broke nearly all the windows and covered the place with soot, and generally gave us rather a stirring up'. Maude wrote of the incident, 'Suddenly the place shook, we thought we've got a bomb on us,' she wrote. In fact it had hit a neighbouring building. 'The only effect in our flat was that clouds of soot covered everything in the sitting room. I spent the whole of the morning with Pat, the maid, in trying to restore a modicum of cleanliness.' The bomb had fallen some ten yards away from their building, but fortunately the Wooltons were on the second floor. But it was, Woolton wrote, 'very disturbing.'

The German Luftwaffe continued to bomb London through the winter and on into the early summer months of 1941.

As Maud recorded, the couple would vacate their London bedroom during German attacks. 'Since the raids have begun we have been sleeping on cushions in our little hall,' she wrote on 12 October 1940. 'We sleep fully dressed, to be ready to get out in an emergency. When the "all clear" goes we undress, and go to bed. Bed does feel nice then.'

Some days later Woolton – as he recorded later in a memoir he wrote in honour of his late wife – was dining with Churchill at Number 10; guests included the King. 'A very bad air raid started and we were all sent to shelters in the PM's basement,' Woolton recorded.

'There was one small shelter and the King went there with the PM who invited me to join them and a secretary who was there to give us a running commentary relayed from the Air Ministry Roof. Quite out of the blue Churchill suddenly said, "Woolton where is your wife?" I said I had left her in the flat and I hoped she was still there.'

The King pondered on this then said: 'Won't she have gone to your air raid shelter?'

'We don't have one,' replied Woolton, who noted that the King and Churchill were 'horrified' by this answer.

'So what do you do in these raids?' asked the King.

'We stay comfortably in our flat and trust to luck,' replied Woolton.

Churchill suggested to the King that Woolton be allowed access to one of the shelters available to VIPs.

'Certainly,' replied the King. 'Woolton, you and your wife

will go to a fortress [one such secure place]. Prime Minister, you will be good enough to see that such accommodation is prepared tomorrow.'

Woolton was embarrassed that his wife's stoic resolution to stay in their flat, while she could have been in the safety of their house by Lake Windermere, seemed to be reflecting on him as a man who wasn't concerned about his wife's safety.

'It was obvious my stock as a husband was in their eyes at zero,' he wrote. 'The atmosphere was strained until I said: "I am grateful to your Majesty for your consideration of my wife – but, Sire, when your ancestors sent their ministers to fortresses they scarcely came out."' The group laughed and then listened as they received an update on the current bombing raid.

When Woolton got home later he found his wife filling a bath full of water and connecting it to a hand pump to put out a small fire in one corner of the flat.

Maud was less than thrilled at the idea of going to an official 'fortress'. 'Bombs have broken water mains and I've heard of people being drowned,' she protested. Privately, Woolton reflected that her real objection was that 'she had scruples about accepting a protection which others couldn't have.'

But while Maud refused to accept the King's offer, she did have another request. 'Fred,' she said, 'I'd like you to buy me a small revolver which I can carry in my handbag. I beg you not to refuse. I don't suppose I will ever need to use it because I am sure we will win the war. But I know that the Germans have a list of people who will be shot as soon as they are captured and you are on that list – and very near to Churchill who is number one.'

Maud, wrote Woolton, 'was very determined that neither she nor her children should fall into the hands of the
Germans'.

'If you are captured I will shoot all three of us,' she said to
her startled husband.

Woolton reassured her that they would win the war and
none of these measures would be necessary. To his great relief
the matter was dropped and Maud never mentioned her need
for a revolver again.

Days later and there was more bombing; the House of
Commons was hit and, as Woolton recorded: 'Big Ben was
considerably scarred – but still working in spite of a very dirty
face.' His car manoeuvred around the wreckage en route to
Smithfield Market to check on rumours that supplies of meat
there had been hit. The rumours were true. 'On Wednesday
morning meat was still burning,' he recorded miserably. 'A
great waste in these times when the ration is so small.'

And while the ministry was apparently safe in Colwyn
Bay, its local food bureaus were not so protected.

In November 1940 Woolton's London staff took him on
a tour of south-east London to check on the operations of
a local food office; the idea was to return feeling reassured
about the running of this complicated operation. But when
they reached Battersea there wasn't an office to look at.

'In Battersea, the town hall, which contained the food
office and all the records, had just been made into a mass
of twisted iron,' he wrote, having picked his way over the
smoking wreckage of the previous night's bombing raid. He
refused to be driven back to Portman Square, curious to see
the wider area. It was a grim hour. 'We motored through

miles of streets in all of which windows were broken, doors blown off, and there were huge areas in which houses had been completely wrecked,' he noted.

Every survivor of the bombing would be hungry, each would need the reassurance of decent food. The heavy bombing raids, particularly over London, had left thousands of people sitting in air raid shelters and getting hungry. While he tried to open feeding centres near such shelters – and encouraged anyone, Dunkirk-style, to take their mobile canteens or coffee stalls to areas in need – he also utilised a 'Food Train' for the London Underground.

On 14 November 1940, the first such tube train ran through the London Underground, stopping to feed people sheltering on the station platforms. The train then ran, during periods of intense bombing, between seven and nine o'clock in the evenings and five-thirty and seven in the morning.

He then turned his attention to the people who, despite being bombed, were reluctant to leave their homes. In the main, wrote Woolton, they were elderly women. To such streets he sent field kitchens, often just portable stoves – braziers – on which soup could be cooked.

And he then went a step further. Spotting a need to boost morale to those returning to their bombed homes once it was safe to do so, he planned a mission of convoys which would be a combined ambulance and food service. There would be 'food supplies, kitchens, and everything that would produce the hot drinks and food that shocked people needed'.

The service would need funding and there was precious

little budget in his department, although he knew he could count on one particular individual to fund a small part of the outfit.

It was the morning of 20 December 1940 when, sitting in his office pondering what was then 'an ill-formed idea in my head as to how to meet this need', he realised that his next appointment was with one Mr Kruger of the British War Relief Society of America. While he had complained much about the lack of official help for Britain from the United States, this private organisation, which provided non-military aid, was a lifeline to him. Kruger, who represented a cohort of wealthy and socially ambitious Americans, was fishing for ways to assist Woolton; so the timing was perfect.

'I have an idea for which I need your help,' he told Kruger. He then outlined his plan for the convoys and listed what each one would need, having sketched it out on paper that morning.

'Each unit would consist of a mobile water-tanker that can carry up to 350 gallons, there would be two lorries each containing 6,000 meals, two kitchen lorries with soup boilers and fuel, three mobile canteens and five motor-cyclists who will liaise between the area in need and the local authority.'

Woolton explained that the convoys would be mostly staffed by women and that the complete fleet would consist of 144 vehicles.

'I'd like you to consider helping to fund the fleet,' Woolton said to Kruger. Kruger nodded with interest. Woolton continued, in a conspiratorial tone: 'I should add that there is one other individual who has pledged to personally fund eight of those vehicles.' Kruger looked on intently. 'And I should say that it might be indiscreet of me to mention who she might be.'

Woolton paused and his eyes flicked clearly to a framed picture on his desk of himself with Her Majesty the Queen.

Kruger understood exactly and, without hesitation, said with considerable zeal: 'Lord Woolton, we will finance the whole lot.' His compatriots back home would relish the association.

That afternoon Woolton went to Buckingham Palace, where he was due to have an audience with the King; it was a regular catch-up (the King, he wrote, 'sent for me from time to time to hear how the food arrangements were going'), and a chance to complete the deal. He mentioned his idea, adding that this convoy might be called the 'Queen's Messengers', because, he explained, 'the women who will take charge of these convoys will indeed be messengers of mercy.'

According to Woolton: 'The King at once jumped up and said: "Come and ask her."' Maud also, having listened to her husband's report of the encounter, referred to the occasion in her diary. '"Let's go along to see the Queen,"' she reported the King as saying, continuing, 'and the three of them stood in front of the fire and chatted for about ten minutes – all very informal. She is a delightful woman and the country loves her.'

Woolton added that they talked 'in a quite domestic way'. 'Food and kindliness indicate the things that Your Majesty means to the people of this country – practical sympathy,' he told her. 'The vast majority of the people think of you as a person who would speak the kindly word, and, if it fell within your power, would take the cup of soup to the needy person.'

The Queen, wrote Woolton, 'was quite taken aback and said, "Do you really think that people think of me like that, because it is so much what I want them to think. It's what I try to be."'

According to Maud, 'When Fred told her how very, *very* much her presence in bombed areas helped people – she clasped her hands together and, with tears in her eyes, said: "Oh. Do you *really* think so? I do hope it does." She is very humble indeed.' Woolton added: 'It was really quite touching, because there was so much depth in it and such obvious sincerity.'

Woolton and his wife saw the King and Queen on many occasions, and Maud would always relay their meetings with joy in her diary. On 11 October 1940, after Woolton had joined the couple on a tour of some of the Communal Feeding Centres, Maud wrote: 'They are so intelligent and keen. The Queen too is so lovely and interested in everything. The appreciation of the women in the centres was delightful. They were so touched by their Majesties' interest, and they crowded round the carriage when they left one centre – one woman calling out "It is good of you to come." The Queen nearly cried, because most of these women had been bombed out of their houses. When F came home at night, six hours afterwards, he was still thrilled by the success of the morning. "They do do their stuff [he said]".'

The Queen, in due course, paid personally for eight of the convoy vehicles and Kruger's outfit funded the other 136. 'The message which I would entrust to these convoys will not be one of encouragement,' the Queen said, when officially launching the fleet, 'for courage is never lacking in the people of this country. It will rather be one of true sympathy and loving kindness.'

The trucks, vans, mobile kitchens and motor-cycles were all emblazoned with the words: 'QUEEN'S MESSENGERS CONVOY' and Woolton had them strategically placed around the country, in his words, 'ready to set off to whatever town in their sections had been visited by the German bombers'. The first convoy went into action in Coventry and over three days fed 12,000 people. These mobile canteens were manned by the members of the Women's Voluntary Service (an organisation established in 1938 by Home Secretary Sir Samuel Hoare which had 165,000 members by the start of the war, and whose unpaid women ran the rest centres that provided washing facilities and clothes to those bombed out of their homes). A leading figure of the WVS was Pearl Hyde, whose vans often appeared in the streets of Coventry while bombing raids were still in progress. 'You know you feel such a fool standing there in a crater holding a mug of tea,' she later said, 'until a man says "it washed the blood and dust out of my mouth" and you know you have done something useful.'

The new Queen's Messengers convoys would usually enter an area as soon as the 'All Clear' was given, which still put them in considerable danger as no one knew how long an 'All Clear' would last. Woolton recognised this by asking that vehicles had their 'battle honours' inscribed on the side. Chevrons were painted on, similar to those worn by soldiers in the First World War, and each time a convoy went into action its record was marked. The convoys became famous, were cheered on as they ploughed and picked their way to recently bombed areas.

Lord Woolton was gratified at a scheme that was feeding the needy, satisfied his love of an entrepreneurial deal, stirred the hearts of the nation and fostered his personal relationship with the King and Queen.

Private American funding for the Queen's Messengers was, as far as Woolton was concerned, a rare example of actual practical help from the United States.

'American sympathy is an amazing thing: newspapers, broadcasts, American conversations, are all full of it,' he confided to his diary on 14 October 1940, 'but they still won't allow their ships to come into England carrying either food or munitions, and [what] they still don't give is one dollar's worth of goods unless we pay cash for them.'

That day he had been invited to join a group of high-powered American businessmen. Towards the end of lunch, it was mooted that he should say a few words. Casting around the room, well briefed by his team, he was well aware that there were, among the tables, a couple of contenders for future President. As he stood up, he thanked this prestigious group of men for the warm support they had given vocally for Britain. They were murmurs of approval. But, the minister concluded, before sitting down, 'what we need is ships, not sympathy.'

This was not the genial, diplomatic schmooze the Americans had expected and they were clearly surprised and taken aback; Woolton left the lunch with that very slight spring in his step he always felt from having lobbed a few well-targeted missiles at a group of people whose vested interests did not coincide with his own.

A month later Woolton, with his wife, were guests at a lunch at the Carlton Club on London's St James' Street. Woolton was a little uneasy at first, sitting between two well-known society hostesses, Dame Margaret Greville and Lady Simon. Aware of the snobbery that abounded in such echelons, he didn't for a moment doubt that some of those at the table were a little sniffy at this businessman, promoted latterly to the peerage. He 'had very much the feeling of being the unknown factor being submitted to close scrutiny', he wrote privately.

His dining companions spent most of the lunch flattering him. 'You are doing magnificently,' said Dame Margaret, 'really, everything you are doing is so perfect.' Lady Simon was equally effusive: 'The public has the greatest reason to be grateful to you and I wouldn't think that anyone could possibly have any reason to criticise you in any way,' she gushed. 'I thought that was very charming,' wrote Woolton, 'but I didn't believe a word of it.'

So Woolton merely nodded in acknowledgement as another guest, Mr Henshall, First Secretary of the American Embassy, added some platitudes of his own. 'You are indeed doing a fantastic job, Lord Woolton, and I should add that I sympathise considerably with the extremely difficult circumstances in which you and your government are operating,' he ventured.

Woolton quickly ascertained who he was and decided it was a perfect moment to trot out his new favourite line when encountering Americans: 'Thank you for your kind words Mr Henshall,' he said. 'But we want ships, not sympathy, from the United States of America. And until you send us some ships your sympathy is not much use.'

History does not record if the smart ladies and others around the luncheon table recoiled nervously, a few moments of awkward silence striking their end of the table at this lapse in good manners. Perhaps Lord Woolton caught the eye of his ever-supporting and beloved wife a few places away, while the ladies muttered to themselves about the stunning vulgarity of this upstart man from the ministry. Doubtless they had heard of how he was argumentative in Cabinet, and less than respectful of the Prime Minister.

But back at Whitehall Court that night, as he wrote his diary, Woolton was resolute. His talk at lunch was, he admitted with a favourite expression, 'quite bald'. But, he insisted, 'I think there's a great danger of the Americans getting carried away in the belief that all these easy conversations of theirs about "Help for Britain" is what matters, and it isn't. It's help we want, not conversation, and it's precious little we're getting.'

There was precious little help from the Irish either, it seemed. Their policy of neutrality remained intact during the duration of the Second World War. Some historians, notably Max Hastings in *All Hell Let Loose,* believe that the then Irish Prime Minister Eamon de Valera had a 'fanatical loathing ... of his British neighbours'; whatever the truth of Ireland's stand, even if it appeared to be supported by the vast majority of Irish people, it did not impress Woolton. He posited that Ireland's position had led to a number of shipping losses. German U-boats were able to lurk around the ports of the west coast of Ireland, for example, and attack passing Allied ships. 'They have always been trying to get something from us and they have never given anything,' he grumbled in his diary on 12 December 1940. He recorded his argument made to Cabinet: 'Mr de Valera might keep his neutrality if he wanted to, but if we are losing ships as a consequence there is no reason why we should bother to feed the people of Eire [Ireland] at the cost of the people of the United Kingdom.'

The government then agreed that the UK would restrict the help it gave in securing imports to Ireland. While they would not limit in any way imports to Ireland occurring on their own account, or to Ireland's ships joining Allied convoys, Woolton wrote that: 'we shall have to reduce the amount of goods imported into Eire according to our necessities.' It was harsh, but fair, he believed. 'This, I think, means that Eire will begin to know the meaning of neutrality and doubt the wisdom of keeping German and Italian ambassadors in Dublin.'

In those dark days of war, Lord Woolton had to dig deep to find his rugged reserve. He was reminded particularly of a book he used to read to his children. Written by General Jack Seely – later 1st Baron Mottistone – who led a famous (and possibly the last) great cavalry charge on his horse Warrior at the Battle of Moreuil Wood by the banks of the Arve River in France in 1918, it related his tales of adventure on 'land, sea and air'. He would sit at twilight reading the book aloud and willing his children to sleep with these tales of derring-do, out of which General Jack always emerged glorious and alive. They were stories of bravery – although, according to one critic, not always factually reliable. But they bore the title of *Fear and Be Slain*. As Woolton considered the mammoth task in front of him, to both administer the ration and distribute food, he took comfort from the romanticism of these tales. 'I knew that feeding the nation against the background of submarine warfare and aerial bombardment was so fraught with dangers, that nothing but boldness could succeed; both for the country and for me in my task,' he confided. 'Faint hearts are no use in government office.'

8

The Battle of the Atlantic

By the winter of 1940 Britain's providers were in a cascade of stress. Hungry children expected of their mothers, husbands of their wives, to put food on the table in the evening. Those women – and let's face it, it was mostly women – relied on their local butcher, the grocer, or some ingenuity that enabled them to scrounge a rabbit or purloin some roadkill.

Those shopkeepers depended on their local food office, who in turn relied on a variety of suppliers. Wholesalers, particularly those waiting on arrivals of items like bacon or cheese or sugar, relied on the merchant seamen who might be bringing the goods in after a perilous trip across the Atlantic. Those ships then depended on their government and the armed forces to defend them. Whatever Lord Woolton could do both to actually get hold of shipping – which involved some serious tussles in Cabinet – and then have them defended, he, in turn, trusted on a bit of luck.

But, by December, there was considerable worry among senior figures in government. Maud noted her conversations with Woolton in her diary: 'Troubles are looming in the food situation,' she confided to her diary. 'We have had very heavy losses of ships,' she continued, 'some including food ones, by submarines and air attack, many ships have been taken off to become troop ships to take men and materials out to the Mediterranean, and quite an appreciable amount of food has been destroyed by air blitz. One of the major stores full of meat has been destroyed and some ships in harbour have been sunk. All this at the beginning of Christmas is hard.'

As the festive season approached, Woolton was enduring a typical week: haggling, cajoling, persuading, making speeches and broadcasts, travelling, attending Cabinet meetings and tentatively eating his way through working lunches and diplomatic dinners. Sat in his Portman Square office on the Friday afternoon, he wondered if he would be able to fend off the demands of his civil servants before they clocked off and a more peaceful weekend might ensue. At around 3 p.m., though, one of his staff entered his office with a grave look on his face; indeed to Woolton grave expressions from some of his staff never seemed far off. Woolton's thoughts were, as ever, to ponder how bad the news was and how quickly he would be able to resolve things. The man carried a note detailing a signal just received from the Admiralty, the body that commanded the Royal Navy. It was not a cheering message. Neither was the second note, nor the subsequent three.

'During the course of two hours that Friday afternoon,' wrote Woolton, 'I received five separate signals from the Admiralty reporting that food ships had been sunk on the Atlantic route.' The sinkings threatened a major British institution: breakfast.

'By some extraordinary misfortune, these five ships were largely stocked with bacon. It was just the luck, or ill-luck, of war,' he wrote. It was never helpful to get this type of news on a Friday, as Woolton liked to think that by the end of each week he would honour the ration. His deal with the British public – that they would abide by the ration and eschew the black market – would collapse if he didn't fulfil his end of the bargain.

So Woolton called in his staff and gave them his usual pep talk. 'We will not fail in the pledge given to the public that the ration will always be honoured,' he said, before adding this time: 'So we need to find some bacon.'

Fortunately such was the meticulous planning of his department over in Colwyn Bay, that his staff identified several warehouses near Liverpool that were housing some large stocks of bacon due to be sent to Lancashire in a few weeks time. Woolton worked out that there was just enough there that, added to the one remaining ship that had not been sunk, he could distribute bacon to the rest of the country.

The only thing was that the bacon needed to be on the counters of the nation's butchers by the morning, as families didn't have the means to store foods in the way we do now. Almost no one had access to domestic refrigeration; by 1948, only 2 per cent of British homes owned a fridge. 'As the one solitary ship that had bacon on board came in to the port of Liverpool, a special squad of men was charged to bring off the bacon with all speed, load it onto lorries and send it straight off into distribution,' recalled Woolton. The system then clicked into place as smaller vans then ferried the rashers out across the country and into the towns and cities. Making such last-minute arrangements often seems tricky enough in peacetime; so it was no mean feat to accomplish it in wartime.

In the early hours of Saturday morning, as the likes of Peter Jennings – the family-run butcher in Twyford (*see* Epilogue) – finished his porridge and thought about firing up the boiler and opening the shutters on the shop, a van from Smithfield market would have pulled up carrying the usual day's approved meat stock. There was the bacon, wrapped in paper. Later in the morning, local housewives would queue up to buy their few rashers to sate the hungry appetites of their family. Little would they know of the midnight drama that only just saved the day.

'We honoured the ration,' mused Woolton that day, whose officials would have been working feverishly to restock the emptying warehouses at the very moment the bacon was being sent out, 'but it was a near thing.'

It would be one of many near things as the war progressed. Both Britain and Germany wanted to be sure that they had learned the lessons of the previous global conflict. As the historian Richard Tames said with regard to the First World War: 'the British Government had given no serious consideration to food policy until the prospect of virtual famine suddenly manifested itself like some malevolent spectre.' Likewise, the scarcity of food that was manifested across Germany during the First World War was cited by many as a major reason for that country's subsequent collapse and defeat.

Like Britain, Germany wanted to secure its own food supplies and deny its enemy's; in addition to competing with Britain to buy food from neutral countries – by whatever devious means possible – Adolf Hitler also vowed to sink as many supply ships to Britain as he could. Britain's proud island status could turn out to be a marvellous weakness, as its food security was remarkably low and every time a submarine sank a ship bearing eggs or grain, Hitler would take another confident stride towards victory.

His order, that German submarines patrolling the world's major trade routes should attack enemy ships without warning, came the moment German troops invaded Poland.

There were fifty-seven submarines under the control of Admiral Karl Dönitz, head of U-boats for the German navy, and his most successful year was 1940. With the help of planes and mines, and the fact that ships had limited radar and submarine-detection technology, the Royal Navy sailed across large areas of sea without any protection at all.

The U-boats were based at a number of French-held ports and their crews returned during what was called 'The Happy Time' triumphant, to be garlanded with flowers and handed champagne for the benefit of German film crews and the beneficial propaganda that would ensue at cinemas across Germany. Meanwhile, survivors who made it back to Britain arrived with horror stories of uncontrollable fires, vessels sinking in the dark, bloodied men and bodies, floating metal and wood, all swilling together in oil-stained seas.

In 1940 some 6,000 British, Indian and African seamen

lost their lives; the death toll between 1939 and 1945 on the Atlantic Ocean of Allied merchant seaman and navy being around 36,000 and 36,200 respectively. As German U-boats became more effective, so the shipping stock became perilously low. Sinkings in 1940 reached 1.8 million tons, and by the middle of the following year, Britain was losing ships three times faster than they were being built.

But Allied attacks on German vessels proved a heavier human cost. Of the 40,000 German officers and men who served in U-boats, just 7,000 came home. The historian David Fairbank White commented that the casualty rate for German U-boat service was 'the highest for any military unit since the time of the Romans'.

For Britain, in addition to submarine attacks on food convoys, 'Air raids added vastly to our troubles,' said Woolton. At the start of the war cold storage facilities had been near all the ports and the Germans, sensibly on their part, had focused on bombing them. 'It made serious in-roads into our refrigerated stocks of meat,' Woolton noted. And so, soon after he took office, he persuaded the Treasury to give his ministry the funds to build a number of cold stores in safer parts of the country and in secrecy. Some were built underground and grain stores were similarly located at suitably inaccessible locations.

Woolton, visiting one such facility during the war, joked to a ministry official that: 'it may well be that people looking at these buildings in a few years' time will wonder why anybody could have been so foolish as to build extensive storages in such inaccessible places and away from the points of either arrival or consumption.'

Once these more secure buildings were constructed, all Woolton had to do was fill them with food. But with shipping being so well targeted, he began to get a little paranoid. 'During this period [the winter of 1940] the shipping position became so dangerous to our food supplies that I created in the Ministry of Food a department which checked the time in port of every ship that carried food,' he wrote.

It meant that if there was any delay in arriving and unloading, an inquiry would be made to the port authorities as to what had happened.

Woolton's food had to travel vast distances over many perilous seas. The Ministry of Food produced a map revealing the miles that foodstuffs had to travel, to drive the point home to householders. It revealed the sardines from Spain had travelled 1,000 miles to the British market – and, in terms of food miles, this was short. The bacon, wheat, eggs, salmon, milk products and dried fruits from America had to travel at least 2,700 miles. Onions were also being imported from the Middle East, some 5,000 miles distant. Coffee and palm oil had a mammoth 9,000 miles trip to Britain while rice, tea, wheat, meat, butter and cheese from the Antipodes were travelling in excess of 11,000 miles.

'In every kitchen there are ways of making these foods go further,' the ministry implored. 'Remember that little economies are multiplied by every home in the land. In this way British housewives can lighten the heavy load of our Merchant Navy.'

For his part, Woolton was in no doubt about 'the unfailing and valorous efforts of the men of the Merchant Navy'. Those who died met a terrible end. For them, wrote Fairbank

White, 'there are no headstones, no markers, no monuments'. Ships would plunge to the bottom of the Atlantic, disappearing often with all hands in a matter of seconds. Others would have perished in that vast, lonely and desolate sea, dying from exposure or starvation in lifeboats or rafts devoid of shelter.

The crews of the cargo ships that made the dangerous journey across that immense sea lived through days and nights of unimaginable stress. One such ship was the *Leise Maersk*, a Copenhagen built vessel completed in 1921. It was 100 metres long, had a diesel engine capable of 10.5 knots and weighed 3,136 tons.

In November 1940, the ship was crossing the Atlantic carrying 4,500 tons of grain and bound for Sharpness, the English port in Gloucestershire on the River Severn.

The shipment had been arranged in part by a group of ladies who sat at the desks and tables in the dining room of the Edelweiss Hotel on Lawson Road in Colwyn Bay; this was the Ministry of Food's bread division. The staff here liaised with the cereal products division run by a Mr Farquherson who, with his team of typists, was located at the Mount Stewart Hotel on the seafront of the town. The ladies in his department had produced a prolific list, hammered out on ancient typing machines, of every flour mill and bakery in Britain. There was considerable pressure from the top to maintain the supply of flour, as Woolton had long insisted that bread should never be rationed. So the departments liaised, hoping desperately they wouldn't fail the minister.

'I was determined to keep free from all rationing, certain food stuffs, notably bread and potatoes, which were energy-giving fillers,' he had said. It meant fending off a great deal of pressure to add it to the ration. To placate a variety of people in his ministry, and around the Cabinet table, he had even gone so far as drafting a bread-rationing scheme – yet he firmly believed the public would not wear it. It would be a ration too far. He said as much to the Prime Minister: 'If the Cabinet feels it necessary to adopt it,' he told Churchill one day, 'then I will not take the responsibility of operating it.' It was a precarious position for the Minister of Food to take, so Woolton had to ensure that it never came to that.

In his favour, he noted, 'there was plenty of wheat in the world; the only question was whether we could get enough ships to bring it.'

It took an average of 16oz of wheat to make a pound of flour, about the right amount to bake a modest loaf. There are 32,000oz of wheat in a ton which meant that, theoretically, the cargo of the *Leise Maersk* could be turned into 9 million loaves of bread.

So quite a few people were hoping it would make it to Sharpness.

On Friday 22 November, the crew of the ship did not have loaves of bread on their minds. They had a vessel to steer and, with hope in their hearts, an end was in sight – in mind if not in vision. There was a wind blowing, the sky was blue and clear to the horizon and the master and crew, numbering twenty-four in total, were not alone. The *Leise Maersk* was part of a large convoy of ships. There were thirty-four in this procession – Convoy SC 11 – and it included the British *Fintra*, a Norwegian ship, the *Brask*, and a Greek vessel named *Panaghis*. Alongside the convoy was HMS *Enchantress*, commanded by Alan K. Scott-Moncrieff, senior officer escort. He was, by one account, 'pleased with the progress of his charges'.

The convoy was heading north-east and, entering the North Channel, finally reaching the last leg of the journey. England was not far off. On board the *Leise Maersk*, third mate H. E. E. Pedersen wondered if they'd almost made it.

Then, as afternoon turned to evening, the clouds gathered. The air turned chilly and rain began to fall. As it lashed the decks, the wilderness of the frothing sea seemed to stretch out to nothingness around them. Then weather conditions went from bad to full gale force. The ships heaved through the growing swell, waves seeping onto the decks, the spray whipping violently against the windows. As darkness fell, so visibility diminished. Worried that in the black of night ships would crash into one another, several made the decision to switch on their navigation lights. So now, across the peaks and troughs of the waves, through the steamed up and rain-lashed windows on the bridge, the crew could just spot the lights of other ships in the convoy.

But as the ships could now monitor each other's progress, so could an enemy lurking amid the stormy seas.

At just after 10.30 p.m., the convoy made an 18-degree left turn to port, cutting through the waves, the rains seemingly more violent. Then suddenly, from out of the distance, came the booming roar of an explosion.

At the back of the convoy, having fallen a little behind, a British freighter, *Bradfyne*, had been torpedoed. Within minutes the smoking hull slipped beneath the waves taking thirty-nine men down with her.

Having scored a first direct hit, U-100, commanded by Kapitänleutnant Joachim Schepke, considered its next target. Commander Scott-Moncrieff was still unaware of the loss of *Bradfyne* and continued to lead the convoy from the front. At 11.45 p.m. there was another explosion; this time, the British freighter *Justitia* was the target. Carrying steel and lumber, she was also well behind the main group of ships and, just six years old, she quickly sank with the loss of thirteen men.

Meanwhile, enjoying his triumph so far, Schepke had radioed to another German submarine, U-93, to say he had found a convoy. The German U-boats then bided their time until some four hours later when, at 3.35 a.m., a smaller Norwegian ship, the *Bruse*, further up the column, just four down from the leader, was struck by a torpedo, which cut through the boat's metal and exploded right in the engine room.

It was Schepke's third triumph of the night. Scott-Moncrieff, now alert to the drama, turned his *Enchantress* round and headed down the convoy. Another explosion thundered as the Norwegian cargo ship *Salonica* took a hit and sank; it was Schepke again. As historian Fairbank White commented: 'He was pumping torpedoes into SC 11 like a sniper with bolt-action reflexes.'

The fifth hit came at ten minutes past seven in the morning. Like all the crews aware of the lurking dangers, seeing with horror ships hit and then sunk, those on board the *Leise Maersk* could do nothing but will their ship on, hoping the next explosion would be someone else's tragic end.

Lying in his cabin, still sleepless in the approaching dawn, was Pedersen. His boat was in the second column on the convoy, third in the line. But suddenly his worst fears came true. There was a slamming shock of a blast. 'I heard a noise like the crack of a gun,' he recalled. Next, he 'felt a terrible shaking and I was thrown from my bunk'.

Pedersen clambered out of his cabin and as the boat began to list he charged up the passage only to find beams and debris from the explosion blocking his path. He finally made it onto the deck where, with other men who had been unable to lower the lifeboats, he jumped into the cold Atlantic water. With seven other men, he spotted a raft which they swam towards and clung to.

The swell of the sea seemed determined to tear the men from their lifeline and succeeded in taking the chief mate who slipped and drifted down into the deep waters.

Two Allied rescue planes sent to find survivors failed to spot the raft. Two ships also passed by, oblivious to the survivors' precarious position in the waves. But after eight hours adrift and marooned, a Dutch tug, *Thames*, found them and picked them out of the water.

While they huddled in the tug for warmth, Schepke was still eyeing up his prey. Now two destroyers in the convoy, *Ottawa* and *Skeena,* were hunting the U-boats, cruising through the waters, dropping depth charges – but Schepke's submarine and U-93 dodged them.

For the rest of the day, as the convoy plugged on, the tension almost unbearable among the crews, there was neither sight nor sound of the German U-boats. But at exactly 8.05 in the evening a huge explosion came from the back of the line. A Dutch ship, *Bussom*, had been torpedoed. This was Schepke's sixth hit. Scott-Moncrieff spotted the submarine and his *Enchantress* surged after it, launching depth charges. But a frustrating hour passed and he gave up his search.

There would be no more torpedoes. Schepke's U-boat disappeared in the darkness of the sea, having sunk six ships in 24 hours. His fellow marauder, U-93, also left but, for some reason, vacated the scene with a tally of zero.

At 4.30 in the morning the convoy was less than 100 miles from Ireland when it came across a final German surprise. The steam-propelled British built *Alma Dawson* hit a German mine. She soon disappeared beneath the waves.

As the convoy reached the Irish sea, the weather calmed and the surviving ships broke off from the line, heading for their prospective ports. Thirty-four ships had joined the convoy; twenty-seven were left. Just after two o'clock on November 25, the *Thames* tug came in to the waterfront of Campbeltown, a fishing port on the Kintyre peninsula, where Pedersen and the other six survivors stepped off the boat and onto dry land. Back there, somewhere in that desolate ocean, were seventeen of his mates, along with 4,500 tons of grain.

News of the sinking was met with grim resignation in Colwyn Bay. Come Monday morning, Lord Woolton looked at the map he had in his office in London. It showed where the main food commodities were being shipped from; if the wheat grain from Canada or the United States went down, at least he could look to India or Australia.

He picked up the telephone to speak with his team in Colwyn Bay. As ever, he was impressed by the contingency plans already put in place, but ships were sinking at an alarming rate. 'The country never realised,' he later reflected, 'how nearly we were brought to disaster by the submarine peril.' The public were protected from the news. Woolton, for example, noted in his diary on 3 December 1940 that, 'We had a Ministers' meeting at which, in great secrecy, Alexander [Earl Alexander of Hillsborough, First Lord of the Admiralty] told us of all the difficulties that the Navy were having in dealing with the U-boats and raiders.'

While his civil servants did what they could logistically, he knew that he needed to get his hands on more ships, and that meant a battle with the Cabinet.

But it was a cold and perfect storm that Woolton faced come the winter of 1940/41. Churchill had ordered that the nation's fastest ships be used to carry troops and arms to North and East Africa, as Italy's entrance into the war that summer had piled the pressure on the Allies as it launched attacks from its colonies in Libya and Ethiopia. With German U-boats effectively closing the Mediterranean to the Allies, Britain had to send troops the long way round, around the African Cape and up the Red Sea. The only ships that could do this quickly were those normally used to carry refrigerated goods such as dairy products and frozen meat. And while they were converted into troops carriers, fifty escort ships were commandeered from protecting North Atlantic cargo to protecting these troops.

On 28 November Woolton had to explain the situation to a very unhappy group of representatives from the fruit and vegetable trade, the Retail Fruit Trade Federation.

'Sinkings have been so heavy from submarines,' he began, '[while] the position is being made more acute by the fact that we have to feed an army in the near east, both with food and with ammunition. The Admiralty has taken the fast boats for this purpose, so that the convoy can move quickly.'

And so came the bad news for them. 'I'm afraid we have no more shipping space to import any more fruits into this country,' he said, 'and apricots will all have to go.' It was ruinous news for some of those who heard his message. He had rejected a petition signed by the federation – which represented 63,000 fruit and green grocery shops – urging Woolton to review his decision to ban the import of the likes of bananas.

He had a similarly uncomfortable meeting with the British Association of Refrigeration. 'Other than oranges there will be no bananas, apples or other fruits,' he announced, later writing: 'And a chilly crowd they were! I felt that their trade had got into their blood.'

But while he could, privately, muster a sense of humour about it, the lack of shipping was piling on the pressure. 'It's going to make my task very much harder,' he wrote.

'No More Imported Apricots, Apples or Grapes,' was the headline in the *Daily Herald* the next day on 29 November. Woolton had explained how 'the refrigerated ships are required for war work'. And in his message he hinted that he didn't want to be seen as the bad guy, he was just the messenger: 'To me has fallen the task of telling the people of this country that for the rest of the war they must change their habits,' he said. He spoke of how fresh fruits were 'a luxury that we shall have to give up'. He also hinted that there might also be no space 'for all the meat we have imported so freely and cheaply in the past'.

He painted a gloomy picture of what would become an

empty fruit bowl in homes across the country. 'Apples, apricots, grapes, bananas – these things that are not essential to the life of a nation at war – must disappear from our tables, while the ships that used to bring them are used to serve the necessities of our forces overseas.'

After the lunchtime announcement officials from his ministry handed out notes to the journalists in attendance so they could advise their readers about getting alternative nutrition. The *Daily Herald* duly obliged: 'To make up for the loss of vitamins contained in the list of banned foods, you should eat green vegetables, potatoes, carrots, tomatoes, wholemeal bread, and as much protective food – cheese, herring, salmon, liver – as you can get,' the paper advised.

Other papers also carried the story, helpfully using Woolton's line on luxury. It would appeal, he knew, to the people's sense of patriotism. The *Daily Telegraph*, for example, reported that the 'Nation Must Go Without Food Luxuries'. The *Manchester Guardian* in an editorial fleshed out the Woolton line, writing that 'It is pleasure rather than nourishment we shall be losing, for even the famous apple a day is called by dieticians an old wives' tale.'

On the morning of 30 November Woolton read a few more stories in the newspapers and breathed a sigh of relief that having lost his internal battle to get more shipping for food he appeared to be winning the PR battle. Then a secretary handed him a letter from Number 10 Downing Street: 'Why are we getting no bananas?' asked Churchill. Woolton was incredulous.

He bit his tongue and saved his ire for his diary that night. 'The trouble with this government is that it isn't one,' he complained. 'The Prime Minister is the War Lord, and is doing nothing to control or guide or influence the members of his government.'

He wasn't impressed either with the then Minister for Shipping, Ronald Cross (the maternal grandfather of this book's author). He was wasting good ships, he asserted. 'Cross', he said, 'tries to frighten everybody into believing that there isn't going to be enough shipping space to bring goods into this country, and at the same time he carries steel across the Atlantic in the roughest weather, so that it tears the ships to pieces.'

But he had no qualms about battling with Cross's ministry: 'I regard the feeding of the people of this nation as equal in importance to the arming of its soldiers and I have no intention of allowing anybody to take the ships that I regard as essential to maintaining the importing of food.'

At a meeting of the Cabinet he talked of his fears and recorded his words in his diary. 'The loss of our ships has damaged our programme for food distribution so badly that I doubt very much whether we can live up to the ration,' he stated at a full meeting of the Cabinet. 'The ration is already so small that, if we reduce it, it will be absurd. I need to know if my ministry will be able to have use of any further ships?' he asked. In his diary he records that this bald question was met with 'vague remarks about secret happenings in the War Cabinet that could not yet be talked about'.

This clearly irritated Woolton, excluded from the elite gathering of the War Cabinet and made to feel like a pesky outsider with his minor food gripes. 'I got very tired of it,' he commented, his code for being utterly furious. So he let rip at his Cabinet colleagues.

'If we are to send troops abroad in order to fight a war to maintain our existence, as a free country, then that's alright,' he told them. 'But my responsibility is to keep the people – who aren't going to fight, who are making weapons for the soldiers – alive. I can't see the sense of defending our country if the troops are going to come back to find its inhabitants dead of starvation.'

Those running the navy were also, he noted in his diary, acting without proper control. 'The Admiralty takes ships, without consultation with anybody, because it wants them for the near East; as a consequence food supplies have to be curtailed.'

In view of the shipping crisis, Woolton decided it would be a good idea if, in a speech about food he was due to make in Cardiff, he explained that extra hardships were on the horizon. His words were, obviously, aimed at being disseminated to the press.

So, out of courtesy, he wrote to Churchill. 'I will like to tell people that they are likely to have to go without things this winter in order that shipping space for things more vital to the prosecution of war than the import of non-essential foods, might be available for war purposes.' In spite of his private views, he was willing to embrace Cabinet collective responsibility and present reasons why there weren't enough ships for food.

Rather than thank him, Churchill sent a letter back which, recorded Woolton, was 'the sort of letter a headmaster might send to a fifth form boy, telling me I had all the powers and to ration'. It showed, he commented, 'that he had completely failed to understand anything about the food situation'.

red's father, Thomas, was the son of a
Lancashire pub landlord. Barely literate, after
work as an itinerant saddler dried up he
never found a constant occupation.

A young Fred Woolton looks confidently
into the camera. After studying to be a
sociologist, he was eager to make his mark
in the world of business.

red would meet his future wife,
Maud, while at university in
Manchester. Bound by religious
faith, Maud would later claim
that a 'higher power' had seeded
them in their actions together.

Woolton joined the retail company Lewis's in 1920. He
would build the firm, owned by the Cohen family, into
a hugely successful national operator.

By the time Woolton entered politics in 1940 he was a wealthy businessman. He had three homes: Hillfoot House in Liverpool, a flat in London and a holiday home by Lake Windermere. Pictured in the formal garb of a member of the Privy Council, with wife Maud and daughter Peggy.

The Woolton family, including Roger in a swimming costume, relaxes in the garden at their home, Fallbarrow, by Lake Windermere, which Fred had bought in 1931.

Woolton poses with his wife, children and the family nanny, along with his beloved pipe, while dressed down in tweed plus-fours.

Prime Minister Neville Chamberlain addresses the nation on 3 September 1939 to confirm that a state of war existed between Britain and Germany. Chamberlain appointed Woolton as Minister of Food in April 1940.

A newspaper seller on the Strand, in London, carries a hoarding pronouncing the declaration of war.

Winston Churchill replaced Chamberlain as British Prime Minister in June 1940. He showed little confidence in his Minister of Food, telling friends: 'We shall have to be ready with a rescue squad for Woolton.'

The German Luftwaffe followed the route of the River Thames in order to target and destroy valuable food and fuel depots.

Warehouses stocking vital supplies of meat burn in the shadow of St Paul's Cathedral i October 1940.

As soon as rationing was implemented in January 1940, queues formed along high streets across Britain.

National Registration Day was declared on 29 September 1939, where everyone – save servicemen and women – filled in forms revealing their personal details and occupation. Ration books and coupons were then assigned to individuals and families, based on age and income.

As the Luftwaffe's bombing campaign of London intensified, the Ministry of Food secretly relocated to the Welsh coastal town of Colwyn Bay. Penrhos College (left) was one of a host of buildings requisitioned by the ministry, in this case used for strategy and planning.

Woolton had a special railway halt constructed so he could alight directly at the Ministry of Food's HQ at the Colwyn Bay Hotel. Here he makes an official inspection of the town's Home Guard.

'OF COURSE I CAN!

I'm patriotic as can be —
And ration points won't worry me!"

The Ministry of Food was quick to issue posters as part of a general media campaign to urge households to become self-sufficient in advance of increasing privations.

Woolton's day was often filled with photocalls to drive home the message of efficient cooking. Here he attends the launch of a V (for Victory) Club Lunch in London's Hackney, showcasing the benefits of communal cooking.

The historic lend-lease agreement between the USA and Britain saw aid – from tanks to food – shipped to the UK. Lord Woolton with the US President's special representative (left) greets the first shipment of food to reach British shores.

Woolton poses for the camera while feeding a group of Bevan Boys; these were teenage lads eligible for armed service but ordered instead to go into coal mines to dig for Britain.

Rescue parties relaxing on furniture brought out from bombed houses are fed from a Queen's Messengers Convoy.

King George VI pays a visit to the Ministry of Food – an event, wrote Woolton, that 'did more for the internal morale of the Ministry of Food than anybody else would have done in a year'.

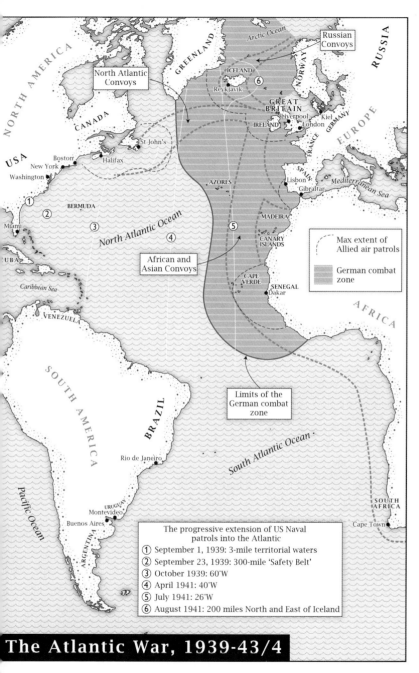

The progressive extension of US Naval patrols into the Atlantic
(1) September 1, 1939: 3-mile territorial waters
(2) September 23, 1939: 300-mile 'Safety Belt'
(3) October 1939: 60°W
(4) April 1941: 40°W
(5) July 1941: 26°W
(6) August 1941: 200 miles North and East of Iceland

The Atlantic War, 1939-43/4

This map emphasises the loss of shipping and their supplies that failed to reach British shores.

Lady Woolton worked alongside her husband to bolster the war effort and the work his ministry were doing. Here she opens up a food centre in Romford (above) and later that same visit hands over the keys of a mobile canteen to the local authorities (below).

Then, as if to rub it in, the following week the Minister of Agriculture, Robert Hudson, and the Minister of Shipping, Ronald Cross, made exactly the same sort of speech he had been planning, but they did so, moaned Woolton, 'without consultation – and apparently without reproof'.

Woolton huffed and puffed about this. 'There is no central-ised government in this country and no control,' he fumed privately.

9

THE PR BATTLE

On 21 November Woolton wrote in his diary: 'Food is becoming an article of so much importance to the public that all the newspapers have now engaged food reporters.' While this would give him a useful channel to disseminate his message to the country, he was also wary. 'They are at once a liability as well as an asset,' he wrote. 'Because, being food reporters, they must get news, and unfortunately stories of failure are better than stories of success.'

In an attempt to garner some control over what they wrote, he instigated regular briefings, a press conference each Tuesday at his Portman Square office. The key writers then formed themselves into what they called the Food Reporters Group. Woolton felt he had some understanding of, and empathy with, the reporters, writing, 'I had some advantage in dealing with the Press in that, at one period of my life, I had been a good deal in and out of newspaper offices and earned the major part of my living as a free-lance journalist. I knew how editors and reporters hated being expected to be the organ of government views.'

At his weekly briefings, he began by speaking on the record 'to enable them to give a favourable background to actions that we have to take in the ministry,' he wrote. If a question then came that he could not answer, because replying would not be in the public interest, he would go off the record and explain why. He realised that simply saying that information was not in the public interest would not put off what he called 'the diligent newspaper-man from searching for information because it might well be that the department was trying to hide its mistakes behind that rather pompous barrier of "the public interest"'. This frankness, he hoped, would keep the press onside.

All the leading newspapers had joined the group, he noted, 'except the *Daily Herald* who prefer scoops regardless of whether they are to the national advantage or not'.

The journalists would gather before their meetings at the Bunch of Grapes pub on Wigmore Street, around the corner from Woolton's office. One writer, Charles Graves, an author and journalist, remembered running into what he called 'The First Eleven of England's food correspondents' one Tuesday afternoon. They 'were drinking mild and bitter in the Saloon Bar,' he wrote in a *Sunday Express* supplement, 'preparatory to attending Lord Woolton's somewhat Rooseveltian Tuesday Conference in Portman Square.' The reporters sipped their drinks and chatted about Woolton. 'He can certainly be caustic when he wants to,' said one. Another joked: 'You can never pull the Woolton over his eyes.'

Graves joined the journalists as they trooped along to Woolton's briefing. He described the minister as having 'good hands, no paunch, grey hair, a pink complexion and bluish eyes'. His voice, he said, 'has the slightly flattish quality of the Lancastrian, but is flexible enough. He has probably had lessons in elocution.' His 'mannerisms', meanwhile, 'include the incessant lighting of a pipe or the removal of his spectacles when his alert brain is concentrating on the easy answer to a hard question. He also has the habit of undoing the bottom button and jigger button of his double-breasted jacket and then doing them up again when in thought.'

Graves also wrote that Woolton 'likes a hostile mind . . . He seldom gets angry. If he does, his mood changes to dry humour and then a dangerous quiet. "Really . . ." is a favourite expression of his, "I am not interested" is another. His day begins at 7.45 a.m. when he reluctantly hoists himself out of bed. He then starts work directly after his bath by jotting down notes on a memo-pad kept in his dressing room.'

As for his team, Graves wrote that Woolton 'seems to be almost worshipped by his staff.' Graves suggested this was due to his being always punctual, avuncular, and because he 'dislikes banquets'. He would return home to his flat for lunch, had working lunches at the likes of Claridge's hotel for business – 'but he prefers home cooking of the simple type like Lancashire hot-pot'. Graves also wrote that, 'His practical and unofficial methods of work are shown by his habit of calling out a couple of ordinary typists to give him a snap judgement on a food poster for women.'

Woolton himself recalled meeting one journalist who was regularly hostile towards him. 'My paper is attacking you every day and we are going to continue to attack you until you have gone,' he told the minister. Woolton asked him which paper he represented, although he declined to name it in his memoirs, writing, 'It was a paper with which I could have had some influence in high places if I had so desired.' But the minister looked at the reporter, suspecting that there was something other than a journalist's antipathy towards a government minister.

'Is anything the matter at home?' inquired Woolton, his Uncle Fred persona coming to the fore.

'What has that got to do with you?' spluttered the journalist.

'I'm only wondering because, in addition to what I view as your errors of journalistic judgement, there must be something which would account for your bad manners,' replied Woolton.

The man looked a little wounded and then, recorded Woolton, 'He blurted out that his wife was going to have a baby and she could not get orange juice and the baby would not be healthy.'

Woolton nodded benignly, noting to himself with some amusement that this panic about orange juice was what he called 'a tribute to our propaganda'. He had used a great deal of energy persuading pregnant and new mothers of the importance, in a food shortage, of giving themselves and their babies things of nutritional value and would help maintain good health. Here was a journalist determined to disbelieve everything that Woolton and his department said, without realising he had himself been swallowing the propaganda.

'Do you think your mother had orange juice before you were born?' asked Woolton. 'I can assure you that mine didn't and both you and I seem quite healthy.'

The reporter nodded, a little humbled. 'But let me tell you,' continued Woolton, 'that when the baby is born it should have the orange juice and I shall see to it myself that your wife and baby get it.'

The journalist's wife and child did indeed, in due course, receive orange juice and, recorded Woolton: 'I thought his articles lost a certain amount of their punch after that.'

When he wasn't schmoozing journalists, Woolton made a point of meeting the more powerful newspaper men: the press barons. On 20 December 1940, for example, he had lunch with the owners of national newspapers including the *Daily Mirror* and *The Times,* as well as regional press bosses such as H. M. Heywood who ran the Kemsley Group of northern papers, as well as Lord Southwood of Odhams Press, who published women's magazines. Also at the lunch was Lord Rothermere of the *Daily Mail.* Woolton wrote that he was 'a keen practical fellow – I should have thought a little light on the trigger as regards judgement'.

Woolton addressed them all as they ate, explaining how he hoped that with the deterioration of the food situation their papers would explain that this was due to war, not government failure. 'I was not asking for any commiseration [or] for restraint of their critics. I was merely anxious that they should know all the facts and then do what they thought right in the interests of the nation.'

The meeting proved useful, as the press barons liked Woolton and several told him that they hoped he would stay in politics after his tenure at the ministry. And a few months later, when Woolton was enduring a rough patch with the press, Lord Southwood gathered a meeting of his press contacts and told them that if they knew of a better man to be Minister of Food then they should suggest it. They didn't and – he reported to Woolton – 'I told them they would regret your resignation and I told them to stop attacking you.' Woolton was charmed but privately dismissive. 'I don't suppose for a moment it will have any influence,' he wrote. 'Newspapers can't keep praising because there's no news in that, and the public loves leaders to be attacked.'

Woolton's regular press briefings made him not just one of the most famous men in politics, but something of a national celebrity as well. Sometimes that fame embarrassed him. On 22 November 1940, after a meeting with his officials in Colwyn Bay, he and Maud stopped for the night at Broadway, a village in the Cotswolds, having booked a room at The Lygon Arms. The couple were shown to their room and were surprised at how good it was. Well furnished and homely, it even had a private bath. Then Woolton noticed some framed photographs about the place. 'It was obviously a personal room and it seemed to have been just vacated.' It then dawned on Maud that this room was the private quarters of the proprietors – a Mr and Mrs Russell – so she prompted her husband to seek them out to insist that this was surely a great inconvenience to them.

'We are just very glad indeed to have the opportunity to show you our appreciation for what you have done for the country and also for us as caterers,' Mr Russell told the minister. It was 'embarrassing', wrote Woolton, 'but very nice.'

Then after dinner the couple moved to the lounge, whereupon the owner came in to introduce his mother, and then his niece, and then a large queue of what seemed endless other visitors.

The next day as they left the Russells refused to take Woolton's money. 'It was our private room, we didn't let it so we can't take payment,' said Mr Russell sealing his argument. 'It has given us great pleasure to have given you the room.'

Woolton left feeling a little embarrassed, but admitting to his wife that it 'was very nice'. But, he wrote in his diary that night not wishing to seem ungrateful: 'I sighed for anonymity.'

At the weekends he would often have to wade through endless newspaper features that mentioned him, or profiled him, or commented on him. 'The cheap Sunday papers seem to think I'm news,' he wrote. And he thought little of some of the columnists – often it seemed authors of light literature – who were sent to interview him. On 8 April 1942 Beverley Nichols, a novelist, gardening writer and later a writer of mysteries, had come to write a profile of him. He wasn't impressed by his visitor and complained to his staff for wasting his time. 'It's amazing to see what poor specimens of mankind these popular authors are,' he commented.

He didn't like watching himself on newsreel either. 'I went to see myself on a film,' he wrote on 22 January 1941. It was, he thought, 'a most humiliating experience. These high-speed cameras strip you and reveal all your weaknesses.

I thought I was quite strong, determined etc.: the creature I saw on the film was quite incapable of controlling the food supplies of the country: the actions were weak and feeble, the voice had quality but no smoothness, and seemed to come in nervous jerks, and I came to the conclusion that this was no work for amateurs.'

Woolton thus employed the services of Howard Marshall, a broadcaster who commentated on major sporting events and state occasions for the BBC. Woolton recruited him to both direct PR operations at the Ministry of Food and give him private media training. Marshall 'spent many patient hours, not only teaching me how to use my voice but teaching me how to write the script for broadcasting,' recalled Woolton. It's not unlikely that, as some contemporary journalists noted, Marshall also gave him some elocution lessons, softening his northern tones, making his voice a tad more acceptable as a member of the British political establishment.

It was that establishment that was very much on show at the funeral following the death of Neville Chamberlain on November 9 1940. The event saw a gathering of the most powerful men in Britain and it gave the Minister of Food an opportunity to reflect on his senior government colleagues.

It was a famously arctic November morning during which mourners had sat beneath the bomb-shattered windows of Westminster Abbey.

'I watched it all thinking of this cold unapproachable shy person,' pondered Woolton on the late former Prime Minister. Chamberlain, he said, had 'few of the attributes for a political life of such great eminence except a personal integrity for adhering to his own convictions'.

He looked about at the assembled Cabinet and other powerful men from the newspaper world as they hunkered down under their thick greatcoats.

'I sometimes wish Lloyd George [Prime Minister from 1916 to 1922] were back in the Cabinet. With his vast knowledge he would make most of these other people look like office-boys,' he wrote. 'There's no allegiance to Churchill: there's nobody in the government whom the public would trust. Halifax [Foreign Secretary] belongs to the Old Munich School [appeasement]: Anderson [Lord President] does his best but it's not much, [he] has no imagination and little human sympathy.' Arthur Greenwood, Minister without Portfolio, is 'an economic philanderer' and Ernest Bevin, Minister of Labour and National Service, 'will blow himself out – he's very vain'. (Woolton was outraged to hear Bevin had eaten at a hotel and ordered champagne for lunch.) and '[Clement] Attlee [sometime Deputy Prime Minister and later Prime Minister] does nothing.'

Next he described Lord Beaverbrook, the newspaper proprietor brought into government by Churchill for a number of senior ministerial roles, as 'a complete egotist' and 'a bully' who 'runs his department by "Giving them Hell" all the time.' He noted simply: 'I don't trust Beaverbrook.'

Lord Reith, meanwhile, the founder of the BBC, 'has more egotism than anyone I've come across'. He mocked how at meetings Reith would grandly offer to jump in and tackle things. 'There were signs that he had done some good work some years ago at the BBC,' he wrote somewhat dismissively of the man widely credited for having established the principles of public service broadcasting, before adding that 'he had never accomplished anything since'.

Woolton's wife Maud had also weighed in on the subject of Reith in her own diary. Reith, she said, 'organised the BBC until neither he, nor the staff, could stand him or it any longer!! He is strange, has queer fits of temper, doesn't know how to manage people – is full of his own opinion. He hasn't made a success of anything he has undertaken since the BBC.' Maud notes that, after a 'succession of failed attempts at running ministries, from Information to Reconstruction', he had been promised a barony. 'He is too conceited to see that he is being shelved. But now he thinks he will be the next PM. God help the country!!'

Woolton made the same point on Reith. Reith, wrote Woolton, 'considers he's likely to be Prime Minister within a reasonable time'. But he's not the only one. 'I notice all these people who get tipped as future Prime Ministers, and who imagine they are going to be, fall by the wayside rather quickly.'

Yet Woolton, too, would be tipped as a future Prime Minister, as he grew in stature both as a politician and a famous figure across Britain. Although he was too wise not to caution himself against holding out for such prospects: 'Whenever I come face to face with the rewards of fame,' he wrote some decades before the real age of celebrity, 'I wonder whether they are worth it.'

He also attacked the department of Lord Leathers, the Ministry of War Transport, complaining that 'the internal transport of this country is in such a jam for the lack of wagons that it cannot move stuff away from the ports.'

Woolton had discovered that there had been plenty of wagons available and that they had stood loaded but idle for a year.

'I find it all very depressing,' he concluded. 'I am trying to play in a team. My temptation is either to leave it, or to do what I would like to more than anything else – and that is to take the gloves off.'

The morning after Chamberlain's funeral Woolton travelled to Liverpool where his views of the wasted landscape that was his government colleagues seemed to be reflected in the aftermath of a Germany bombing.

'The whole of the centre of the town had been completely wrecked by a bomb. Rows and rows of houses and shops had just been razed to the ground in a heap of brick, stone and rubble,' he wrote. 'Water mains and gas mains had been broken: great torrents of water were flowing through the streets. It was a desolate mass of destruction.' But, he added, 'the people were not looking too depressed.'

He was further cheered the following day – when he addressed a meeting in Manchester of what he called 'the principal citizens' of that city at the Reform Club.

He talked again about why food was being restricted and was impressed by his audience. 'It was interesting to see the way in which these hard-headed men in Manchester sat and watched and listened without any emotion on their faces,' he wrote. 'It was clear they wanted hard plain speaking, and it was also clear that they were a little curious to know whether this local businessman who had become a inister of the Crown would give them the real ministerial sort of stuff, or whether he was just a plain businessman.'

So Woolton did what came naturally and went off script. 'I

defined the attitude of the government without any consultation with my colleagues or the Prime Minister,' he wrote. 'I felt it was time that somebody came out with a story that the way to win a war was to attack.'

Woolton finished and the dour men of Manchester got to their feet and cheered him to the rafters. 'They were very appreciative,' he wrote modestly, adding that he was mobbed as he left the hall. 'The police escorted me out of the town.'

Woolton felt he was doing a good job of slaying those weak ministers. But then he found another enemy: farmers, although Woolton had always been clear in his message that, after the Royal Navy, the Army and the Royal Air Force, agriculture was the country's fourth line of defence. For some time they had been gently rocking his cage. In mid September 1940, one farmer, a Mr F. Ashley from Irlam in Lancashire – who served on the National Farmers' Union council – reported to the Lancashire Executive on a recent meeting with Lord Woolton. 'We gave the minister a sound dressing down,' he told a room full of tub-thumping farmers and a journalist from the *Daily Despatch* who reported on the meeting the following day, 16 September. 'But,' added Ashley a little sombrely, 'he didn't seem to take a damned bit of notice of what was said to him.'

But on 9 December 1940, Woolton had to confront a larger number of them, face to face.

It was a lunchtime meeting, and escorting him into a hall in Whitehall was Norman Vernon, director of Flour Milling, who reported both to the Ministry of Food and the Ministry of Agriculture. Vernon briefed Woolton as they walked along in the chilly winter air; 'This union is an extraordinary body,' advised Vernon, 'one of the most powerful organisations in the country.'

'Yes,' Woolton nodded. 'But are they a positive force? The union always opposes,' he said. 'And they have a destructive power.'

'Indeed, Lord Woolton. And they can destroy ministers. They have managed to ruin the careers of every Minister of Agriculture I can think of,' said Vernon.

He went on to explain that the current Minister of Agriculture, Robert Hudson, had sworn not to be taken down by this union; he had spent months working for their approval, but it appeared that he was doing it at Woolton's expense. 'He needs to have these men on his side,' explained Vernon. 'It's vital for Hudson, for example, that they understand why grain is priced the way it is. Flour has to be universally affordable and as you know only too well the government does not want to add bread to the ration. Of course this means that farmers are not earning as much as they would wish and they resent that.'

Woolton nodded, understanding the challenge. Then as they reached the location for their lunch meeting, Vernon stopped by the stone steps of some faceless government building. 'The farmers seem to be supporting Hudson,' said Vernon gravely. 'But if things go wrong on prices and if they look for a villain, the way things stand, it will not be the Minister for Agriculture who will be to blame – Hudson has seen his predecessors stumble and has vowed they will not have his scalp – it will be the Minister of Food.'

Listening to what Vernon was saying, Woolton took it all

in; then, looking up at the building where the lunch was and wherein lay the next challenge, he breathed deeply. Then he skipped up the steps to the door. 'As far as they are concerned, I am Public Enemy Number 1,' he would write in his diary later that day. Nothing could cheer him quite like a little afternoon tussle with a bunch of farmers.

Inside he found a large number of men standing around and clearly waiting for a fight. Vernon introduced Woolton around and he shook hands with the union president, the chairman and other senior members. He also met the editor of the farming periodical, the *Farmer and Stockbreeder*, in whose pages Woolton was attacked month after month.

'I was right in the enemy's camp,' Woolton reflected. And while he wore an air of confidence, he noticed that the farmers seemed less self-assured. 'They were rather uncomfortable,' he recalled. Doubtless – and having never met Woolton – these men were ready for a bruising fight, prepared to take, head on, yet another aggressive minister. And they knew from past experience that when they met fire with fire the minister soon wilted. They'd get rid of him and then wait around to clobber another.

But Woolton was different. There was no hint of aggression from him. In fact his approach totally disarmed them. 'I treated them with the affability I reserved for my dearest friends,' he said. As they settled down for lunch, Woolton stood and addressed them. 'Gentlemen. In this room are many men with many grievances and there are others who bear me less ill will. But let me make one thing very clear to you all. Whether you choose to attack me or not attack me is a matter of entire indifference to me, so long as the country wins the war. To this end you have a job to do. You must assist in feeding our country and feeding cattle and sheep and tending fields and harvesting crops. That is your job. Your job is not to get exactly the money you believe is owed to you for everything that goes to the market. Your job is not to hustle for every last shilling out of the Treasury. And I will not waver for one second in my duty, which is to keep our nation fed.'

The farmers looked astonished at Woolton. Here was a man not pleading for their support so he could keep his job. And here was a man who talked to them with an honesty that they did not expect from politicians. 'The atmosphere completely altered,' wrote Woolton later. 'These men seemed to like the perfectly bald statement that I made to them.'

As lunch ended the men got up from the table and gathered around Woolton to talk to him personally. 'You're very direct with us,' said one, 'and that means we can just get on and have a business conversation with you.' And what was destined to be a difficult few hours became, according to Woolton, 'a very pleasant afternoon. I think I buried most of the suspicions of the Farmers' organisation.' They no longer suspected him. They knew just what he thought.

Shortly before 4.30 p.m., when Woolton had to leave, several senior union members approached him and engaged, he said, in 'a deliberate breach of confidence on their part'.

'They assured me they would give me their support.' They then explained their irritation at how Robert Hudson, earlier in the year, had 'taken all the credit for getting a big increase in prices for them from the Treasury'. But what he had not told them was that this increased amount was to last for just three or four months during the winter. Furthermore he had then made it clear that any further reductions in prices for their commodities would be the doing of Lord Woolton. 'He left it clear that the Minister of Food was the fellow who was going to adjust downwards.'

The Minister of Agriculture's attempts to curry favour with the farmers at the expense of Woolton had backfired. As Woolton himself wrote: 'Hudson has spent so much time trying to get the Farmers' Union on his side that it is perfectly clear they have no respect from him. They regard him just as a politician out to make a name for himself.'

Woolton returned to his office emboldened about his own principle of plain speaking. Two days later he let rip at what he called 'hoarders'. The *Manchester Guardian* reported on a speech he made in Portsmouth. Woolton had taken Sir Henry with him as the man had hailed from the city. The idea was to launch a 'Food Economy Plan'. Sir Henry appreciated measured speech, and liked to discuss the quotes Woolton was thinking of dispersing to the waiting press. The following day's *Manchester Guardian* included talk from Woolton that was clearly not words chosen by Sir Henry. 'It is against the law to hoard,' said Woolton. 'And if I find any hoarders I will deal with them remorselessly, ruthlessly, and with immense pleasure.'

Despite becoming used to his minister, Sir Henry may have cringed. But Woolton was true to his word – although on one occasion he may have been a tad overzealous. Word reached his ministry that a large house on the banks of the Severn Estuary in Gloucestershire was hoarding vast amounts of food. Woolton was keen to jump on any examples of the privileged classes abusing his ration system, so he approved an aggressive search by his agents.

After the event Woolton was summoned to the House of Lords to listen to a question raised by a Conservative politician, Charles Bathurst, the 1st Viscount Bledisloe.

The property belonged, in Bledisloe's words, to 'Colonel Sir Lionel Darell, D.S.O., Deputy Lieutenant of the County of Gloucester, a county alderman, and for at least twelve years chairman of the local bench of magistrates, a man well known, respected and indeed beloved throughout the county, devoting his energies in his retirement from the Army to unpaid public and philanthropic service of varied descriptions.'

Having ransacked the house – turning over beds and bed clothes, opening every trunk, suitcase and ottoman, looking in every kitchen jar and in old boxes in the dustiest corners of every outhouse – the inspectors had found nothing.

A tip-off had alleged the hoarding of vast amounts of honey, jam and biscuits. The men had also interrogated various members of the Darells' domestic staff, including their chauffeur. 'Have you seen large quantities of honey enter this house,' a ministry agent asked. 'No', was the chauffeur's emphatic reply.

It seemed that a nosy and uncharitable neighbour had watched some lorries moving what were boxes of accumulated piles of paper gathered by the village – and stored by Sir Lionel – for the benefit of the Red Cross. Also spotted were the comings and goings of a van transporting the belongings of a friend of the family's whose London home had been blitzed. Sir Lionel, pillar of the community and his wife Lady

Darell, had offered their house as a refuge for this man and his wife.

The couple's reputation, said Bledisloe, had been besmirched, they had been distressed and humiliated, and he attacked Lord Woolton whose officials had acted without 'a shred of evidence'. He also complained that 'the powers claimed by a certain government department and their mode of execution would appear to be in violent conflict with the traditional sanctity and privacy of the homes of British people.'

Woolton had tried to defend his ministry and wrote in his diary: 'We had had pretty good grounds for making the search but had not been able to find the food that we had been told had been hoarded.' Thus, he added: 'We weren't on a good wicket. I got away with it, but I don't think it left a very good taste in the mouth of my fellow Peers.'

The Lords attack

If he found the senior politicians in the Commons tiresome, he also saved special ire for those in the second chamber. On 19 December 1940 he attended the House of Lords to talk about bread. 'It really was an important speech,' he wrote in his diary. 'There were seven people there, not very heartening.'

It seemed the very building depressed him. 'The House of Lords is the dreariest thing that someone could imagine,' he wrote, 'and its dreariness begets dreariness.' He loathed the place when it was insultingly empty. But he didn't like it much when it was full either.

As thunder and rain poured down onto the London streets

in mid-July the following year, dramatically breaking a short heatwave that saw temperatures reach the low 30s, Woolton took his seat in the Lords.

Viscount Dawson of Penn, who had been doctor to the late King George V, had put down a motion to stress the necessity of providing milk, particularly for children. Dawson had evidence that the production of milk was falling dangerously. It also gave his fellow peers a chance to weigh in on the subject of food and to attack the minister of that department.

'Are the active adult population to be deprived of this essential food?' asked Dawson. 'What folly, at a time when the maximum of health and strength is required.' In a long speech he set out his concerns. 'The production of milk is like a reputation, very easy to lose and very difficult to regain,' he said. 'That is one of the reasons why I am venturing to press your Lordships as I am doing, because it is our one hope at the present time. At this late season of the year, if we are not going to be face to face with great difficulties in the coming winter, we must act here and now to try and prevent that reduction of the production of milk which so seriously threatens. Milk I would rank as a munition of war,' he said, before adding, almost as an afterthought, that 'we must have more eggs.'

Woolton, he admitted, 'has a large and extremely difficult task,' but, he continued: 'He is sometimes let down by the imperfect implementing of his policy. He is at times called upon to make bricks without straw, and I hope that the result of this discussion will be to give him a larger ration of straw.'

If the first peer to speak had a vein of kindness towards

Woolton, the next certainly did not. Lord Davies, a Welsh former Liberal MP, rose to make several general points about food production before addressing the issue of the black market. 'It is very disquieting to know that in regard to this matter there have been and apparently still are so many attempts at evasion,' he said. 'Black market activities were going on in Germany and other countries,' he said, adding that that 'is only natural and just what we might have expected'. But now, 'I venture to suggest that this sort of thing going on in this country must cause us a great deal of disquietude and alarm.' It was, he said 'un-British [and] a sort of disease. It is, moreover, a very infectious disease, because when one section of the community discovers that sums of money have been made by flouting these food restrictions and regulations, it means that others are tempted to do likewise.'

Davies then turned to Lord Woolton, sitting listening. 'One cannot help feeling that this foul growth should have been nipped in the bud by the Minister of Food when he discovered that huge profits were being made in this way. He ought to have put his foot down at once and prevented the disease from spreading.'

Next up was Lord Addison, who had been both a Labour and Liberal MP and a one-time Minister for Health. Addison was a frequent critic of Woolton, often attacking him on subjects like jam, sometimes strawberries, other times fish. The pair once had an altercation on the subject of boiling sugar. Such was Addison's keenness to talk about the availability of sugar and the boiling of it to make jam that Woolton joked that he 'intended to have a private still in his garden'. Addison was furious. 'The noble Lord must not misrepresent me,' he said demanding that Woolton 'repudiate' his statement.

'The Ministry of Food,' Addison asserted, 'for some reason have, I think, been infected with some kind of disorder in the last few weeks.' The ministry issued orders, he argued, without insuring that they could actually be complied with. 'The community has been presented with a succession of quite needless blunders and is being exposed to serious and unnecessary hardship.' Addison talked of the 'propaganda department of the Ministry of Food' being run by people who 'seem to receive very large salaries: I wish they took a bit more trouble to know something about their jobs.'

He then turned to potatoes, which, he argued, had been in such plentiful supply that 'the farmers did not know what in the world they were going to do with them.' But he stated: 'it is due, I am sorry to say, to gross mismanagement that we should now see people standing in queues a hundred yards long outside greengrocers' shops to buy potatoes.'

Next he tackled an issue of bureaucratic management that had affected the distribution of tomatoes. Addison told the story of a shopkeeper who had ordered a box of tomatoes from a wholesaler in Reading. The tomatoes were brought on a van to the shop from Reading – some twenty miles, but, said Addison, 'the shopkeeper was informed that although the tomatoes had been carted twenty miles all he could do, by order of the Ministry of Food, was to look at the box. The driver was not allowed to take the box off the cart and give it to the shopkeeper. He was instructed to take it back to Reading.'

Woolton, listening to the speeches and planning to address

each issue when he was finally able to make his own speech, could not keep quiet at this point. He rose and asked, 'Was that by order of the ministry?' 'He has said so,' replied Lord Addison. 'I do like to be precise,' said Woolton, clearly angry. 'This is a serious matter. Does the noble Lord seriously suggest that somebody should cart a box twenty miles and then take it back again?'

'I do,' retorted Addison. 'I am stating the facts. I am going to urge that the noble Lord should restrain the zeal of his subordinates in these matters and not let himself in for this kind of misfortune.' He then said that there was 'no earthly reason why these things should occur, but I am coming to two which are much worse'.

He then described how a scheme to get villagers to contribute fruit for jam-making had collapsed. 'It is worse than failure,' he said and Lord Woolton had been 'asking for trouble' in launching it. Part of the plan involved village women getting loans to set up jam-preserving centres with equipment such as oil stoves, preserving pans and jars. But, said Addison, 'the scheme has broken down, I do not know of a single village where there is a centre working [and] whoever drew it up had not the faintest idea of what life in an English village is like. The scheme is a failure and masses of fruit will be unused as a consequence.'

Addison then moved on to the subject of eggs, which was where, he said, he needed to 'press the minister to mend his ways'. The egg scheme had been launched in June of that year. Any keeper of poultry who had more than twelve birds had to sell their eggs through packing stations, and needed special permission to retain any for their own consumption.

But, Addison alleged, the scheme had been started before the packing stations were organised and so, he explained, 'there is no channel between the local producer and a packing station of any kind and the result has been that of course you are interrupting the supply between the producer and the consumer.' And where there were packing stations, distribution had not been organised so that thousands of eggs had been left sitting there and going off.

In order to avoid being subject to the scheme, many poultry smallholders simply reduced their flocks by a bird or two – meaning there were less eggs in the system. Thousands of hens, for example, in Devon were slaughtered. Lord Addison spoke of 'three maiden ladies' that he knew personally who kept hens. 'They had been frightened,' he said, 'by the propaganda department of the Ministry of Food. They had got it in their minds that somebody was going to come into their garden and count their hens and they were not going to be left with more than a dozen.' So the maiden ladies wrung the necks of thirty-five of their hens. Their actions were foolish and unnecessary, said Addison, 'but it was the exploits of the propaganda department of the noble Lord that made those women kill those hens.'

Lord Woolton, according to Lord Addison, had created unnecessary suffering. He implored Woolton to check the operations of his ministry. 'If there is one thing that is likely to undermine the public morale it is needless hardship in connection with the daily supply of food.' The public, he continued, were willing to participate in any inconvenience which they knew was necessary but, he added gravely, 'what they do and will resent – and I implore the noble Lord to remember it – is any needless hardship, any foolish interference with their habits.'

One can only imagine the frustration Woolton felt; here was a man whose very passion was social service, whose motivation was an understanding of poverty gained from an early age. No one felt the pain suffered by the public at his own administered privations as raw as he did; it was a major motivating factor for him. Yet he had to sit and listen and be lectured to by his peers about the job he was virtually born to do.

But before Addison sat down he had one final anecdote to share. A few days previously he had been driving through a local town where he saw a line of people outside a greengrocer's shop. 'The queue consisted of perhaps eighty or a hundred women, who were marshalled in double rank by a police officer. I suppose that they were waiting for potatoes or tomatoes.'

At which point one lord piped up 'Cigarettes perhaps,' to the delighted chuckles of peers keen for some light relief.

As Addison watched the queue he saw a woman arrive at the shop in a car. 'She was evidently a favoured customer. She got out of the car and went into the shop in front of the queue. Shortly afterwards she came out with a bag of potatoes and a parcel of tomatoes. What happened then was that the women in the queue fell upon her, scattered her potatoes and tomatoes all over the road, and tore her dress. I rather think that she deserved it. I do not think anybody would sympathise with her very much. Undoubtedly she should not have done what she did.'

Having told his anecdote, Addison then twisted the knife

into Woolton with his analysis. 'The point I want to emphasize to my noble friend is that that kind of thing is very dangerous and most undesirable. Any step that can be taken to avoid such happenings should be taken, and should be the subject of adequate and careful forethought.'

Addison was telling Woolton, the House of Lords, the press and the public, what the minister knew only too well. It was what kept him awake at night and the fear of which tore into the deepest recesses of his soul. If he didn't provide the nation with the basics, such as eggs, there would be anarchy.

There was a further speech before Woolton would get the chance to answer these charges. Liberal peer Lord Teviot complained about how new centralised systems, which enabled the Ministry of Food to quantify provisions of food, meant that a friend of his who grew tomatoes had to send them to London, before they were checked and then returned to his own local town for sale 'employing petrol and transport'. The consequence, he said, was that local people 'get hardly any tomatoes. I live very close to the town in question, and I cannot buy tomatoes at all.' There was, complained Teviot, 'too much control'. Woolton, he said, 'seems to have got into rather deep water, and I think it is due to over-legislation'.

Finally Woolton was able to get to his feet and speak. His aim, he said was to 'put these problems into perspective'. The things that had been discussed, milk aside, were 'jam, tomatoes, new potatoes and eggs'. Yet, he explained, 'how fortunate we are that it is these things that are causing concern in the country, because it might indeed be, after twenty-two months of war, that other things were causing concern.'

He told the Lords that a senior Cabinet colleague had chastised him the previous day, telling him that 'as Minister of Food I was failing in my job because I was not letting the country know how well we were provided with food.' He told him that the morale of the people would be sustained if they knew what the situation really was. He was reluctant to follow that advice, 'because the truth is that if we try to tell the public what we have done, then there immediately comes to some people's minds the charge of complacency, which is, of course, the latest of modern crimes.'

Woolton then referred back to what was his natural territory. 'Before the war,' he said, 'there was no acute consciousness in this country of the fact that so many hundreds of thousands of people were suffering from malnutrition. It was not one of the subjects they read about daily in the newspapers – that there were, before this war broke out, very many thousands of children in the country who had not enough to eat.'

Woolton had heard the charges about over-zealous regulation, problems with petty bureaucracy but, he said, 'I wonder whether they are really sufficiently aware, when we discuss food questions, of the fact that they are largely determined by war conditions.'

He went on to explain that if he could trade with Denmark or Holland there would be no problem with milk, cheese, butter or eggs, that if he had the Channel Islands there would be plenty of potatoes, and that 'if the Battle of the Atlantic had not been raging day by day, noiseless and unseen, for the most part unappreciated by the people of this country, we should have had very few difficulties with our supply of meat.'

Compared with the last war, problems with food supply were of greater complexity and difficulty yet, he said, 'in spite of all the nervous strains of air raids, as a nation we are fit and we are well.'

Indeed, he argued, 'there are fewer people who are suffering from malnutrition now. We have come through the winter, we have had plenty of milk and bread in abundance. Whilst our rations have not been on a generous scale, they have been taken up by the people of this country, thus showing that the food that we have prescribed as a fair share for everybody has been of such amount and at such a price that everybody could get their fair share.'

It was Woolton's passionate belief that 'Before this war started it would not have been possible to say that nobody in the country wanted for food. As a result of the policy of organisation of the distribution of food, and of selling it at a price within the reach of the ordinary housewife, we can say that many people in this country are more adequately fed now than they were before the war started.'

Woolton went on to defend the distribution system while apologising for the occasional local and 'ridiculous error'. 'I am sure there have been many such mistakes made,' he said. There would always be critics, as 'the system arouses all sorts of opposition among people who have been trained in another school of experience.'

As for the tomatoes, he explained that the point of controlling the numbers was 'to secure that a smaller quantity shall disappear down a multitude of throats rather than a comparatively large quantity shall disappear down the throats of fewer people.'

And when it came to eggs, he said that 'all my political instinct warned me to leave eggs alone, but the shortage of eggs represented a serious problem in the nutritional diet of the town dweller.' They also needed to be subsidised as the price producers required was more than most consumers could afford. He batted off criticism about the packing stations, saying that they were in the hands of private companies and 'I do not think they are any less perfect since they accepted instructions from the Ministry of Food, but they are doing a much larger job than they ever did before.' He accepted that there may have been delays in distributing eggs around the country, but more people were getting hold of them than had previously. 'This is not,' he added firmly, 'a story of universal delay all over the country or of universal confusion.'

As to the apparent failure of the jam scheme as highlighted by Lord Addison, Woolton said he was 'unconscious' of it, stating there were 5,667 centres established for dealing with the problem. Lord Addison then intervened and said, 'I am well aware of the number of centres. I say they have not made the jam; that is the trouble.' Woolton countered saying that there had been a very small fruit crop that year and that the scheme had been run by a group of women who oversaw the women's institutes and that 'It is not fair, is it, to say they do not know anything about rural life.'

Lastly he answered the criticism regarding the zeal in which his staff went about ensuring their regulation was administered and adhered to. 'Lord Addison has asked me to curb the zeal of my staff,' he said. 'I do not desire to curb the zeal of people who are doing all they can to try to help in this war effort.' It was a stinging rebuke; his staff were simply being patriotic, the inference being that to criticise them was to be unpatriotic.

As Woolton sat down he hoped that would be the end of the debate. But he was not so fortunate: more peers were lining up to criticise him.

Lord Perry argued that as tomatoes were never a poor man's food, it was unnecessary to curb their availability to some and widen it for others; and the men who policed his eggs policy represented, he said, 'the growing up of this "Gestapo" ... the minister ... has a number who might perhaps be described as "snoopers"; personally I would call them agents provocateurs.'

'No,' cried Woolton, 'I have no agents provocateurs in the employment of the ministry.'

'We will let it pass,' said Perry.

'It is not true,' Woolton cried.

Next the Earl de La Warr, whose full name was Herbrand Edward Dundonald Brassey Sackville and who in the course of his political life served both Labour and Conservative governments, attacked Woolton for 'unnecessary and artificial shortages created by departmental mismanagement'. Woolton had failed to fully answer 'hardly a single question' he said, adding that 'the country as a whole, both consumers and producers, is profoundly disturbed about the present handling of the food supply of this country.'

At home in Whitehall Court that night, Woolton penned his rather more forthright thoughts in the pages of his diary. He cast the lords as wealthy, privileged people out of touch with real life and only able to take an interest when they were personally affected. 'It wasn't a debate,' he wrote. 'The truth is that even the wealthy are now not getting all the things they want to eat, and that rouses them to speech.'

Woolton, for all his titles and ministerial clout, still felt very much the outsider with his fellow peers. 'I think it's pathetic that, at a time when we are in a war on which depends our very existence, the Noble Lords should spend their time calling attention to the fact that tomatoes are in short supply,' he wrote.

The House of Lords was also, according to Woolton, at its worst in the aftermath of the death of the Duke of Kent, the fifth child of King George V and Queen Mary, in August 1942. Prince George, the young brother of Kings Edward VIII and George VI, died with fourteen others when a flying boat he was travelling in, possibly on a military mission to Sweden judging by the currency he was carrying, crashed into a hill in Caithness in Scotland. The death of the thirty-nine-year-old prince saw tributes given by members of both houses. Woolton was not impressed by the lack of sincerity that emanated from all sides: 'It doesn't seem to me that there is really anybody who was very sorry,' he wrote. He noted that the radical, anti-coalition Independent Labour Party, 'which started out with so many ideals, should have descended so completely as to be prepared to make political capital out of a death.'

The former Prime Minister, Herbert Henry Asquith, who became first Earl of Oxford and Asquith, had also contributed some thoughts. But the words washed over Woolton who struggled to pay attention. 'I often wonder whether he speaks at home with such slow deliberation as he speaks in the House,' he wrote, 'If he does it must be very dreary.'

The other House wasn't much better and he was pretty

disparaging about the entirety of MPs, penning his thoughts one evening after some disgruntled members had spent the afternoon attacking his ministry. He had been required to sit in the gallery above and listen to the speeches. 'I thought they were a miserable crowd,' he wrote. 'I wondered how the country could wage a war successfully with a House of Commons like that.'

Woolton was in fact despairing at the whole political class. One afternoon he had a meeting with the Liberal MP Tom Horabin. 'He used to be at Lewis's,' he wrote, referring to his retail business. 'And he wasn't any good. So I sacked him and he went into politics.'

He also recorded with glee an occasion in November 1942 when Labour MP Philip Noel-Baker came to see him on an issue relating to food hygiene. 'I've come to talk to you about rats,' announced Noel-Baker, a serious and rather glum British Quaker and an earnest campaigner for disarmament. Woolton looked at him steadily. 'Do you mean agricultural or political?' he said. Noel-Baker just frowned. 'He didn't like it very much,' Woolton confided to his diary later.

He relished a fight too with the government department that dealt with the colonies of the British Empire. For example, on 28 June 1942, he alerted the Colonial Office that the people of Malta were suffering from food shortages and something needed to be done. It was four o'clock in the afternoon and the message came back that officials would be happy to deal with it in the morning. 'I was furious,' he noted, 'and asked what was the matter with today.' In fact, he added, 'you might have to work all night.' His edict did not go down well, but Woolton couldn't care less, writing in his diary almost happily that 'I don't think the Colonial Office like me.'

Woolton realised of course that all countries were governed by individuals and Britain probably had just as many tiresome officials as the enemy. 'Fortunately Germany is subject to the same personnel difficulties in government,' he wrote on nearing Christmas in 1940. And he remained certain that a great many people of his nation showed the same steel that he had seen among those businessmen in Manchester. 'It isn't the government of this country that's going to win the war – it's the people.'

10

THE BLACK MARKET

Christmas 1940 was, according to Maud, 'very happy . . . the pleasure being increased by having, for three nights, no air raids. Whether it is the weather that has put off the enemy or a spirit of Christmas, we don't know.'

Both daughter Peggy and son Roger were with their parents and the family stayed in London. 'It doesn't matter where we are, so long as we are together,' she wrote, commenting that Roger 'seems to be very happy [down from Cambridge], but we wish he would work more than he seems to.'

But whatever happy conversation the family had over Christmas, Woolton told Maud about his political worries. 'F has been worried lately about the direction from the top,' she wrote. 'There seems to be very little co-ordination between the various ministries, in fact sometimes there is definite antagonism.'

Woolton had written to the PM, because, in his words, 'he really ought to know a little more about the food position,' and was promptly invited to Chequers on Boxing Day. 'I saw a new Winston,' he wrote, 'in the midst of his family, where the relationship was obviously that of the father and not of the Prime Minister.'

Woolton set out a list of grievances and Churchill listened intently. The Home Front 'was not good enough for the job it had to do', the Economic Policy Committee 'under the presidency of [Arthur] Greenwood [a Labour Party politician] came to no decisions and had delayed my shipping programme for weeks', 'the Food Policy Committee under Attlee also came to no decisions, and ... the latter was so weary that he had great difficulty in keeping awake – and didn't always succeed.' He also blamed Churchill because 'he had taken food ships which were bringing meat, to send them to the Near East and that this had caused the trouble that was blowing up regarding the meat ration.'

Woolton was having to reduce the meat ration – discerned by price rather than weight – by a third, from 1s 10d to 1s 2d – hardly the Christmas present the nation might have wanted

In spite of his frankness, Churchill on this occasion, among his family, 'was receptive and helpful', wrote Woolton. The PM sent out an immediate order that a group of ministers convene 'to discuss the food problem'.

Maud gave her own account of the meeting, based on her husband's report. Woolton was 'very pleased', she wrote of the invitation to Chequers, 'because with the PM you never know whether you get snubbed or not.' She described the Chequers scene as 'a very cheery and friendly ... family party. The PM wasn't at all petulant as he often is – he doesn't like being told things aren't going well – but when he has once got over his petulance, he does get things going.'

(While Woolton talked frequently of Churchill to his wife Maud, she did not often find herself in his company, so she made a point of describing an encounter she had with him in April 1942. 'We were invited to lunch with the Prime Minister at 10 Downing Street. It was very interesting for me as I had never met him except to shake hands with, before,' she wrote. 'He is much more benevolent in looks in his own home than one gets the impression of in pictures – but he is difficult to talk to as he hasn't any small talk to get things going.' But his wife was considerably easier: 'Mrs C is delightful – charming – full of fun, and very vivacious,' Maud added.)

A few days later, as a result of the Chequers meeting, a 'Production Executive Committee' was formed under the chairmanship of Bevin. Churchill also moved Greenwood to look after post-war problems. But this committee formation didn't please Maud. She was allergic to committees, writing that 'one of the failings of the Labour Party was its passionate attachment to committees. It's a vice of democracy.'

She felt that her husband's beef was that there were already too many committees and they weren't working together effectively. Politicians always create committees, she said, 'to investigate whatever problem arises ... [but] in practice it wastes an infinite amount of time.'

A week after Woolton's meeting with Churchill, Maud noted that this dreadful new committee had not been 'fully constituted' and 'it does seem awful that still another committee has to be formed.'

Woolton's other problem was to, as he put it, 'check profiteering'. On 6 January 1941 he wrote that 'a large number of people have come into the food trade buying up articles and selling them again at higher prices.' So he issued a 'Standstill Order', so that prices could not be any higher than they were on 2 December. 'People who had been speculating during the interval have had their fingers burned,' he wrote gleefully.

It was a rare reference to the black market, because Lord Woolton liked to think the British food market was a closed shop and, with him as manager, there was little chance of impropriety. In summing up the food situation in early January 1941, Woolton again referenced the black market saying that it irritated the public but the amount of food affected was small and most of the people responsible were, as he put it, 'having a diet at Wormwood Scrubs' (the prison in West London).

It was only many years later, on a summer's morning in 1958, that the Minister for Food finally laid bare his thoughts on the subject of the black market. Woolton, by then the first Earl, was seated in his grand house near Arundel. The library where he worked at Walberton was quiet. A large Persian rug added some colour to the room's conventional cream walls. He was proudly positioned behind a large estate desk, there was a dark leather sofa, and books were set into shelves on three walls. Between each bookcase were arched recesses hung with gentle watercolours. The shelves below were decorated with clocks, small lamps, little figurines and such things as a cigarette box.

On the walls, in this room and all over the house, were the attractive, but safely formal, paintings of mainly landscapes by English watercolourists such as Copley Fielding, John Varley and Peter de Wint. These paintings Woolton had bought (along with antique furniture that he and Maud had gathered) to help confirm the wealthy status he had gained by his middle age.

Walberton served as a place to entertain friends – many of whom were politicians – and such accoutrements were vital for their socialising. And so important was the society that the couple kept, once Woolton had become an established businessman and politician, that Maud recorded some 100 names of those they regularly came into contact with on the first page of her diaries. She writes her 'List of people who have come into our "orbit" since we came to London' and they include businessmen, senior civil servants, politicians, diplomats and aristocrats. There are the names of the wartime American Ambassador, John Winant, one-time head of the Civil Service Sir Warren Fisher, as well as the Dukes and Duchesses of Buccleuch and Devonshire.

High above the fireplace, below the coving, hung proudly the family crest. An ornate mirror was secured above the mantelpiece which itself displayed framed photographs of men such as Churchill. Chintz curtains were gathered by a large window and light flooded the room. On Woolton's desk were positioned more framed photographs. There was a fading wedding photograph of himself with Maud. Another saw him dressed in a dark suit, standing next to King George

VI who was dressed in the khaki uniform of field marshal, the pair examining a map which detailed the country's emergency food storage areas. The King leans over the table, studying the map diligently, while Woolton holds his glasses in his right hand and looks relaxed and confident in the company of the sovereign. Woolton remembered the conversation on 8 May 1940, which had taken place in the Food Ministry's chart room. As the pressman flashed his camera, Woolton was explaining how local food offices were organised and the exact time of day that divisional food offices reported on the local situation.

Another photograph showed him in black tie with the Prime Minister of the late 1950s, Harold Macmillan. There was also a picture, a personal favourite of his, showing him at a lectern at the Conservative Party conference in Bournemouth in 1955. It was three years previously and he was giving his farewell speech as chairman of the party.

Directly in front of Woolton on the desk was a pile of neatly stacked papers. He looked at it contentedly. It contained several hundred sheets of his neat handwriting. This was his current piece of work, his memoirs, and come Monday his secretary would begin to type up the papers.

There would be no clever name, no snazzy title. He had long resolved with his publishers, Cassell & Company, that it would be entitled *The Memoirs of the Rt. Hon. The Earl of Woolton C.H., P.C., D.L., LL.D*; his name, title, awards and doctorates being quite sufficient to herald its contents.

He was almost halfway through writing it; the day before he'd just finished putting in neat order his recollections of how he had managed the internal distribution of food across

Britain. This morning he had just one final bit to add to that chapter; it would merit just three paragraphs and would have a small subtitle – Black Market.

On this subject the first earl was adamant, unequivocal. He set about writing it and within a mere fifteen minutes had concluded all that was needed to be said.

'There was little or no black market in Britain,' he stated. It was, he firmly believed, 'a tribute to the British people which I hope the historians of this period will proudly record.'

He glanced at the image of himself delivering that final speech in Bournemouth and composed the next few sentences as if he were to deliver them forcefully from that same lectern.

'It was, of course, nothing more than the normal operation of the British people, their attitude to the law of the land, and their sense of fair dealing with one another.'

Yet it was not just the resilience and character of the British people that had created this singular absence of a black market; Woolton was resolute that some of the credit should go to himself. He remembered very clearly his thinking at the time. There would always be criminals, there would always be unscrupulous foreigners – both breeds not at one with British values – and so he would have to set up a system of harsh penalties that would deter those most insistent on profiteering illegally from the scarcity of supplies and the rigidity of rationing. He was not worried about small-scale, petty offending; the housewife who got an extra ration from a butcher who had taken a shine to this young woman whose husband was away at war, the boys selling a few apples scrumped from an orchard.

'What mattered,' resolved Woolton, 'was to be sure that there could not be a "market".' And so he would put in place such measures as to prevent that. 'Now and again a combination of people – very often people who had hailed from other countries and [who had] not got accustomed to the British way of life – made such efforts,' he wrote. He would stamp on such villains with punitive legislation, encouraging Home Secretary Herbert Morrison to increase penalties for black market offences. Jail sentences would be dished out and fines paid that amounted to three times the value of the capital involved in the dodgy transaction.

Judges would relish the power Woolton's special legislative orders would give them. 'The penalties for infringement of the food regulations were literally ruinous for the people convicted of breaking the law,' he said, 'and the consequence was that, however great the temptation to make money in this illicit manner might have been, it became so perilous an occupation that few indeed dared to embark on it – and most of those who did so subsequently had plenty of time for reflection, away from temptation.'

If you crossed Woolton you were going down. And alongside his fines and threats of incarceration was a PR plan that, whenever possible, he would front. He would go on the radio, would make speeches, would pen articles, ensuring that the British public would come to understand that his ration system was both fair and correct.

As he wrote, he took great pleasure in recounting the time when an Ambassador to one friendly allied nation had once asked his wife: 'How does your husband account for the fact that there is so little black market in this country?' The man had, reflected Woolton, 'been here a long time, but he had not learned to understand the British character, for the answer to that question was because the British public disapproves of black markets.' And that was that.

But what Woolton failed to mention, either deliberately or through ignorance, was another side to the story.

Take Billy Hill, for example. Hill was a dapper gangster from London's Seven Dials, by Covent Garden, an area police once described as having more pickpockets per square yard than anywhere else in the world. In the late twentieth century it became a fashionable place; but in the 1940s it was an area of destitution, crime and general low life. Hill would become a leading figure of the wartime underworld, and later a notorious gangster operating in everything from smuggling and protection rackets to forgery and ostentatious robberies.

Within weeks of rationing being introduced, Hill, born in 1911, was exploiting the need that rationing threw up. He had spells in prison throughout his life and, after the war, was a prosperous individual. Hill talked proudly of the war years decades later to his biographer, Wensley Clarkson: 'So that big, wide, handsome and, oh, so profitable black market walked into our ever open arms,' he said. 'Some day someone should write a treatise on Britain's wartime black market. It was the most fantastic side of civilian life in wartime. Make no mistake. It cost Britain millions of pounds. I didn't merely make use of the black market. I fed it.'

Convinced his call-up papers would arrive at his home in Camden Town sooner or later, he got busy the moment war broke out to take advantage of a nation's security services focusing on an enemy rather further afield. Amid rumours that he had bribed his way out of the forces, no papers ever arrived, although in his autobiography he insisted he was as baffled as anyone as to why he was never called up.

He quickly realised that storage depots were easy pickings and started stealing and selling whatever he could. 'Four or five smash 'n' grab raids in a week were nothing unusual for Hill's mob,' wrote his biographer Wensley Clarkson in his book, *Billy Hill – Godfather of London*. He also developed a nice line in robbing post offices. When he wasn't selling the likes of fur coats, stolen from warehouses free of alarms or guards and always under the cover of darkness thanks to blackouts, he was selling whisky; with supplies scarce there were numerous small-time illegal distilleries selling danger-ously unsavoury spirits. Hill was disdainful of this hooch and realised there was a market for the genuine article. 'I liked to think that if I was crooked, at least I was bent in an honest way,' he reflected many years later. 'I sold only real whisky. Good stuff at that.'

So with his gang he identified and raided facilities that stored whisky, later selling barrels for £500 each. There seemed to be no shortage of people willing to pay a lively price. Similarly he got hold of and sold sausage skins to butchers, and in the early years of the war was making between £300 and £400 a week from his trading. He man-aged to evade the law even if he did occasionally drink with those seeking to catch him. One night Scotland Yard's chief inspector Peter Beveridge called into Hill's local pub in Camden. 'Make the most of it while you can because when I feel your collar, you're going to stay nicked for a long time,' he told the criminal. 'Well, guv'nor,' replied Hill, 'you can't blame me for everything. I've got to earn, and you've got to catch. What you havin'?'

He was incarcerated in Chelmsford Prison in 1940 after a jewellery heist, but served barely twelve months, returning to his wife Aggie back home in Camden Town who, he noted admiringly, had been pretty diligent herself in his absence. Her kitchen was filled with fresh eggs and butter and a number of other things the ration card wouldn't have permitted.

He quickly returned to what he casually described as his 'bread and butter' – the food and drink black market – and also started hitting sub-post offices again where he stole cash as well as stamps and money orders. Blacked-out windows added to the ease of the jobs, as it meant that passing police patrols couldn't see the criminals working inside with their flashlights. Hill then rented a large barn near a big, yet remote, air base at Bovingdon in Hertfordshire, where he stashed everything that was in short supply during the war years: whisky, clothes, towels, bed sheets, furniture, food, silk, tobacco, jewellery and petrol. It was to the barn that Hill and his gang would ferry unopened safes where they could safely, out of earshot, blow off the doors.

By the time war ended, Hill was in Dartmoor prison having been grabbed by the police while escaping from a botched job knocking a postmaster on the head in Islington. But the end of the war didn't mean the end of the black market. Rationing would continue until 1954 and many goods remained in short supply. It was a time, wrote Clarkson, when 'black marketeers scoured the countryside, buying up broken-down horses which would later be served up as choice rump steak in high-class establishments.'

Of course Billy Hill was not operating alone. The onset of war and implementation of rationing saw a surge of black market operations. In 1939 just twenty people were convicted of black market offences, described technically as 'Persons found guilty of offences against the defence regulations.' In 1941 the figure was 13,580, in 1942 the number leapt to 30,309.

They were figures that caused alarm among those who constantly niggled at Lord Woolton and his ministry, namely peers in the House of Lords. On 15 July 1941 Viscount Dawson of Penn, the King's doctor and regular critic of the minister, accused Woolton of neglecting the issue. Lord Dawson spoke of his disquiet at discovering that so many people engaged in black market activity.

'This sort of thing going on in this country must cause us a great deal of disquietude and alarm, because it is un-British that in a time of crisis anyone should endeavour to evade the regulations and restrictions,' he said. Dawson likened it to a disease and 'moreover, a very infectious disease, because when one section of the community discovers that sums of money have been made by flouting these food restrictions and regulations, it means that others are tempted to do likewise.'

He then socked it to Woolton. 'One cannot help feeling that this foul growth should have been nipped in the bud by the Minister of Food when he discovered that huge profits were being made in this way,' he said. 'He ought to have put his foot down at once and prevented the disease from spreading.' Woolton felt that he had put a stop to such antics with his Standstill Order of 6 January 1941.

Later that year, in May, he wrote of the stern briefing he gave to those officials who were responsible for catching those who profited from rationing. 'I had our Enforcement Officers at a meeting in the ministry and told them we must get this black racketeering stopped.' On 13 June he decided to reprimand the whole nation via BBC radio. 'I broadcast to the people of Britain,' he wrote that evening. 'I told them it wasn't any use them getting all worked up about the newspaper stories of profiteering whilst they themselves helped the profiteer to live by buying his goods.'

In fact the evidence points to there being rather fewer Billy Hills and rather more of what has been termed the grey market. According to historian Ina Zweiniger-Bargielowska, whose book *Austerity in Britain* analysed rationing, controls and consumption during the Second World War, 'There was no large-scale organised black market in Britain.' Instead, she wrote, 'It operated through widespread infringement of the regulations by producers, distributors, and retailers, ultimately sustained by public demand.' Hence Lord Woolton's admonishing of the general populace.

To make it quite clear what he meant by the black market he ordered his ministry to print leaflets defining it. Widely distributed and often visible in shops, the pamphlet described the black market as 'attempts to distribute foods in short supply through abnormal or unauthorised channels with the object of securing profit out of all proportion to the services rendered'. Those who worked the black market were 'unscrupulous men' who worked to obtain 'more than their fair share of goods in short supply'. Those who profited were 'the unscrupulous individual, the trader anxious to build up stocks unfairly'. The language was all about right and wrong and fairness. It was a moral issue.

Working to detect illegal trading were enforcers at the Ministry of Food run by a Director of Enforcement. There were regional teams who collaborated with the police, and local food offices tasked with dealing with minor offences by retailers and the public. The efforts were beefed up in the middle of the war after a report by divisional food officers in April 1943 stated that it 'was obvious that many black market operators worked on a national scale and a co-ordinated effort was needed to defeat them'.

Thus the figures for convictions peaking mid-war can be explained by more rigorous enforcement demanded by politicians such as Woolton, and the fact that recorded crime in general dramatically increased during that period. Some ten years later, criminologists, making a study of the 1940s, pointed to how society erred towards wrongdoing during the war. Family ties were loosened, consumer goods were scarce, bombed-out houses made it simpler for looters, supplies of guns and ammunition were easy to come by and deserters, who lived on the fringes of society without official documents, tended towards criminality. And the general lack of trained police officers and other officials who were abroad fighting meant that law-breakers could often get away with it.

As for the grey market, it was widespread. Katherine Knight recorded some voices for her book *Rationing in the Second World War* which included the following:

'We never had anything extra – except sugar. Don't quite know where it came from, but my mother kept it in the airing cupboard.'

'My father came back from the farm with a big bit of butter about once a fortnight.'

'My father was a Church Warden but we once had a whole side of bacon from his cousin in the country.'

Likewise Lizzie Collingham's *The Taste of War* records a conversation between Vera Hodgson and her grocer in February 1941. 'Went for my bacon ration and while he was cutting it had a word with the man about the Cubic Inch of cheese. He got rid of the other customers and then whispered: "Wait a mo." I found half a pound of cheese being thrust into my bag with great secrecy and speed.' It was nothing more than normal civilian behaviour, it was just that war and rationing had made it an infringement if not actually a crime.

Meanwhile food producers themselves employed a variety of tricks to enable them to keep back food for themselves, or others in their communities, if not for actual illegal profiteering. Farmers could simply fail to register a small fraction of their livestock – an animal here and there – or those at the slaughterhouse could weigh a carcass with its head on, so that the equivalent of the weight of that head could be kept back for an illegal sale.

Yet those members of the public who took a little extra here and there did think that Lord Woolton overstated the case when he denied that a significant black market was operating. In June 1943 a Gallup poll of the British public showed that 72 per cent thought that Woolton was exaggerated in his view that this market was virtually non-existent. Still Woolton claimed there was massive public hostility to the black market – through speeches and via guilt-inducing posters. One advertisement he published, for example, on 14 September 1941 – across the country in national and regional newspapers – featured an illustration of an eyeglass and spoke directly to the readers: 'Ask yourself these 5 questions,' it said in tones of George Orwell's ever-watchful Big Brother. 'Do you ever try to get more than your ration? Or accept more if offered?' It's unlikely that a wave of guilt swept across the nation.

Yet his constant insistence that the public was hostile to the black market was a successful piece of propaganda. And it came hand in hand with very heavy penalties; Woolton relished every time he got legislation through that inflicted harsher punishments on illegal trading. On 17 December 1942 he primed a peer in the House of Lords to ask a question about penalties for those people 'trafficking in the black market', noting in his diary that this enabled him to announce that, 'in addition to the present maximum penalty of £100, people can be fined three times the value of the goods involved in the transaction or three times the price at which they were offered, even if the transaction did not eventually materialise.'

He was pleased with the response to his words. 'The press took up the story very well,' he wrote, 'and it rests with the magistrates to enforce the penalties. The newspapers and the public have consistently blamed me for not making the punishment fit the crime: they forget that I am powerless to enforce the law.'

He was similarly charged up the following February. The harshest month was as grim as it could be, with freezing temperatures and snow on the ground that did not exactly leave the capital looking like a winter wonderland. 'London has had a very heavy snowfall and it is so cold that everybody looks miserable,' Woolton wrote. 'I've never seen a town look so dirty as London does with dirty half-melted snow piled in the streets. There are few men to clean them, and even the shopkeepers seem to be so shorthanded that they do not clean in the front of their shops.'

But Woolton had a tonic that would at least warm his cockles. This time he had the Billy Hills of the black market in his sights, or at any rate those of his ilk who had bank accounts.

He organised a meeting with Sir Eric Gore-Brown, a partner of the banking firm Glyn Mills & Co., a private bank that dated back to the 18th century and had been sold to the Bank of Scotland. Sir Eric was a distinguished soldier and was well respected in the banking industry. 'I want him to persuade the banks to help us in tracing the people who operate the black market,' wrote Woolton.

Sir Eric was, said Woolton, 'a modest and delightful fellow' and the moustachioed, round-spectacled city gent took his seat in Woolton's office.

'The banks must have, in the operation of their business, knowledge of people who are using large amounts of cash, instead of cheques, with which to conduct business,' Woolton asserted. 'The black market is operated on a cash basis, and if we could be supplied with the names of the firms who are handling large amounts of cash and notes, we might get on the track of some of the larger operators.'

This government intrusion into the confidentiality of private bank accounts was met with simply a stalling nod from

Sir Eric. He said he would look into the matter. But there is no record of him making any progress, nor of Woolton having further meetings on the subject.

A fortnight later he had another go, this time pushing through a harsh law that delivered a maximum sentence of fourteen years' penal servitude for black market trading. 'People will think twice about continuing their practice,' he muttered to himself as he penned his diary on the evening of 2 March having announced the measure that day.

Although when he made tough announcements it didn't always please Winston Churchill. Back in February 1941 Woolton had issued new regulations for hotels, culinary establishments and canteens. The *Evening Standard* focused on the penalties Woolton announced with a headline that spoke of 'Imprisonment or fine' and talked of 'Prison if you eat meat or fish, egg or cheese.' 'The PM was furious,' Maud wrote in her diary, 'and sent a "snorter" to F objecting.'

Woolton recorded the details of the 'snorter' in his diary. 'I could have wished that this class of announcement should be referred to the Cabinet before it was made public,' he recorded Churchill as writing.

'F got annoyed,' commented Maud, 'and sent a similar one back indicating that the person to grumble at was the Editor of the ES. The PM cannot bear these food restrictions!!'

Churchill was also irritated at the press coverage Woolton had generated on 18 February, after he had made a speech in the House of Lords 'warning the country that the effects of submarine and air attacks would inevitably mean restrictions on food.' The speech, he noted in his diary, 'had a very good press'. There had been a leader in *The Times* and, wrote

Woolton, 'several members of the government congratulated me on my courage in making it.'

But, just as he was savouring his good PR, 'The Prime Minister sent for me at night, and warned me against the dangers of being drawn into political rationing.'

Then on 2 March Churchill reprimanded him again. 'Perhaps before you have any other important announcements to make, you will consult the Cabinet, and then the Minister for Information who will be able to make sure the right emphasis is put on the orders before the news is given to the newspapers,' he wrote, as Woolton recorded in his diary.

Woolton reflected on such admonishments saying: 'I always felt like a little boy when the Prime Minister used to reprove me for having taken action without consulting either him or the Cabinet, and I had to acknowledge my error and faithfully promise that I would try not to do it again.'

Ten weeks later on 12 March and the pair met again. They discussed food supplies. 'He was in great form,' wrote Woolton, 'and when he had finished making a general attack on me, he said "I have said what I wanted to say: now you go for me" – which I did but in the same mood. I fortunately knew the answers to everything that he had raised, and was able to assure him that everything he had proposed had already been done months ago. It was a good meeting, and it didn't do him any harm to know that his Food Minister neither resented attacks, nor wilted under them.'

Woolton now had in place severe punishments: fines at three times the value of the goods traded, £500 fines for some offences (bear in mind that the average male wage was just over £6 per week) plus incarceration; any non-payment would lead to a bankruptcy order on the culprit's business.

However, Woolton's problem in tackling the bigwigs was that they didn't rely solely on food profiteering. The likes of Billy Hill were into everything from petrol to cigarettes, so they had money to fund fines and could diversify away from food if they guessed their collars were about to be felt. But when it came to controlling the black market in alcohol, Woolton was less concerned. There was a shortage of whisky, for example, not surprisingly and Woolton acknowledged that this enabled those who had it and were selling it to do rather well. 'Large profits are being made by the sale of black market spirits,' he wrote in November 1941. But, he added: 'Personally I am not interested: if people like to be swindled into paying these extortionate prices for spirits, which are totally unnecessary as a luxury, I should let them be swindled.' His department, he felt, had better things to do. 'I see no reason for a government with a war of this nature on its hands spending its time trying to protect people who are foolish enough to pay "through the nose" for liquor.'

Woolton's own tastes and stomach issues meant he was naturally contemptuous of what he saw as luxury foods and alcohol. But he must have ultimately understood that if the housewife was to be thrifty as she sought to care for her family, she might also seek a little extra here or there. And while he liked to claim that it was the British character that lessened the extent of black market trading, it probably has more to do with the fact that Woolton and his ministry held a very tight control over the production and distribution of food. At every stage there was tough enforcement, so criminals actually found it quite hard to get a look in.

Yet Woolton's punitive views were not quite as strong as those of the Paymaster General, Sir William Jowitt. While Woolton was arguing for a maximum fourteen-year term, Sir William announced in a speech he gave at his former constituency Ashton-Under-Lyne, the market town in Greater Manchester, that that those who indulged in black market practices ought to be brought before a war court and then, if found guilty, be sentenced to death before a firing squad.

Sir William's entry into the debate came after a new swindle came to light that month involving the substitution of foods in cans, packages and bottles. The fake food concerned dodgy surrogates for the likes of eggs, onions, oranges and milk. A newswire story on 26 February 1942, revealed that 'egg substitutes were 90 per cent wheat flour with the addition of dye and gum.' It reported a product that described itself as a 'perfect substitute for lemons' and 'contained only citric acid and starch', while 'one common milk substitute was composed of flour, salt and sweetening.' The same thing was happening with other household goods with an item described as mascara being nothing but shoe polish and some rouge-coloured paint powder. The CP cable wire service reported that 'Manufacturers of many of these items have been arrested.'

Sir William's remarks were welcomed by several newspapers who argued that, if sailors had risked their lives in bringing cargo in from overseas, then those who stole it should lose theirs. The same newswire story mentioned the following occurrences: '240 tonnes of molasses stolen from a Thames wharf went into the black market; 144 cartons of tomato puree, stolen from a bombed warehouse, were sold for more than three times the controlled price; 18,000 eggs and 50,000 chickens were sold above the maximum price.'

Yet Sir William's part in the debate was quickly curtailed when a little bit of black market shenanigans was discovered on his own doorstep. Woolton merrily recorded it in his diary: 'it transpired that he had a country estate and has been receiving feedings stuffs above the ration from supplies that had been stolen.' Sir William was prosecuted later that year for buying animal feed without the appropriate coupons for his farm in Kent. He had been zealous in the prosecution of exactly such offences, but in court claimed that he employed a bailiff to run the farm and had no knowledge that the offence was being committed. The court accepted his explanation and he got away with it. And so, by and large, did Billy Hill.

11

REGULATION AND AUSTERITY

On 21 March 1941 Woolton was summoned to Chequers, the Prime Minister's rural retreat in Buckinghamshire.

Chequers, a well as being a haven from bomb-torn London, was a refuge from the ration. Churchill, disparaging of the system, thinking it over-complicated and lacking a bit of common sense, liked to base his views on first-hand experience. He had written to Woolton a few days earlier – on 2 March – complaining about a new system of regulating foodstuffs, whereby consumers had to choose between fish or meat. 'I should have though that an exhortation not to leave anything on the plate, and to take small portions, with, if necessary, a second helping, would be a wise step.'

For Woolton such advice was just Churchillian eccentricity. But clearly that was how Churchill managed his own personal ration. He cleared his plate and then had a second helping if he felt like one. After all there was no lack of food at Chequers or 10 Downing Street. Churchill told his personal staff to write to the Ministry of Food; but not to Woolton. The letters, containing requests for extra ration books, points or whatever was needed, would always be addressed to more junior minions who would not query demands from the Prime Minister.

For example, on 24 June 1940 Churchill's private secretary John Martin wrote to one R. P. Harvey at the ministry to say: 'Both at Chequers and at No 10 Downing Street the rationing restrictions make it very difficult to entertain officially to the extent which the Prime Minister finds necessary. Mr Churchill has asked if an arrangement could be made whereby in both instances extra rations could be supplied to cover official guests.'

Likewise in the same month there was a letter from the Downing Street cook, Georgina Landemere, asking for extra ration books. Other staff, such as Kathleen Hill or Elizabeth Layton – assistant private secretaries – wrote frequently during the course of the war to say they had 'exhausted' their supplies and to ask for extra coupons for meat and cooking fats and tea as well as cheese and butter vouchers. One private secretary wrote to the Army & Navy Store in London asking for extra sugar for 'bottling' at Chequers. Similarly those who had to entertain Churchill – if he was due for a weekend house party, for example, or just coming for lunch – would write to the Ministry of Food.

On 14 November 1940 John Martin put in another request, this time for extra coupons for the chef at Ditchley Park, in Oxfordshire (where Churchill often stayed and sometimes held important meetings).

There is also a record of a telephone conversation between Martin and a ministry official on 20 November 1940, in which the official confirmed that there would be 'no difficulty' in using special diplomatic food coupons at places, other than Chequers, where the Prime Minister might spend his weekends. While Britain had to tighten its belt, it seems Churchill merely loosened his.

But Woolton would not raise his eyebrows at the food on offer at Chequers that evening in March 1941. He had more pressing arguments to make and, not having suffered a bout of illness for some time, rather relished the prospect of a decent dinner. He detailed the events of the night in his diary.

He was told to dress appropriately for it, in black tie and dinner jacket. Churchill himself, who had spent much of the afternoon and evening asleep, shunned that garb, coming downstairs instead in that 1940s equivalent of the onesie, his blue siren suit. Woolton was hungry and they tucked into fish and then cold, rare beef.

Woolton had two helpings. 'Because I actually live on the rations I prescribe for the country I am hungry,' he said to Churchill and his fellow guest Robert Hudson, the Conservative Minister of Agriculture, as he popped another pile of reddish, thinly cut beef onto his plate. 'I think it's important that I get more meat.'

'You're too much like a dictator,' Churchill scoffed, 'you keep wanting to send people to prison.' It had not escaped the Prime Minister's notice that Woolton had administered harsh penalties and threatened prison to those who made minor domestic errors. Just a month earlier, on 25 February, Churchill had written to Woolton saying: 'I must say I do not like all this rather dictatorial publicity. I do not think anyone ought to be sent to prison merely for making mistakes.'

So for the rest of the evening Churchill referred to Woolton as 'General Goering'. After dinner the PM put on some very loud marching music. 'This music does us good,' he yelled above the din of the gramophone record, as he started marching about the room. 'We must have lightness in life as well as food and this music stirs the blood.'

Amid the crashing symbols, drums and bagpipes, Churchill received the news, from a member of staff who seemed quite used to the scene, that two German battleships, the *Scharnhorst* and the *Gneisenau*, were steaming towards the French port of Brest, their guns loaded, ready and threatening. Churchill got on the telephone to Bomber Command and, as the marching tune ploughed on, ordered them to go and bomb the ships. 'We saw the War Lord in action,' wrote Woolton, 'and it was very good action too.'

Come midnight, Churchill suggested they get to work discussing the country's slaughter policy for cattle. Two hours later and they were discussing the issue of ships. 'You have taken my ships that were bringing food into this country and sent them to the Middle East without any reference to the consequences to the food position,' Woolton complained. 'I must have some of them back.'

'It was 2.30 in the morning,' wrote Woolton, and Churchill, having put on another record, 'resumed his parade around the room and told me he would give me 2 million tons of extra shipping.'

'That is only one half of what I need,' Woolton said, almost shouting to be heard above the music.

'So I will give you some refrigerated tonnage to bring in meat,' Churchill shouted back, pausing and standing bolt upright by the fireplace. 'But I want another 2 million tons in addition to that,' said Woolton. 'You're being difficult,' Churchill told him. 'We should go to bed.' Churchill then walked him to his room and told him to look him up before he left in the morning.

'I will,' said Woolton. 'But I shall tell you now that I need 15 million tons of shipping,' and in saying that he presented a formal note of his demand. Churchill, says Woolton, 'was not too pleased, but accepted it and a few days later sent out a directive saying that I was to have what I wanted.'

As Woolton closed the door of his bedroom, he breathed a sigh of relief at the prospect of a few hours of peace, privacy and some sleep. He lay in bed that night pondering on the events of that evening: the marching music, Churchill ordering British planes to rally to the cause and bomb those German ships, his extraordinary suit, those rare cuts of beef. As he drifted to sleep he was sure he could hear the Prime Minister barking out more orders somewhere in the house.

'He works in his own way,' Woolton reflected, 'and consequently it isn't easy to work with him but he continues to be perpetually animating.'

Britain Eats Out

Some five days later, in late March of 1941, *The Times* reported the news of 'British Restaurants In Over 100 Towns.' A banner headline on the same story also announced: 'Emergency Centres Renamed'.

Woolton had been working on a scheme to launch some 10,000 state-run cafes. These were not-for-profit eating centres and Woolton's request to Churchill to approve the plan had not been one he expected to have any difficulty with. The Prime Minister did indeed give Woolton the go-ahead, but in a memo he stipulated one proviso: Woolton must abandon his plan to call them 'Communal Feeding Centres'. 'It is an odious expression, suggestive of Communism and the workhouse', he wrote. 'I suggest you call them British Restaurants. Everybody associates the word "restaurant" with a good meal.'

Woolton didn't argue, made a press announcement and *The Times* duly reported that '"communal feeding centres" is too cold and dreary a name for the new eating houses for all the people which are being started all over the country.'

Woolton also wrote to local authorities around the country, asking that they support his plan for the restaurants. Diners would not have to flash their ration books and, he said, 'If every man, woman and child could be sure of obtaining at least one hot, nourishing meal a day at a price all could afford we should be sure of the nation's health and strength during the war.'

In fact, 79 million meals a week were eaten by civilians outside their homes in May 1941 with the figure rising to 170 million by December 1944, equivalent to an average of some four meals a week for every man, woman and child. These British Restaurants were opened across the country, often officially by Lord Woolton, and frequently in his absence by his wife Maud, something she mentions in her diary. 'I can't speak with authority,' Maud wrote, 'the Ministry of

Food wanted to take responsibility for what I might say and I don't want to talk about F all the time. However, I generally manage to say something fairly innocuous without being too dull.'

The Ministry of Food came across some apathy from boroughs unaffected by air raids, and there was some hostility from commercial caterers worried about the detrimental affects to their business from this subsidised dining. But while Woolton didn't manage his ambition of 10,000 cafes, by 1943 there were 2,160, serving 650,000 midday meals as well as breakfasts and suppers. Most were in areas not served by factory canteens, and often located in town and village halls, serving food consisting of meat, fish, vegetables, soups, puddings, tea and coffee. One such establishment in Liverpool, the Byrom Street Restaurant, sold main courses such as fish pie, beef and dumplings or minced beef with carrots and parsnips, as well as currant or milk pudding. Main courses cost 6d (around £2 in today's money), soup 1d and puddings 3d. Tea, coffee or cocoa was priced at 1d.

There was also a British Restaurant that the Ministry of Food and locals used in Colwyn Bay. The establishment, seating 150 people, opened on 10 January 1942 and was located in the Congregational Church Lecture Theatre on Sea View Road. There, the ministry's civil servants could get a shilling lunch; for that, you could get soup, roast lamb, vegetables, a pudding and a cup of tea of coffee. To ensure no one left carrying any of the cutlery or crockery it was all stamped 'Colwyn Bay British Restaurant'.

Surveys done during the war tended to give these restaurants a reasonable rating although they were not to everyone's taste. One diner, Frances Partridge, a Bloomsbury group writer and more regular habitué of London's The Ivy, wrote of her visit to a British Restaurant in Swindon: 'a huge elephant house, where thousands of human beings were eating, as we did, an enormous all-beige meal, starting with beige soup thickened to the consistency of paste, followed by beige mince full of lumps and garnished with beige beans and a few beige potatoes, thin beige apple stew and a sort of skilly [thin porridge]. Very satisfying and crushing, and calling up a vision of our future Planned World, all beige also . . .'

Woolton would, of course, have eagerly dismissed such pompous scribblings. He was happy that these restaurants, in his own words, 'served an urgent need'; people were having their tummies filled, whatever the colour of the food. Not that such places were always above criticism; he often noted, privately, instances of poor cooking, particularly for workers. On 15 October 1942 he had inspected a factory canteen newly opened at the Port of London. 'It is a first class affair from a structural point of view,' he wrote, 'but I thought it shared the usual fault of these places that the food was badly cooked. I'm not a bit convinced that they are as good as they ought to be. To spoil food in the cooking in these days of scarcity is a social crime.'

It was an unusual fact of the Second World War that a very large number of people stopped eating meals in their own homes – and not just because they had been bombed. As John Burnett, author of *England Eats Out*, wrote, 'One of the strange ironies of the Second World War is that more people ate out than ever before and, probably never again, until the most recent years.'

But while the general populace lived with rationing and had regular hot meals in such places as communal halls, it wasn't a picture of unadulterated austerity. Smart independent restaurants or those in halls still operated, albeit with somewhat straitened menus. With Woolton as head of the Ministry of Food however, the world of gastronomy could not count on support from his department; Woolton was not a fan of anything that even nodded to the concept of richness.

On Thursday 15 October 1942, for example, he was found sitting at his desk looking distinctly off colour, feeling in turns sick, guilty, remorseful and cross. And he was tired; he hadn't slept well, his weak constitution having been tested beyond measure. Even his treasured pipe tobacco tasted off.

Lunch the day before, to which he had taken Maud, had been at the Russian Embassy, a grand, gothic building in the smart and exclusive confines of Kensington Palace Gardens. There had been course after course, endless drinks and, as he ploughed his way through the meal, he wondered half-joking if the whole event was some kind of set-up. Perhaps word had gone around diplomatic circles that the current Minister of Food disdained ostentation and a few mischievous individuals determined to make light of it. When he and his wife were finally able to leave the lunch and were putting on their coats, the American Ambassador had turned to Maud and said sarcastically: 'I hope your husband appreciates the austerity under which we ambassadors live.'

The Wooltons were not amused; Maud forever fussed about her husband's delicate constitution, and this lunch was decidedly unhelpful. Indeed, Woolton's groaning stomach had deterred him from returning to the office; he'd gone home instead and straight to bed. He hadn't even had the strength to write his diary.

The following morning at his Portman Square office he, somewhat painfully, recorded the details of the previous day's gastronomic adventure. 'We had lobster and vodka – I tried to pass on both – followed by grouse with potatoes and a salad followed by a soufflé, by cheese straws as a savoury, grapes and coffee: cigars and four different sorts of liqueurs, and of course there had been a choice of two wines.' He called his secretary into his office and demanded he scrutinise the schedule. He didn't want to see the inside of an embassy or a smart restaurant for at least the next forty-eight hours.

The previous day's banquet aside, he was simply not a fan of fancy dining establishments. They served their purpose when it came to entertaining influential newspaper barons, or if he was seeking to persuade a political ally or enemy, but his dislike of large and long lunches or dinners was not a pose for the benefit of the press. He was certainly known by the head waiters of places such as L'Escargot, and the dining rooms of the Savoy or Claridge's, but anything too fussy and rich and he regretted it badly during the subsequent hours, days even. And as Minister of Food he shuddered when he saw anything that came close to waste.

On 22 May 1940, addressing a lunch attended by leading British caterers, he touched on this subject. 'If you knew the amount of time, trouble and anxiety that some of us have gone through to secure the bread supply,' he said, 'you would know what feelings are when I see a waiter, clearing a table, take a roll of bread that has not been eaten and put it in an ash-tray.'

Yet while many might have expected him to put smart restaurants in the firing line – after all he had all but banned ice-cream and jam – he was reluctant to interfere with this field of private enterprise. 'The question was repeatedly raised as to whether hotel and other restaurants should not be closed down during war-time on the grounds that they constituted "luxury feeding". This was not right: people needed relaxation,' he argued. 'I said I did not defend luxurious living, but if I could give to the hard-working people of this country – and those returning for brief periods from overseas – something of happiness, it would be a contribution to national work.'

But Woolton wanted to vanquish any perceptions that smart restaurants continued to operate normally, feeding their customers with whatever they wanted. 'There were the restaurants, and particularly the luxurious ones, which were popularly supposed to have all the food their clientele demanded,' he wrote. 'It was not true: but it was a political issue which, with all the egalitarianism of rationing, could not be ignored.'

There were agitators, for example, such as the Stepney Young Communist League who, on the evening of 14 September 1941, marched down the Embankment towards the Savoy, encouraged by their beloved *Daily Worker* newspaper. 'If you live in the Savoy Hotel you are called by telephone when the sirens sound and then tucked into bed by servants in a luxury bomb-proof shelter,' went one editorial. 'The people must act,' it demanded. So the group trooped to the front door of the hotel and made it inside the lobby, where a strange thing then happened. According to one hotel guest, Constantine Fitz-Gibbon, who witnessed the scene: 'The demonstrators were so awed by the Chaldean splendours of the hotel that they soon forgot to shout their slogans.' The hotel staff breathed a sigh of relief as the gathering was ushered out and dispersed. The establishment did not want untoward publicity; it retained much of its smart clientele and certain pre-rationing standards in the restaurant, and the last thing it needed was any public scrutiny.

As a parry to this threat, the hotel decided to release a set of photographs that showed business as usual in the face of war. Pictures showed sandbags at the front of the hotel, a diminished-looking dining room and off-duty soldiers dining modestly.

Woolton did not want to curtail absolutely the operations of smart restaurants because, while conspicious consumption would not go down well with the British public, the message that one could still eat well in the capital's best dining rooms had its uses in the face of the enemy. As Matthew Sweet wrote in his book, *The West End Front*, 'If Hitler could not disrupt the business of dinner, then what chance did he have against shipping or heavy industry.'

Sweet also mused on the PR tightrope that such establishments walked; normality in London's grand hotels being perceived as 'proof that all were not equal under fire'. If the likes of smart restaurants put out the message that normal service had resumed, 'it represented something less attractive,' he wrote: 'the tenacity of privilege during wartime.'

Woolton though wanted restaurants to behave modestly,

telling the *Daily Express* on 4 July 1940 that he wished to cut out 'ostentatious eating'. At a press conference in Manchester the following day he said, 'We are going to have to be content to live a harder life gastronomically,' but, he added, 'We shall not be the worse off for it.' So Woolton never threated restaurants with closure – instead he hit them with regulations.

Throughout the war there came a stream of orders from the Ministry of Food. Meat allocations to commercial caterers were restricted, restaurants were first encouraged to voluntarily restrict meals to one main course before being ordered to limit it to one main dish of meat, fish, poultry, game, eggs or cheese (soup didn't count). Icing sugar was banned, as was the manufacture of cream, not more than a twelfth of an ounce of butter could be served with a meal, the use of milk in cakes, biscuits and ice cream was banned, as was white flour and white bread, and in September 1942 the manufacture of ice cream itself was prohibited.

It was the limitation on meat and fish, and the disappearance of butter and cream, that most vexed the chefs, although it wasn't just their ingenuity that would be tested. As the home cook used a little creative cunning, so too did regular restaurant-goers, who with a nod and a wink from the manager could get around some of the regulations. At the Savoy, for example, while Crêpe Suzette fell foul of the rules, a diner could order a pancake then ask separately for some brandy and a box of matches, before flambéing the dessert themselves at the table.

Chefs, meanwhile, added a little magic to their meagre offerings by dressing them up in French on the menu. 'Le

rable de lièvre à la crème' was a saddle of hare in a cream-
less white wine sauce at the Savoy; Madame Prunier's, in St
James's, offered 'Moules Chowder' with mussels replacing
the American clams and 'Croquettes de Pommes Land Girl',
which was simply mashed potato with dried egg powder.
The Royal Court Hotel had 'Saumon Florentin' (tinned
salmon with spinach), while Simpson's-in-the-Strand played
a straight English bat, as ever, offering a 'Simpson's Cream
Spam Casserole' (potatoes, tomatoes and Spam) as well as
'Simpson's Spam Pancakes', a dish that merits no explanation.
The case was the same for restaurants across Britain. At the
Bristol Grill in the centre of that city, for example, the menu
offered 'Blancmange Vanois', or jelly as they called it in the
kitchen.

Yet many chefs also took advantage of the fact that seemingly up-market delicacies such as lobster, shellfish, hare and
game were not rationed. The wealthy clientele of the grander
hotel restaurants were known to check in with a suitcase in
one hand and a brace of pheasant, a whole salmon or a haunch
of venison culled from their own estate in the other.

The Grosvenor House restaurant offered game in the form
of 'Rabbit Campagnade' and many menus featured wood-
cock. The Savoy also served roast kid and pigeon pie, which
became so ubiquitous that Nancy Mitford named a novel
after it. However, actress Jean Kent recalled a date she had
one night with the producer Jack M. Warner – son of the
film studio founder – at a West End restaurant, where she
ordered a dish called 'Chef's Surprise'. 'I should have known
better,' she later said. 'When it came it was a puff pastry case
with a turnip inside.'

But it was not just the ration that threatened restaurants. The Blitz, between September 1940 and May 1941, made many diners fearful of venturing out. The Savoy was bombed three times, for example, although its mid-war refurbishment came with added attractions. The River Room's roof was re-enforced and favoured couples were given curtained cubicles where they could dine and then stay the night, a post-dinner late night walk home being deemed too dangerous for favoured customers. The society pages reported the Duke and Duchess of Kent slept one night behind one of these curtained recesses.

The fashionable Regent Palace Hotel in Piccadilly, with its Grill Room and cocktail bar, was bombed twice; the Ritz kitchens attempted to cook on radiators after the gas main was damaged by bombs; both the Langham and Cavendish hotels were attacked; and one night at the Café de Paris, as a large crowd of people danced to 'Snakehips' Johnson and his band, a bomb scored a direct hit and killed eighty people.

Yet Lord Woolton would have been irritated had he made some late night forays to some of London's most famous restaurants. One diner at The Ivy in 1940 recalled that the establishment was full of 'prosperous-looking people as usual, all eating a whacking good meal ... and a delicious creamy pudding'. But while that West End haunt was offering smoked salmon, grouse and chocolate mousse in 1942, its menu was looking a little depleted by 1944 with just oysters, some elderly hens and a distinctly average Algerian wine.

Early in the war Sir Henry Channon, the politician and diarist known as Chips Channon, commented on the fact that not everyone seemed to be struggling. He lunched at the Ritz in September 1939 and said the place had become 'fantastically fashionable. Ritzes always thrive in wartime, as we are all cookless,' he wrote. 'Also in wartime the herd instinct rises.' Twelve months later he recorded that, while dining at the Dorchester, he discovered 'half of London [society] there'. On 5 November 1940 he wrote of the same place: 'London lives well. I've never seen more lavishness, more money spent or food consumed than tonight; and the dance floor was packed. There must have been a thousand people.'

When these places weren't cowering from bomb attacks they were also struggling to maintain good levels of service. Many of their experienced waiters, being Austrian, Italian or German, were interned for the duration of the war. Ferrucio Cochis, for example, was the general manager of Claridge's and had worked at the hotel for twenty-one years when he received a letter on 24 April 1940 ordering him to vacate his quarters. The missive was from his employers, on the advice of the government. It wasn't just that he was Italian, though; the British secret service had been advised by US agents that Cochis was in the pay of Rome and alleged that he had, among other things, once bugged the room of a US Under Secretary of State. He was offered a month's pay and, it seems, few staff protested at his departure on account of his ferocious temper.

It was a similar story for Loreto Santarelli, restaurant manager of the Savoy. On 25 June 1940, as trays of high tea were brought to guests in the lobby, two men from Special Branch arrived. They searched his rooms, confiscated his passport and marched him off to a cell in Brixton Prison.

They took two other Italians as well: the assistant banqueting manager, Fortunato Picchi, and his boss Ettore Zavattoni. They were removed, as were so many others, under Defence Regulation 18B, which allowed internment of people if they were suspected of being: 'of hostile origin ... [or] to have been recently concerned in acts prejudicial to the public safety or the defence of the realm.' 'They came,' wrote author Matthew Sweet, 'for waiters and wine butlers and cooks and restaurateurs across London and delivered them, without criminal charge, from hot kitchens and mirrored dining rooms into police cells and holding camps across the country.' Many so-called aliens remained interned until after the war.

Santarelli attended a hearing on 23 October 1940 in front of a committee which decided to revoke the order and free him, while insisting he attend a local police station each week. He returned to the Savoy but his old panache was gone. His hands trembled as he poured drinks, and before he reached the age of sixty he had a heart attack, collapsing and dying on the soft rich carpet of the hotel one morning before the war was over.

Having defended the private operations of restaurants, Woolton also found himself having to shield another British passion: beer. On 12 May 1942 Woolton had to attend the House of Lords to listen to an assault on the idea of beer consumption.

Lord Arnold, a former Liberal and Labour politician and a pacifist who had supported appeasement towards Germany, got to his feet to express his disbelief that beer was still being sipped across the nation: 'It is indeed almost incredible,' he said, 'at a time when nearly everything of universal consumption is rationed or is going to be rationed, and when we have fervid appeals on the wireless to do with less of almost everything of general consumption, that nevertheless the consumption of beer should remain, and should have remained throughout the war, at about the highest point for the last ten years.

'Now I come to the Minister of Food himself,' continued Lord Arnold who looked down at Woolton, sat on the benches listening diligently while wearing his favourite non-committal and benign expression. 'Only a few weeks ago, he [Woolton] said: "The time has come for a call for great personal austerity, austerity in living, austerity in working, and austerity in thinking." I do not quite know what that means, but that is what he said, and he went on: "I shall have to give you many opportunities for practising austerity." Yes, my Lords, but there is not to be austerity in beer drinking.'

As Lord Arnold sat down Woolton got to his feet and began his reply. 'I was among those – not with such extreme views as, in my opinion, the noble Lord had – who were very anxious to see some reduction in the amount of excessive drunkenness that there was, particularly among the poorer section of the population, in the slums of this country twenty-five years ago. Then the thing for which all of us begged and prayed was a light drink which the working people of the country might have that would give them more pleasure and satisfaction without the bestiality that followed from excessive drinking. We have got that beer now, people are enjoying it, and it is doing them at any rate very little harm.'

Lord Arnold was not satisfied with the reply: 'We have had the usual unsatisfactory and disappointing reply from the noble Lord. It is exactly what I expected,' he said.

Woolton shrugged his shoulders, said nothing more but did commit his thoughts on Lord Arnold that night to his diary. 'He's a bigoted teetotaller of the worst variety and made a speech that was little short of offensive ... I suggested to the House that at a time when we were calling for the maximum physical effort from the working man it was unfair to deprive him of his glass of beer if he wanted it.'

Whatever Lord Arnold's alcohol-free tipple might have been it was not something that provided him with longevity. Within two years he was dead.

Press difficulties

Lord Woolton was glad that he somehow managed to retain a sense of humour. On 1 May 1941 he spread on his large desk in Portman Square the morning newspapers and some others from that week. 'Mayday, Mayday,' he muttered.

Woolton considered himself rather of a master of PR, a genius in messaging, a man with a knack for judging the public mood and getting favourable press coverage. It was something that doubtless irritated his Cabinet colleagues but it deeply gratified both himself and his wife Maud. Good editorial helped to justify and sustain the minister in his Cabinet battles, those fights with farmers, the doubting public. But on this Thursday morning he was wondering if he'd lost his touch.

He picked up the *Daily Herald*. 'M.P.s attack Ministry for Muddle,' the headline screamed. The paper commented on the previous day's proceedings in the House of Commons, when a report on the state of food in the country had been presented by his parliamentary secretary, the MP Gwilym Lloyd-George, a younger son of the former Prime Minister David Lloyd George.

Lord Woolton had sat in the peers gallery and listened as MP after MP lined up to attack Major Lloyd George as he attempted to outline how the control system had kept prices down, how bombs and population movement had made food distribution difficult, how emergency feeding centres had been set up and how the ministry had by that time opened 299 'British Restaurants.'

The *Daily Herald* talked of 'seething attacks on the Food Ministry'. One MP, Eleanor Rathbone, said she had 'the carking nagging feeling that it was the poor who had to bear the burden'; another, John Clynes, attacked fish prices and claimed the ministry was allowing traders to profiteer and escape punishment.

Woolton then turned to the *Daily Telegraph*. Here there was an assault of a very different tack. 'Lord Woolton & Lewis's – "No Connection"' read the headline. The paper reported on how the MP for Dumbarton, Adam McKinlay, had alleged that Lewis's had been able to sell cooked meats while its rivals had none. 'Where did they get it?' he had asked. 'Supplies of cooked meat were being diverted from working-class districts throughout the west of Scotland. It is strange that in every industrial part of Britain it is common talk that if you want anything in the food line you should go to Lewis's.' The insinuation was clear. 'I cannot explain to all the public outside that it is only a coincidence that the noble lord who presides over the ministry was at one time connected with Lewis's,' he stated, putting the scurrilous idea out there without himself making a firm allegation.

The paper's front page story continued inside and talked of 'startling allegations against the firm of Lewis's, of which Lord Woolton, the Minister of Food, was formerly chairman'. Woolton read the rebuttal that he had agreed the previous evening. An official had stated: 'Lord Woolton has no connection with Lewis's and has had no connection with them since he took office. Any suggestion that Lewis's either in Glasgow or elsewhere have had special treatment is entirely without foundation.' As he scanned through the piece, his eyes picked up the sub-heads with words such as 'Scandal' and 'No Control'.

He pushed the paper aside and looked at another. It was from the day before yesterday. Political commentator Maurice Webb's weekly column, 'Inside Politics', was headed: 'This Woolton Wobble Can't Go On.' Webb was anticipating the publication of the ministry's report. 'Ominous clouds are gathering over the handsome head of Lord Woolton, Commander-in-Chief on the Food Front,' he wrote. 'They are the sort of clouds which, when seen in the vicinity of a Minister, usually signify that his life in Whitehall is moving inexorably to a close. Not long ago Woolton's stock stood high. Today it is on the slide and worth little.' Woolton had read these words several times and could almost recite them. They cut deep.

'On all sides the critics are in full cry,' Webb continued, 'not least in his own department, where responsible administrators make no secret of their dissatisfaction with the way things are handled on top.' This hurt Woolton particularly as he had gone out of his way to make personal connections across the ministry. But with thousands of them in Colwyn Bay, he would never be able to maintain perfect relations and engender a universal understanding of his methods.

'In Parliament powerful voices are to be raised against "Woolton wobbling" over food distribution,' wrote Webb. And of the coming debate: 'The affair will be anything but a love feast. It will leave Lord Woolton in little doubt as to his present standing with the backbenchers. The people most closely in touch with this food business say that the root cause of much of the Food Minister's tenderness is his trading interest. He has a touching faith in the goodwill of big business, which no amount of obvious huckstering seems to disturb.'

Webb's article wounded Woolton on several fronts. He prided himself on the way he conducted himself, that he worked the ministry as a businessman, that it was his 'trading interest' that meant he did deals that others wouldn't, but that he had secured supplies because of it.

He knew he had political enemies but he didn't like the idea of it being written about and discussed in public. And as for the idea that his career in Whitehall was approaching its final chapter, he felt he still had much to do. He resolved to rise above the criticism. Politics was a rollercoaster ride and while these were bad days for his PR he had had much better ones and hoped he would again.

But the many papers that had so warmly welcomed him to the ministry in the spring of 1940 began to play a rather different tune twelve months later. On 9 April 1941 the *Daily Mail* had the headline: 'Woolton gets "ultimatum"' and it told how poultrymen from Lancashire were furious with the minister. Woolton had decided to lower egg prices that month; the men told the *Daily Mail* that this would force small egg producers out of business, and that 'by July there will be a famine in home-produced eggs.' The result, they argued, would be that 'in Lancashire eggs will disappear from the open markets and be sold "back door".'

The egg saga would disturb much of his summer – and he endured torturous attacks on the subject in the House of Lords. 'My press conference today was confined by the subject of eggs, of which I am heartily sick,' he wrote on 17 June. The afternoon had been spent thrashing out a scheme whereby the country's hens got enough food to produce the number of eggs he had undertaken to control and to work out, how, in his words, 'we could tie the producers so that we got the eggs when they were produced by the hens.' The meeting lasted well into the evening after which, he wrote, 'we all felt that although we were hungry we never wanted to see an egg again.' The following day he had to meet a deputation of egg producers. He wrote wearily after: 'I'm very tired of eggs.'

On 26 April the *Daily Herald*'s headline had been a little more strident: 'Woolton Must Go', it said. The paper reported on a delegate at the Scottish Trades Union Conference in Dunoon calling for 'immediate action' to get rid of Woolton because it alleged his ministry did not administer an equitable supply of meat across the country.

Days later, on 30 April, the *Manchester Evening News* reported: 'A move appears to be afoot to oust Lord Woolton from the Ministry of Food.' Within the month it repeated the story, talking of how 'recently the Food Minister has been criticised from many quarters and in Parliament,' and mentioning 'public dissatisfaction with the distribution of non-rationed foodstuffs'.

Woolton attempted to wrest back control of the agenda a few days later on 7 May when he travelled to Colwyn Bay to make a speech to journalists. It was a pleasant day so he decided to speak outside. 'I addressed a meeting on the pier,' he wrote; 'people were standing eight deep all round the place and apparently a large number of people on the pier to whom my speech was relayed. It was very enthusiastic.' He attacked those who tried to play the system and attempted to thwart the ration. Afterwards, returning to his car, he was accosted by a group of women who told him that they thought someone ought to thank him and so they had come to do so. 'I was told that the women of England were against me,' he said jocularly. 'But I see now that I can be assured that the women of Wales will support me.'

The women laughed and chorused back: 'But we come from Lancashire!' The encounter cheered him, but he was more concerned at how his speech would be portrayed in the press. The *Daily Post* duly reported on Woolton's robust message. 'Food Gamblers And Cheats', the paper wrote; 'Lord Woolton's Final Warning.'

The Post told how Woolton had warned people who thought they could make a little extra profit out of gambling in food that he was 'on their tails'. 'They must remember,' Woolton told the assembled throng, 'that he knew something about commercial life, and he recalled the speculation in turkeys last Christmas, when he suddenly dropped the price when they were high and caused the speculators to lose

The ration book can be likened to a passport that enabled you to get enough food to eat. With an individual serial number, it was posted to everyone who could receive rations, including members of the Royal Family. It was as vital to grab your ration book as your gas mask when the siren sounded in the event of an air raid.

The basic food stuffs two adults in the British Isles would have been entitled to in a weekly ration.

Woolton was keen not to ration bread, although he had drafted a scheme, as he felt the British public would not wear it. Instead he urged people to fill themselves up with 'energy-giving' potatoes.

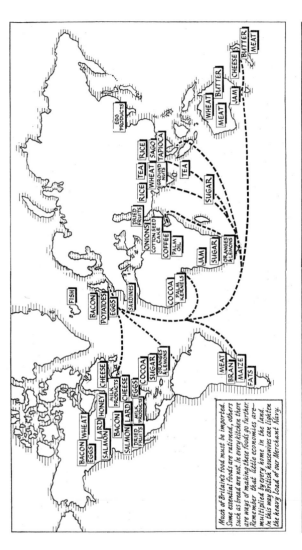

THE FIGURES BELOW GIVE SOME IDEA OF THE GREAT DISTANCES WHICH THESE SUPPLIES MUST TRAVEL
BEFORE THEY REACH YOUR TABLE

Much of Britain's food must be imported. Some essential foods are rationed, others such as bread are not. In every kitchen there are ways of making these foods go further. Remember that little economies are multiplied by every home in the land. In this way British housewives can lighten the heavy load of our Merchant Navy.

Bacon	2,700 miles	Egg Products	2,700–13,000 miles
Bran	6,200 miles	Eggs	2,700–2,760 miles
Butter	13,000–13,500 miles	Fats	6,200 miles
Cheese	2,700–13,500 miles	Fish	1,000 miles
Cocoa	3,000–4,000 miles	Ground Nuts	11,000 miles
Coffee	9,000 miles	Honey	2,760 miles
Cotton Seed Cake	9,000 miles	Jam	6,000–12,000 miles
Dried Fruits	2,700–12,000 miles	Lard	2,700–2,760 miles

Maize	6,200 miles	Sago	11,200 miles
Meat	6,000–13,000 miles	Salmon	2,700 miles
Milk Products	2,700–13,500 miles	Sardines	1,000 miles
Onions	5,000 miles	Sugar	4,000–11,200 miles
Oranges & Lemons	1,500–6,000 miles	Tapioca	11,200 miles
Palm Kernels	3,000 miles	Tea	11,500 miles
Palm Oil	9,000 miles	Wheat	2,700–11,000 miles
Rice	11,200 miles		

This chart, distributed by the Ministry of Food, hung in the Portman Square office of Lord Woolton. It was a

A typical Allied convoy heading across the Atlantic, their precious cargo and merchant men guarded by the ever-vigilant Royal Navy. Despite chronic losses to German U-boats in the early years of the war, the convoys still managed to bring Britain invaluable supplies.

The merchant navy would lose over 3,500 ships to the U-boat scourge, with over 36,000 seamen and 36,000 sailors of the Allied navies dying in their bid to get supplies to Britain.

Supplying Britain with food was just one of the major tasks
Woolton faced. Equally vital was the job of maintaining a supply
line to British forces overseas, in the Far East, for example. Here an
Allied convoy makes its way through the Suez Canal.

Moving food stuffs around the British Empire was integral to
achieving victory. Above, stores of rice are loaded onto a ship in the
Indian city of Bombay.

ord Woolton was always keen to showcase the latest Ministry of Food campaign to the
ation in order to promote both healthy diets, as well as fostering a community spirit.
ere he is seen with the Queen as they warm their hands on a winter's day while viewing
e arrangements of a field kitchen.

On leave from the Royal Air Force, Woolton's son Roger relaxes with his parents at their flat, Whitehall Court, in Westminster.

Victory is ours! The crowds come out to celebrate VE Day in central London. Happiness at the end of the fighting in Europe would soon be tinged with frustration for many, as rationing continued to bite for the foreseeable future.

Rationing would continue for the next several years as the country slowly got back on its feet. It would officially end in July 1954, when meat was finally taken off the rationing card. Cheese production would take decades thereafter to recover due to the ministry enforcing only one type of 'Government Cheddar' being made, thus setting back indigenous cheese-making for years.

Lord Woolton would enjoy a successful political career after the war, helping to guide the Conservatives back to government in the 1950s. Here he is seen in 1957 with his old colleague Sir Henry French (centre) at an official government function.

Woolton may have crossed swords with Winston Churchill during the Second World War, but he proved an invaluable ally to him in his post-war political comeback. Here, the two elder statesmen enjoy a quiet word at an official engagement in 1963.

money,' the paper quoted Woolton as saying. 'I am watching some of them now and this is the last and final warning they will get,' he added. The paper also described how Woolton had been asked by a journalist how it was that such people still managed to exist despite the laws he had put in place. 'They are allowed to exist because they are like worms of the earth. They slither along and go underground, and it is not very easy to catch them all the time, but we are digging for them and we are catching them.' Having used his worm analogy he then paused before adding: 'I apologise to the worm, which, I believe is of some use in agriculture, but I have not found use for the people I am talking about.'

Back in London he relished seeing these quotes. He loved it when he was hitting targets hard and he certainly enjoyed seeing his fruity language in print. But while an opinion poll published later that summer in the *Manchester News Chronicle* gave him an almost 60 per cent approval rating ('Fifty-seven per cent of people replied "Yes" when asked "Do you think Lord Woolton is doing a good job of work as Minister of Food?"'), the press were still on the attack.

Woolton despaired as the coverage that summer of 1941 just seemed to get worse and worse. 'The ministry's press has been bad recently,' he admitted in his diary on 28 May. 'We are being attacked on several scores.'

He was also feeling the strain of real attacks. On 16 April he recorded that he and his wife had lain awake as they listened to hundreds of German planes flying overhead and dropping their deadly parcels across the capital: 'It was a terrible night. 500 machines over, and from 9 at night until 4.30 the next morning they dropped bombs and land-mines and did a great deal of damage from blast. The Strand the next day looked as though it had been put out of business. In the Ministry of Food we had not a window left in the place and most of the walls went.'

The bombs were getting uncomfortably close to his flat at Whitehall Court. 'All this, as the crow flies within a few hundred yards of us,' he wrote. Then on 10 May he recorded: 'We had one of the worst air-raids London has had: bombs were dropped indiscriminately over all districts and it looked as if the whole of London was ablaze. We got a direct hit at Whitehall Court, which started a small fire in our flat, but we managed to put it out ourselves.'

It was, wrote Maud in her diary, 'one of the worst blitzes. It was a terrible night and in the morning London was burning so badly that although I believe it was a lovely day, we never saw the sun because of the pall of smoke.'

At the same time bombs had rained down on Liverpool, causing considerable damage to the headquarters of Lewis's. The couple drove there and, wrote Maud, the building 'looked like the Roman Colosseum. It was roped off and F stepped over the rope to get near and a soldier said: "Have you any business here?" and F looked at him and said: "I had."'

On 17 April he went to work. On the way there, he was impressed to note generally that 'I thought Londoners looked as happy this morning as though they had all the excitement of a cup-tie! There was very little feeling of fear about, but everyone passionately hoping that they would get it [retaliatory action] back that night – which they did.' 'The Ministry of Food office was a sight: I decided that I could not do any real work with the office in that state, so I'd better go round and cheer people up, and so I went round every room and had a word with the staff.' But, he added happily: 'They didn't want cheering – they were all very cheerful.' Then he added a sour note: 'The amazing thing to me was that French, as Head of the Department, had not been round. These civil servants never seem to be taught anything about human relationships.'

Of the many newspaper attacks, Woolton recognised that he was on thin ice when the stories were about profiteering. 'They are on a good story in regard to profiteering – because there's no doubt it exists, as does the black market,' he wrote in his diary on 28 May. Yet he continued to believe it was not particularly widespread. The problem was identifying it and prosecuting. 'It is very difficult to put a finger on it. We are prosecuting when we get the evidence, and the number of prosecutions has increased, but governmental machinery grinds slowly, and unless it's very sure it doesn't grind at all.'

That day he had attended a lunch with the Newspaper Society; a group of owners and editors. 'These fellows,' he wrote of them, 'who are short of sensational news in a war that isn't very active at the moment, pick on profiteering incidents and write them up as evidence that the ministry is sitting back and allowing the public to be exploited.'

At the lunch he changed the message he had planned to give. 'I had intended to talk a news speech to these people,' he wrote, as – doubtless – Sir Henry had also intended, 'but I was feeling very sick about them and I got on to my feet and hit them hard.'

'If you have evidence on which you base your stories it is your duty to the nation to give it to us so that we can stop it and protect the public,' he lectured the gathering. 'And if you haven't got that information then you are doing the public a disservice by agitating them about profiteering.' Woolton glared at the assembled throng. 'So either produce your evidence or stop your perpetual sniping.' The lunch over and Woolton considered the effect of his hectoring. 'I think I impressed them,' he noted that night. But it made scant difference to the headlines.

A couple of weeks later, on 13 June, he tackled the public on the subject. As he put it: 'I broadcast to the people of Britain. I told them it wasn't any use them getting all worked up about the newspaper stories of profiteering whilst they themselves helped the profiteer by buying his goods.'

He then decided to toughen his stance with his regular group of food journalists and then meet their bosses, the editors and owners. As they trooped into his office, their pints duly sipped, for their regular Tuesday afternoon briefing on 15 July 1941, he was without his usual affable air. 'It was,' he wrote, 'a period of adverse publicity and I thought I might put them in a better frame of mind.'

With the food reporters sat around his conference table he stood and told them directly: 'You are not representing the view of the average citizen who is satisfied at what he or she can get. This food question always appeals to the man in the street, as there isn't much else to write about. So you work up stories about shortages and queues and bad administration and profiteering. You know that the situation is nothing like as bad as you are making out and that the general situation is very good. But in what you write you are doing no good service to the country.' He finished and then dismissed them.

As they filed out of his office, he retreated to his desk and opened the top drawer. Sitting there was an item he had been sent that day – and it wasn't something he was going to share with the reporters. The post that morning, he reported in his diary, 'brought me a mysterious parcel'. At the time, due to an administrative error, some fruit and vegetables had been wrongly overpriced. 'The result of which,' he noted, 'was that the housewives of this country were being asked to pay up to 1s 6d per pound [7.5p, but, in real terms, some £5 today].

'My parcel contained a large onion with the following note: "I am sending you this onion as a gift. After paying sixpence for it (you will see it weighs half a pound) I had not the heart to cook it. I hope it will bring tears to your eyes, as it did to mine."'

Woolton noted that the 'grim sense of a humour' came from a 'citizen' of his neck of the woods: Manchester. But, he wrote in his diary (with a straight face), 'I had the onion situation in hand.' An Order was effected, and the prices dropped a few days later.

As for the press, that night he complained to his wife that, 'I am suffering from the lack of a good public relations officer. The result is we are being badly put across to the public. It's an annoying situation.'

On 5 June, in the midst of his stormy summer, he was asked to see the Prime Minister. Churchill asked him straight whether, wrote Woolton, 'I was tired of being Minister of Food and asked me if I'd like to take another job.'

Woolton pondered on this because he was not having an easy time. 'Truth to tell, I'm a little tired of it myself,' he wrote, 'but I don't think it's a good thing to take another job just because you're tired of the one you've got, unless the new one is one for which you've a special qualification or desire.'

Churchill raised the idea of Woolton running another ministry but he declined. 'I think it's a good thing to have continuity of control in food supplies during a war,' he told the PM. His job was far from done.

That evening he made one of his occasional visits to Colwyn Bay where he found Sir Henry French. Tired from another day of meetings and the stresses of his work, he told Sir Henry that Churchill had mooted the idea of him leaving the ministry and moving to head up another.

'Although I must have given many headaches to French,' wrote Woolton, 'he said he was delighted that I had decided to stay.'

Woolton pie

On the same day that the *Daily Herald* was reporting demands from the Scottish TUC that 'Woolton Must Go', there was a rather softer piece of PR in *The Times*. 'Lord Woolton Pie', the paper stated on 26 April 1941: 'The Official Recipe'. 'In hotels and restaurants, no less than in communal canteens, many people have taste Lord Woolton pie and pronounced it good,' the piece read, sounding like a public service announcement.

The recipe for the dish had been distributed around the country over the previous month, having been unveiled on

18 March at a lunch at the Savoy hotel. The occasion was organised by the Pilgrims Society, whose raison d'être was to promote goodwill between the United States and Great Britain and who had a tradition of holding a lunch to welcome a new American Ambassador. The latest incumbent was John Winant and, as he was led to his table in the ballroom by Winston Churchill and the Earl of Derby, around him was gathered the most powerful figures in Britain: the elite of the business world, most of the Cabinet, leading military figures as well as newspaper owners and publishers.

For Winston Churchill it was the opportunity to make a great speech. The BBC carried it and he was at his best as he told his ally: 'Mr Winant, you come to us at a grand turning point in the world's history. We rejoice to have you with us in these days of storm and trial because, in you, we have a friend and a faithful comrade who will "report us and our cause aright".'

For the Ministry of Food it was the opportunity to launch a new pie. Or rather dress up an old one and give it a new name. The ministry had tasked Francis Latry, the hotel's chef – a man with short legs and an even shorter temper, by all accounts – to create a pie that made a virtue of vegetables. His recipe was duly printed in *The Times*; it was a mixture of diced and cooked potatoes, cauliflower, swedes and carrots, some spring onions, a little vegetable extract ('if possible') and a tablespoonful of oatmeal. Once cooked and cooled, the mixture was placed into a pie dish, sprinkled with chopped parsley and covered with a crust of potato or wholemeal pastry. Once baked until brown it was served 'hot with a brown gravy'.

If a gathering of the most powerful people in Britain – and the new American Ambassador – could happily dine on Woolton pie at the Savoy, it was surely good enough for men, women and children across Britain. Such initiatives were often launched from smart hotels, so that the public might get the idea that the food of the rich was just as proscribed as that of the poor. Indeed ordering Woolton pie when it was on the menu in restaurants, and then pretending to enjoy it, offered the middle classes the chance to demonstrate their virtue. 'It was the equality of suffering, conjured in root vegetables,' wrote Matthew Sweet who studied in detail the food of London's grand hotels.

But there was one aspect to the pie-launch story that was not reported. While Lord Woolton wrote in his diary that the pie – his first taste of it – 'was extremely good', it fared less well with Churchill. 'When it was offered to the Prime Minister he sent it away, and asked for some cold beef,' Woolton wrote. He further recounted, in an interview with the *Star* newspaper, that when the waiter placed a portion of the pie in front of Churchill, he asked: 'What is this?'

'Woolton pie, Sir,' said the waiter.

'It is what?' barked Churchill.

'Woolton pie, Sir.'

'Bring me some beef,' he said pushing the plate away from him.

Woolton spotted his actions during the lunch but said nothing, not wishing to draw anyone's attention to Churchill's less-than-helpful contribution to his latest PR wheeze. As the lunch ended Woolton quietly cornered the PM. 'I thought you treated my pie with less than respect Prime Minister,' he said. 'Yes,' replied Churchill, 'I thought it was one of your synthetic productions.'

As ever Churchill was keen to prick the Woolton ego bubble whenever possible. Still, Woolton pie became famous and it grew to be a symbol of British resilience as well as a memento of rationing for decades to come. The dish may have been something of a joke but, as Woolton himself wrote in his memoirs: 'The public was either going to laugh or cry about food rationing, it was better for them that they should laugh.'

He did, however, get a little fed up with being offered the dish on rather too many occasions. On opening a British Restaurant in December 1941 in the London borough of Hackney he was given Woolton pie but spotted that it contained sausages, 'which wasn't Woolton pie at all'. He then had his office send the cook, a Mrs Amy, the official recipe so she could get it right next time.

The restaurant opening was not a great success as there was a large group of media in attendance about which Woolton moaned he hadn't been warned. With the 'bevy of pressmen ... it was impossible for the people to be informal.' He didn't hold out much hope for the ensuing coverage. 'The film they took won't turn out very well,' he said. 'It isn't easy to be informal when you know that pictures of you are going all over the world.'

The trip to the new Hackney restaurant ended at one o'clock and having spurned the Woolton pie it was 'too late to have a proper lunch and too lightly fed for the rest of the day – so I came back to the office and had some sandwiches.' A mundane note in his diary, but comforting, nonetheless, to hear a man in high office, during the Second

World War, uttering a sigh that can resonate with our own twenty-first-century daily moans.

The weight of celebrity was causing him discomfort. He once panicked after a photographer took a picture of him backstage after a trip to the theatre. One of the chorus girls joined him just as the pictures were taken. 'She was dressed in little more than a couple of feather plumes,' he wrote. His office later came to the rescue: 'I believe the ministry bought the copyright of one in order to protect the marble-white reputation of one of its ministers,' he commented.

The Times, doubtless having witnessed him eating his eponymous dish on countless occasions, cruelly noted on 22 September 1944 – as he yet again was faced with his pie – that 'There may have been those who were not convinced by the smile [of Woolton], the look of relish directed at the morsel on the fork.'

But that damn pie kept Woolton's name in the public conscience, even in the decades after his death. Although, frankly, it's a grim and dull pie and, as a famous British dish, a white flag of surrender against any advancing legions of French gastronomy.

The pie also reflected on how Woolton managed to create a warm image of himself to the public. From his radio and television broadcasts (the former, such as the regular broadcast *The Kitchen Front* – often presented by him – sometimes pre-recorded on a gramophone record for occasions such as Christmas Day), he came to be seen as a member of one's family who could be relied upon and trusted, who had everyone's interests at heart and who would treat each person fairly but, if need be, with a firm hand; 'Uncle Fred'. In tandem with his own broadcasts he enlisted the help of Walt Disney himself to create characters to help him urge the nation to Dig for Victory, the campaign to plant vegetables in order to become more self-sufficient. Disney created three carrot characters for the ministry's advertisements and then, as a gesture of good-will, wrote Woolton, 'presented the copyright to us.'

Family matters

Woolton wrote in his diary in early July that his son Roger arrived a day late from a ten-day holiday on a houseboat in Windermere. 'He should have arrived last night, but had succeeded, when leaving the houseboat, in falling into the lake, suitcase and all, and had had to spend the night with friends of his in Windermere so that he could be dried out.'

It was not an episode that seemed uncharacteristic for poor Roger. Perhaps his father gave him one of his haughty lectures on his return. The previous year, when Roger had left Rugby, Woolton decided to give his son a pep-talk on succeeding in business, an episode he recorded in his diary. 'You have concentrated on classics at both your prep school and public school,' he said, 'and if you now go into business you will be able to forget that training. An unbiased mind can concentrate on making money. I have observed that the people who make the most money are the people whose minds are not unduly embarrassed by either education or ideas.'

Roger nodded diligently at this hinted suggestion that he need not therefore go to university, especially if he, as was expected, were to follow his father into Lewis's. Then

Woolton added: 'But I beg you to do one thing for me. When I am dead do not get up in their Lordships' House and seek to guide the nation into its political destiny on the experience of a self-made man.'

His son looked disconcerted. 'The effect of this on Roger was so demoralising that he said if I would like him to go to Cambridge he would be very glad to go.'

So, in order to avoid what seemed endless opportunities to let his father down, Roger duly went to Cambridge. Then, on 16 April 1941, he reported for National Service; Woolton noted the occasion in his diary. His son reported at Acton, in West London, whereupon he was told to go to Waterloo and take a train to Fareham, between Portsmouth and Southampton. Woolton felt they might have saved him his journey in the first place.

But he found time to say goodbye in person. 'I went to see him off. It seemed to me that he was old enough to go and do a job,' he commented, 'but he seemed to me to be ridiculously young to go and fight.' Woolton wrote that he sensed no nerves in his son other than 'feelings ... that he experienced when going to a new school – rather exciting. He showed no fear at the prospect of a new environment.' Possibly he had no desire to join the Navy but didn't want to disappoint his father, who was clearly so proud of this progression in his life that he had made the journey south to wave him off. And if he felt some trepidation he wasn't going to let his father see it.

But just one day later Roger turned up at the family's London flat. 'The medical test revealed a slight colour-blindness which they said would prevent him from ever having a commission in the Navy,' wrote Woolton. 'The only thing that might happen is that I could become a steward,' Roger told his father. 'The officers have given me four days leave to come home and discuss the matter with you.'

'So do you want to be a steward, Roger?' asked Woolton.

'No,' he replied. 'And I don't want to be a land officer in the Navy either.'

Father and son discussed the issue and, Woolton wrote: 'He has decided that he would like to go to the Air Force.'

Three months later there was a setback with this new plan. On 9 July 1942, Woolton wrote that his son 'has gone to consult a Harley Street man about his stammer'. It is not clear whether this condition was a recent phenomenon or an issue since childhood. But it adds a devastating note to the picture of this hapless young man and the stammer that would stay with him for the rest of his life.

The Royal Air Force were not sympathetic when they came to interview the twenty-year old as he stammered through his answers. He made several attempts to enter the Service; on one occasion, on 8 July, Roger spent a whole day being medically examined. Woolton reported that he 'had a most unpleasant day, being buffeted about from place to place and being described as a "bloody menace" by a medical officer'. Towards the end of the day, 'he eventually came across another medical officer who suggested that his stammer would be a disadvantage to him in the Air Force.'

If he had treatment for it, he was told, he might have a chance. Perhaps Roger endured a tortuous merry-go-round of Harley Street professionals who would have put steel marbles in his mouth and implored him to enunciate his words better.

The situation is never mentioned by Maud in her diaries. But in April of the following year Woolton wrote that he travelled to Manchester to see Roger off, this time on a ship bound for Canada where he was to get training overseas for the Air Force. It seems either his stammer receded or a more understanding officer agreed to accept him.

Almost a month later Woolton recorded news of his son: 'We heard today that Roger had arrived safely in Canada, which was a relief.' With his personal knowledge of how precarious the journey was across the Atlantic, the couple must have been very relieved indeed. His training was a success and he was accepted into the Royal Air Force. His was the most basic aircraftsman rank of A/C2. And he attained a small measure of celebrity in that his friends in the service, with a distinct nod to his father, nicknamed him 'Rations'.

Less problematic was the Wooltons' daughter Peggy. She was a diligent school worker and progressed through the ranks of the Auxiliary Territorial Service – the women's branch of the British Army – during the Second World War. The only time Woolton made a note of any difficulty regarding her was when, on 6 February 1942, he was passed a copy of *Tatler* magazine. Within its pages, charting the social goings on of Britain at war, was a photograph of Peggy. Rather than feel pride as some parents did, and have done ever since, at their daughter appearing in such a magazine, Woolton was cross. 'Nice people don't seek this type of publicity,' he thundered in his diary. It was, he said, 'impertinent that a photographer should supply a portrait that is a private property'.

Autumn

By the end of August, Woolton noted a dramatic change in his press coverage. 'We're having a period now when our publicity is very good,' he wrote, almost surprised. 'We are doing almost everything that's right and indeed are described as a ministry with a vision, doing a difficult job extremely well. Only a few weeks ago, to judge from the press, the ministry was a collection of absolute nit-wits, who didn't even think before they spoke, and who hadn't anything to think anyhow.' He pondered on this turn of events before adding, 'We can't be very much different from what we were two months ago! Popularity's a fickle jade.'

Woolton was more concerned about government policy. He was still arguing with senior ministers about getting his hands on more ships; on 2 October he recorded a frustrating discussion with senior ministers. 'I asked flatly if it was a fact that we could not rely on having the ships: there were vague remarks about secret happenings in the War Cabinet that could not be talked of etc etc. I got very tired of it.'

Government policy was, he then reflected later that day, 'signs of the "war lord" at work. Look after the troops, feed them, transport them, and generally give them first place in every possible way. It's all right, and it's got to be done, but it cannot be done at the total expense of all the other people.' Woolton was irritated at the continuing 'lack of real cooperation in the government'.

'We must win the war,' he wrote, 'we all hope it will be won abroad – but I see no sense in winning it abroad and losing it at home.'

Woolton's grumblings continued into the winter months of 1941. On 10 November he listened to a speech Churchill made at the annual Lord Mayor's lunch at the grand Mansion House, the Lord Mayor's eighteenth-century Palladian official residence in the City of London. 'Winston,' he wrote, 'made an excellent speech about very little: he has an amazing facility for using words and whilst he said nothing . . . that he hasn't said before it went very well.'

Woolton, meanwhile, had been preparing the ground for the next big initiative in rationing: the Points System. It was an adjunct to rationing but he still needed the Prime Minister's general agreement. The problem though, Woolton wrote on 28 November, was that Churchill 'wanted as little rationing as possible. He's not very good in his judgment on these home affairs: he doesn't seem to understand that nobody else wants rationing any more then he does, but that there has to be rationing when there are short supplies.'

The Points System was introduced on 1 December 1941 as a way of limiting the purchase of items like canned meat, fish or beans. Such things were not as sparse as meat or butter, so simple rationing would have been overkill. Yet they still needed to be limited in a way that was measured and practical. Woolton was well aware of the gloom that had been cast across the country when, in July 1940, he had banned the making and selling of iced cakes.

At first every person was given sixteen points a month. The selected range of foods were then given a points value. This could change according to its availability: in the early stages of the system, a can of peas, corn, tomatoes or green beans weighing 1lb 4oz was worth sixteen points. A larger can of pears weighing 1lb 14oz, was twenty-one points, pineapple twenty-four, grapefruit juice was worth twenty-three points and tomato juice weighing 1lb 7oz was thirty-two points.

The number of points also varied, reaching a high of twenty-four per month in early 1942 and mid 1944.

As time went on, more goods were added to the Points System and they included rice, dried pulses, canned vegetables, condensed milk, breakfast cereals, oatcakes, syrup and treacle. The system did give individuals a touch of liberty because they could be used in any shop that had the goods and were happy to sell them – unlike with ration coupons where you could only shop in premises where you had registered. You could also choose whether to splurge one month on some peaches, or play it safe with some spinach and corn.

Woolton wrote that, ironically, it was 'a system that we borrowed – and, I believe, improved – from the Germans'. He described it as 'a sort of 'Stock Exchange'. The articles that were in the shortest supply cost the largest number of points and vice versa. 'If we found, for example, that we had a considerable quantity of sardines, then we advised the shopkeepers that they were in good supply and presently we reduced the number of points for which they called,' he explained.

But to make it work he had to exercise fierce control over the system. 'The whole scheme depended upon the success of the first two months and on this I took no risks,' he recalled. Several weeks before the scheme came into operation he reduced the supply of all the extra goods to be added to the Points System. Meanwhile shopkeepers were asked to build up heavy stocks of these items but 'on the strict understanding that they were not for sale until released by order of the ministry'.

This required a considerable degree of honesty on the part of the shopkeepers who had to somehow keep the deliveries and storage a secret from their regulars, doubtless among them many beady-eyed and gossipy shoppers. Sometimes gossip and rumour led the public into making rather unusual shopping purchases.

One of the non-food items that Lord Woolton had to control was soap. This became a real scarcity in the war and Woolton did not want to create a soap-related panic. So to avoid any leaks about his impending plans to ration it, the files of papers at the ministry containing soap-related arguments, distribution schemes and much more were given the codename of 'Nutmegs'.

Woolton planned to announce his soap rationing on a Sunday, a practice he used relentlessly with the Points System as, on the Sabbath Day, the shops would be closed and there could be no mad rush to purchase, with people instead thinking things over and planning their points spending. As to the soap plan, he wrote, 'there was no sign of any leakage of information on this subject until the Saturday afternoon.' Then, somehow, word got out. Or, rather, the wrong news did, as reports suddenly came into the ministry that there had been an extraordinary rush in the shops that day on nutmegs. 'I wonder what happened to all the nutmegs [bought by] the credulous people who cleaned up the market on nutmegs on that Saturday afternoon,' he later mused.

As for the real build-up to points items, on the whole the shopkeepers of Britain managed it and, reflected Woolton, 'with great patriotism they legitimately kept these goods "under the counter"'.

'The Points Plan gives you freedom,' he announced after lunch on Sunday 21 November 1941 on the BBC Home Service radio. 'You can buy these new goods where you please in the four-week period. You're free to spend your Points on any foods that you choose on the list and you can go to any shop you like on the list. Everyone doesn't want the same thing every week. We want variety.' Benevolent Woolton was at his affable best selling his scheme to the nation; they, on the most part, cheered him on. His department even issued a new book, available at one's local food office, coloured in a dainty pink. The points came in the form of coupons which were each dated and were only valid on the date printed and, if unused, could not be carried forward to the next month.

The Points System was up and running but Woolton received no thanks from the Prime Minister. He soon discovered that he wasn't the only one disgruntled with Churchill. On 7 December, Woolton and Maud spent the evening with Alan Lennox-Boyd and his wife Florence.

At the time Lennox-Boyd was in the Navy (and would later become a member of Churchill's peacetime government); he had been Woolton's parliamentary secretary when he first became Minister of Food, so he was keen to hear about his career progress and how he was now getting on in his new job in the Navy. But, Woolton admitted, 'I was more interested in the things he told me about the feeling of the House of Commons.' By which he meant the feelings of MPs about Churchill.

'He was very frank about Winston, and told me that the House was beginning to be critical about some of the PM's actions and decisions,' he wrote. It tallied with Woolton's thoughts. 'We are not making headway anywhere except in Africa, and this will be a temporary success,' he commented. 'The German general, Rommel, is clever and we shall have trouble there. The PM is trying to run a one-man show: he has a war Cabinet in which none of the Service Ministers operate, he being Minister for Defence, and accepting responsibility for all the war strategy. This may be all right if the strategy succeeds, but the people won't care whose responsibility it is if we keep on having defeats as a result. They are being urged to work and save for Victory, and soon they'll want to see some.'

On Saturday 13 December 1941 Lord Woolton had set aside some time to write a speech that he was due to give the following Monday when opening a new canteen at a Nottingham colliery. The press had been invited and it was to be a chance for some positive words; this was a new facility for hard-working people; the photographs would show white teeth shining out of the blackened faces of gritty British miners. Woolton would be at his magnanimous best.

But he was struggling to write the speech he wanted to give. 'Japan has declared war on us, and Germany and Japan have declared war on the United States,' he explained, the official declaration of war by the Empire of Japan having been published on 8 December. As the text from Emperor Hirohito read: 'Our Empire, for its existence and self-defence has no other recourse but to appeal to arms and to crush every obstacle in its path.' Woolton felt mournful:

'Practically the whole world is now in the war, and these latest developments are going to make things very difficult,' he wrote.

For Woolton that meant more political difficulties. The supply routes would be further squeezed and that would inevitably mean even less food imports. 'I shall find great difficulty,' he explained, 'because, in the first place, the Pacific will no longer be safe as the Japanese submarines are operating there, and in the second place America will probably need for her own use much of the food that she has been sending us.' Woolton's options were diminishing. 'The closing of the Pacific route will mean a great loss to us, because our meat supplies from Australia and New Zealand have been crossing from those countries to America, and then coming across the Atlantic,' he lamented.

As the press were due to assemble at this Nottingham colliery, he felt it appropriate to make a speech in which he would warn that further privations were coming; that the ration would be squeezed. He had written to Churchill during the week asking him to clear his message. 'I indicated to the Prime Minister that, in my speech on Monday, I wanted to announce the withdrawal of the extra sugar and fat rations that were recently given and to reduce the meat ration. But without the go-ahead from Churchill the hour he had set aside to write the speech was wasted. 'I cannot prepare my speech because I have had no reply from the PM,' he recorded crossly.

The following morning, Sunday, he decided to go to the office and see if he could chase the reply he wanted. Ever the stickler for the best decorum and behaviour, he called at Buckingham Palace on the way to wish the King a happy birthday 'as a good Peer to the Realm to His Majesty'. At the office he saw that a letter had been delivered from Number 10. It was not the answer he wanted. 'The PM's reply had come,' he wrote; 'it was, as I suspected it to be, an unqualified negation to any reductions in the ration.'

Woolton was angry. 'He's not a good home minister,' he ranted. 'In the early days of the war he said that there was no need for any rationing system in this country, the British Navy would keep the seas of the world open to Britain. Fortunately nobody took any notice of him then, or we would now be in a parlous condition.' Woolton firmly believed that he had no option but to make these reductions to the ration – yet here was Churchill vetoing the idea. 'In spite of all the experience we have had he just sets his face against any reductions, regardless of conditions of necessity.'

The public was aware that Japan's entrance into the war would impact their lives so Woolton reckoned that he should take advantage of their being pliant on the issue. 'It's a great pity he has taken this line,' he wrote. 'We shall have to reduce the rations, and that soon, but people are expecting it now and would take kindly an action that they realise is inevitable with a fresh war zone with which to cope. The longer we delay the announcement, the less kindly they will take it.'

So Woolton went to Nottingham that Monday and made his speech. 'It was received well,' he noted, 'although there was really nothing in it.' He cursed the wasted opportunity. 'I had to say that there would be no immediate change in the rations, and this was a pity because we shall have to do it quite soon.'

Within the month Churchill had relented and Woolton announced that as a result of the opening of the war front in the Pacific there would be a reduction in the ration. He made the announcement as a postscript to the BBC news at one o'clock on 11 January 1942. It was a day in which he confided to his diary that 'the war situation is very depressing. The lack of success we are having, and the ever-widening war zone, seems to have little effect on the complacency and lethargy here.'

Yet his words were not just targeted, as they usually were, at the government and Churchill. While Hitler's planes seemed to have paused from their incessant bombing raids a new mood appeared to have crept over the country. 'In this period of freedom from air-raids, life in England seems to have gone back to almost normal,' he wrote incredulously; 'restaurants and theatres crowded; West-end hotels full; nobody seems to care very much about getting the war moving.'

Woolton didn't like it. 'On the continent people are literally dying in their thousands from starvation. The food situation in Greece is desperate: these people, whose heroic resistance to an enemy superior in numbers and equipment delayed the German progress in Europe for many weeks, are starving.

'I've told the Cabinet that I will take the risk of depleting our food stocks in this country so that we shall send them food,' he continued. 'I cannot bear to think of people, at whose expense we've had weeks of respite from attack, dying from lack of food whilst we've had some in the cupboard.'

Doubtless the Cabinet and Churchill sighed wearily at

Woolton's latest pleading. Even when things were looking up, the tiresome Minister of Food seem determined to deliver his gloomy assessments and decrease the ration.

As ever, Woolton was just as dismissive about his colleagues as he was Churchill. 'I wish that in these Cabinet meetings I saw more of the evidence of the will to win the war,' he wrote on 22 December. 'I'm afraid that some of my colleagues are more concerned about their careers than about England.'

12

Demand Runs High

As warring Britain welcomed in 1942, the Minister of Food saw little signs of optimism about him. With the Japanese gaining ground in the Pacific, Woolton looked at the map of the trade routes for food in his office and groaned at the prospect of fewer items such as cheese, butter and meat arriving in Britain.

'The war situation is very depressing,' he wrote that day not relishing the task of relaying yet further news of belt-tightening to the country. Meanwhile Maud was spending her days at South Africa House, a grand building on Trafalgar Square which acted as that country's high commission and consulate. 'I spend most mornings helping to pack parcels and do all sorts of food jobs,' she wrote. From the packing room where she worked, were dispatched parcels of food, clothing and cigarettes. She was, she said, 'the only English person there . . . However they have taken me in and I enjoy the work very much.'

It served as a positive distraction from the realities of the war, about which she ruminated in her diary. 'At the present moment we are almost as much in the depths of woe about the war news as we were at the time of Dunkirk,' she pondered in early February 1942, adding: 'nowhere are we being successful. It is devastating. I don't mean to say that we are down and out – not by any means, but we are sick about these things and dread to think of what is happening in Singapore.'

Maud wrote of her husband's state of mind. 'F is very disturbed,' she noted. But at least the couple could seek some solace in attacking the man in the charge.

'He thinks that the PM is making a muddle of things, because he does see himself in the role of a war lord and strategist,' she wrote, adding that 'rumour says that he wants servicemen about him who are "Yes" men. He can't bear contradiction, and he does insist on keeping everything in his hands. It isn't possible for one man to do all he attempts to do. He really ought to keep an eye on all departments but only in a way of a guiding and co-ordinating hand. Instead he goes into minute details of things he's keen about, and allows some departments to get hopelessly muddled.'

The pair had discussed whether it should be Woolton who should take a stand and publicly criticise the Prime Minister. 'F feels that someone ought to make a protest and wondered whether he ought to be the one to do it as he isn't a politician.' Of course it would mean he would have to quit and so Maud had counselled against it. 'It would be a pity if he'd retire as a protest as his department is talked of as *the* one which is properly run.'

Churchill, sensing grumbles among colleagues, held a three-day debate in the House of Commons on the 'Motion of Confidence in the Government'. He won it of course – on 29 January by 464 votes to 1 – and Woolton was a little cynical when contemplating it in his diary on the day the Prime Minister opened the debate. 'He knows that his personal popularity will secure the vote for him, but it's dangerous and a foolish thing to do, and I think he'll lose reputation through it.'

Woolton didn't hear Churchill's speech, though received word that it had had a 'tremendous reception'. 'But reading it,' he wrote, 'I didn't feel it was that strong.'

February came with a dump of snow and an affliction for Woolton of colitis. He lay in bed for a day but then dragged himself to a meeting to discuss imports. 'It is so important that we import the amount of food that we must have for safety that I dare not risk any decisions being taken in my absence.'

The meeting over, and Woolton looked out of his office window across Portman Square. People, wrapped in their coats and scarves, walked quickly along the pavements, finding paths where the snow had been cleared to stay dry. Cars and buses passed beneath his window and opposite he could see a sentry, who, shivering in the cold, guarded the sandbagged doors to an office on the other side of the street.

Woolton puffed on his pipe – it often seemed the only tonic to his stomach pains – and considered a major problem with rice supplies raised at the meeting of the Import Executive which had just ended. The impending fall of Singapore was affecting imports. Rice may have been a comparatively small part of the diet of the British people, but he had a problem in Ceylon. The Indian population there, which made up a large proportion of the naval base, were refusing to eat wheat and were threatening to leave the colony unless they could get adequate rations of rice. It wasn't just the people in Portman Square who relied on Woolton.

But where on earth was he to find a new supply of rice? His global hunt for this vital commodity was proving fruitless. A shortage of rice in India closed that option, and his contacts in Brazil had assured him they had none. His sources in Egypt told him they had exhausted their exportable supplies, but Woolton had a hunch there was more if he looked hard enough. As he considered these difficulties, there was a knock on his office door and one of his two secretaries announced a visitor. 'I'll be seeing him on his own,' reminded Woolton. This meeting would be private; no notes, no records, no memos. Officially, it wasn't taking place.

The man coming to see the minister was civil servant Harold Sanderson, who, Woolton later wrote, 'seemed to me to have knowledge of all the rice fields of the world at his finger-ends'.

'I have a problem that is more serious than I am able to tell you,' Woolton told his visitor. 'All I can say is that I need rice and I need you to go to Egypt and see what you can find.'

'I'll go without delay,' replied Sanderson.

'Thank you,' said Woolton. 'This will be a difficult job but I know I can rely on you. Whatever you do and however you do it you'll have my support. I know just a little about the Eastern ways of negotiation, so if some issue arises that is beyond your authority do not feel the need to consult me. Using telephonic communication will only involve delay and no assured security. My confidence in your judgement is such that you are at liberty to make any statement or decision that you believe would represent my views.'

Woolton's guest thanked the minister and got up to leave. But as he reached the door, Woolton called out to him: 'Oh by the way Mr Sanderson, don't come back without 200,000 tons, will you?'

A few weeks after Harold Sanderson's brisk meeting with Woolton, the Ministry of Food's Head of Rice was to be found in Cairo, drained and wearied. As he pushed his way through the teeming streets of the city, this Englishman's nose found nothing appealing in the combined smell of exhaust fumes, donkey manure and incense. The road bobbed with fez hats and turbans. But in addition to his own panama there were the berets and khaki caps worn by the variety of allied troops who had now, in their thousands, joined the million-plus Egyptian inhabitants of the city.

As he crossed the street looking for respite at the grand nineteenth-century Continental Hotel, he had to dodge a mismatched chorus of scrawny-looking sheep, tiny Fiat cars and British army motorbikes.

He had had another frustrating morning and it felt like he had exhausted all the usual avenues as he negotiated for rice from a crowded office in the British government's Cairo HQ. What deals he had failed to seal on the telephone were similarly futile as he met his contacts on the hot and dusty back streets.

Passing a small market he mused on how simple it would be if he were only tasked with buying seasonal supplies for a few families. In comparison with cold and dreary war-torn London, Cairo was bursting with produce. There were the stores owned by Greek immigrants, for example, whose shelves heaved with sugar, butter, eggs and soap. Greengrocers were bulging with mounds of every kind of bean as well as maize and cabbages, cauliflowers and toma-toes. Small butcher shops heaved with live poultry and there were other individual stalls selling grapes or eggs. He passed piles of dates and oranges and let out a sigh; his task, his mission for Woolton in which failure was apparently not an option – quite easy to bark out in an office in London, another thing to actually succeed on the ground in Egypt – was overwhelming him with apprehension.

Off the street and into the cooler, more serene confines of the Continental bar, Sanderson ordered a cold glass of South African white wine and moved to a quiet table in the corner. He had no energy to involve himself with the cheery British officers standing at the counter. Their tasks, involving things like blowing up bridges to cut enemy supply lines, seemed a damn sight simpler than his job. And as far as he and Woolton were concerned they were, quite frankly, considerably less vital for the war effort. As he sipped on his drink, he considered what he had secured so far. His contacts had agreed to sell him 100,000 tons of rice; it was a solid order, but only half of what he needed to satisfy Woolton back in London. The white wine cooled his throat, invigorating him a little.

But he had another problem which was a touch more personal. He'd felt some unusual pain in his stomach that morning and, in spite of the heat, he felt a little chilled. He was definitely tired also, an unshakeable malaise which had lingered ever since he disembarked from the overlong and rough journey by ship he had endured some ten days previously. What worried him was the talk of bugs swirling round the city. Sanderson hoped to hell he hadn't caught anything. The next drink he ordered was water.

His night, back at the Services Club on Ezbekieh Gardens, was a terrible one. That slight chill had turned to a fever, the stomach pains into severe vomiting. The next day, pale and ill, the staff called him a doctor. 'I'm afraid you have dysentery, Mr Sanderson,' the doctor told him. 'You should leave Cairo and go back to London.' Sanderson said he couldn't, he had work to do.

Concerned for his wellbeing, some officials from the Egyptian government with whom he'd had some dealings, also came to visit. They told him the same thing. 'Cairo is not a good place to be if you have a sickness like this,' he was told. Furthermore they had a plan to ease his passage home. This time there would be no ship. 'You must go home, Mr Sanderson,' they said. 'We have provided a special plane for you to take you back to England,' they said. 'If you stay here, the doctors say you will die.'

'I'm not leaving until I have another 100,000 tons of rice,' Sanderson replied weakly from his bed. 'My country and her dependents are facing a grave threat and I would rather die in Cairo than face my minister having failed in my mission.'

The next day he dragged himself from his bed and, having made some telephone calls, went out to meet some contacts. Four days later Sanderson took the plane and returned from Cairo. He was very weak and went straight to bed. A few days later he had recovered sufficiently to be able to report to Woolton back in his office on Portman Square. The minister rose from his desk as Sanderson entered the room; noting how ill he looked he eased him into a chair.

'My poor fellow, you didn't need to take my word literally,' said Woolton. 'But I gather that you did get 100,000 tons.'

'I got a damn sight more than that,' replied Sanderson, then, surprised at his own language, added a deferential 'Minister.'

Woolton looked at him, surprised and impressed. 'You did?' he asked.

'I got you the required amount. Yes, and a little more.'

'Well, I thank you in the name of the British government,' Woolton said.

Sanderson nodded appreciatively. But then sat in silence, somewhat awkwardly, for a few seconds. He then breathed in deeply, looked at Woolton and said: 'By the way, Minister, do you remember that you told me before I went that whatever I did that I thought right would have your support?'

'I certainly remember it and I meant it,' replied Woolton.

'Well, as you know, Egyptian standards, both of trading

and respect for government decrees are not quite the same as in this country. So I hope you think it's alright that I bought an extra 130,000 tons of rice on the black market. I hope that you think that was alright.'

'Sanderson,' replied Woolton coolly, 'I shall remain completely ignorant of such things. I do not understand anything about the existence of a black market in Egypt.' He paused before adding: 'And I shall remain so.'

After Sanderson had left the room, Woolton walked over again to his window and looked down at the people in the street below, a smile growing on his face.

'Just how he got the rice out of Egypt was something into which I never thought it necessary to inquire,' he wrote later in his memoirs, noting also that a few years later Sanderson would be awarded with a knighthood for his courage and negotiating skills. 'But they were very grateful for it in Ceylon,' he added. He then considered how some in his team had scoffed at the idea of Sanderson being successful in his mission. 'It showed how unwise it was to believe anything about the "impossible",' he wrote.

While things like rice disturbed Woolton, the political situation was unnerving him. 'I had spent a more or less sleepless night thinking about the state of England,' he wrote on 13 February 1942, 'and I came to the conclusion that it might be my duty to resign from the government in order to break it.'

Churchill, he wrote, 'is not a good strategist: we never seem to have a sufficient force of men or materials to defend ourselves and any efforts we have made to conduct an offensive seem to result in dismal failure. Winston insists that nobody but he can direct our defence policy; from what I hear he treats his Chiefs of Staff with little consideration, sending for them at all hours of the night as well as the day, and, when times of crisis come, issuing orders himself. It isn't reasonable to expect people to work with clear minds when they cannot have a decent night's sleep, and it isn't reasonable to expect clear judgement from anyone who smokes twenty large cigars a day as the Prime Minister does.'

Woolton felt that the Cabinet underestimated the strength of the enemy ('In the East the Japs are just running all over the place') but there was no obvious replacement for Churchill or his colleagues. 'If I were clear that we had personnel to replace the present Cabinet I would myself resign in order to break the current one. There's little talent,' he complained.

Woolton pondered on possible successors. There was the newspaper proprietor Lord Beaverbrook (formerly Max Aitken) who he distrusted and said, 'was always at the Prime Minister's elbow ... and one wonders how much his judgement affects Winston's. I cannot imagine the Beaverbrook judgement having any good influence in the strategical conduct of the war: he's a bully, and you can't be a successful bully when you're smaller than the other fellow and have no weapons.'

As for other senior Cabinet members, 'Attlee [then Lord Privy Seal] does nothing; John Anderson [at the time Lord President of the Council, later to become Chancellor of the Exchequer] does his best but it's not much; Bevin [Minister of Labour] talks all day about mobilisation of labour, whilst people who are willing to work can't get themselves into jobs.' So would Woolton make the bold move? He was in a quandary. 'I am concerned about the situation,' he wrote, flustered, 'and I don't know what to do about it.'

Two days later, and not only was there a row about how a number of German battleships had managed to escape along the English Channel under the noses of the British in an episode later called the 'Channel Dash' – but also Singapore had finally fallen.

Woolton wrote that Churchill made a broadcast that night – 15 February – at nine o'clock. 'He made the most of all the possible excuses,' wrote Woolton. 'Then he went on to say that the only crime would be disunity in the country, and indicated that anybody who dared to criticise him or the government was a Quisling [an enemy collaborator]. It was a foolish and unpleasant speech. He referred to the vote of confidence that had been given to the government, when he must have known his own attitude had made it impossible for the House not to give the vote, but that the giving did not represent a whole-hearted agreement with it. I don't know whether he was deliberately lying, or whether his personal vanity causes him to believe that the House and the country are at one behind him.'

For her part Maud wrote that 'the Sunday newspapers were distinctly critical of the PM yesterday [15 February] but he cannot bear criticism.' She too noted that Churchill's broad-cast said 'people who criticised were guilty of spoiling the war effort – and thereby becoming almost quislings. He is most unfair.' She continued that Churchill 'has got this awkward faculty of taking criticism personally.' He had, she also felt, a loyalty to certain colleagues that she called 'schoolboy loyalty; when the country is in danger that sort of loyalty has to go, and your colleagues if they are not competent, must be cut adrift.'

According to Maud, her husband had discussed this lack of constructive criticism with both Lord Kemsley (the owner of the *Sunday Times* and *Daily Sketch*) as well as the senior Labour peer and publisher Lord Southwood. 'They are both worried,' she wrote, 'and feel that criticism is needed.'

Since Woolton was plotting this criticism, he felt the prospect of being accused of disloyalty with anguish. Both Woolton and Maud had been listening to the broadcast at home with some fellow politicians, one of whom was a close colleague of Churchill. 'When he finished speaking there was a complete silence, which I felt was that of courtesy [to the aforementioned guest],' commented Woolton; 'it was a little uncomfortable.' But his wife rescued the situation: 'Maud burst in with a denunciation of Winston's comment about critics being Quislings, and that lightened the atmosphere.'

Woolton was, as they say, considering his position. 'The use of words won't win the war,' he wrote, 'and I'm afraid that feet of clay are being discerned.'

Churchill was looking weak. But what would Woolton do about it? A few days later, he reported a conversation with Lord Rothermere. 'He told me that the press were very worried about the present situation: he told me that my position in the country was second in popularity to that of the PM. He thought that if I resigned from the Ministry of Food and went into private life again it would not be long before I was recalled.'

'You could have any position you liked,' Rothermere told Woolton. 'It's all very flattering,' Woolton reflected in his diary, but, he added, 'I don't want any other job.' Woolton maintained his only ambition was that the war be conducted with more vigour.

Woolton's next meeting with Churchill was in early March. 'When I went into the room the PM was scowling,' he wrote, 'and asked if I'd been flogging anybody that morning. The remark was occasioned because the *Daily Mail* had come out with a headline saying that I had asked for the "cat" [a particularly unpleasant form of whip] for black market racketeers.

'So I said "No",' wrote Woolton, '"we'd had a morning off."'

A few days later, on 19 March, after what Woolton called 'a very bad attack of colitis in the night' he attended a meeting of the Privy Council, 'wondering how I would manage to stand through it [as was the custom]. I managed – but only just.' According to Woolton: 'After the meeting the King took me to his room: he immediately said I didn't look very well, and pulled up an easy chair for me to sit in.' The pair chatted about rationing and the importing of produce. 'He talked very intelligently about the food situation, and very frankly about my colleagues,' he recorded. 'He spoke of Bevin [Ernest Bevin, Minister of Labour and National Service] – and mentioned in passing that when he (Bevin) sat in the chair in which I was sitting he bulged all over the sides. He said that Bevin had no understanding of the mind of the people, adding, "Neither has the Prime Minister".'

Woolton enjoyed this indiscretion, writing that 'The King has been brought up to do the industrial side of the Royal job, and he knows more about working men than the Minister of Labour.'

Later that year Woolton also gleefully recalled a dinner at Buckingham Palace given by the King and Queen on Saturday 24 October 1942 at Buckingham Palace for the

US President's wife Mrs Roosevelt. Woolton noted that Bevin, in his behaviour and conversation with the King, 'was overstepping the limits of courtesy. He then accidentally broke a glass and the King rebuked him saying: "Now what have you done?"', with Woolton commenting: 'I thought [the King treated] him rather like a child who really doesn't know any better.'

The Colwyn Bay Propaganda department

In mid May 1942 Woolton spent two days at Colwyn Bay. There was something about the place that depressed him – the drab seaside town with all those Victorian houses crammed full of civil servants. Usually he would sit in a room in the Colwyn Bay Hotel and delegations from the town would visit him. On this visit he decided to stir things up so, as he wrote, 'instead of sitting in my room and people coming to see me I went in detail through three divisions.'

One of his three stops was the building that housed what Woolton's House of Lords detractors called his 'Propaganda Department', This was at Merton Place on Pwllycrochan Avenue; there a team, having intensively researched the subject of food and gathered evidence from a specially selected band of elite scientific advisors, had the job of convincing the British public that the sparse diet of the ration was in fact good for them.

Those advisors included Lord Horder, physician to the Royal Family (a man whose middle name was Jeeves and whose roles included President of the Cremation Society of Great Britain), Sir Henry Dale, President of the Royal Society (a notorious participant in the 'Brown Dog Affair', a scandal in 1903 involving the vivisection of a terrier) and Professor Jack Drummond, Professor of Biochemistry at University College London and an expert on food contamination (later brutally murdered along with his wife and daughter, apparently without motive, while on holiday in France).

Woolton had explained that however useful the advice of his scientific advisors, what he needed was a small group of women to sell his schemes to the housewives of Britain; at this meeting he would inspect the work of the ministry's latest recruits. Already he had hired Marguerite Patten, who perfectly fitted the mould of what he had in mind. A sensible-looking home economist, she had already proved her salt by working as the face for both the Eastern Electricity Board and Frigidaire. Her job, she once recalled, had been to fulfil the 'thankless task of persuading people to buy fridges when they all thought the pantry was quite good enough'. So convincing British cooks to revel in the prospect of making marmalade with carrots or replacing steak with whale meat, would not, perhaps, be so hard a task.

Woolton recruited her as a regular presenter for *The Kitchen Front* on which he himself sometimes appeared. It was a daily radio broadcast, just five minutes long, during which Patten would teach the arts of thrift and of making food last. After radio came pamphlets, then books (such as *Feeding the Nation*), then short films, including the two-minute *Food Flashes* that aired in the cinema and whose introductory voiceovers sternly preached epithets like: 'Don't waste food. It doesn't grow in the shops you know.'

Patten urged women to plan their menus, and then stick to them when they went shopping. It would be a habit that diligent British housewives would then be reluctant to break for decades after, ignoring any fresh produce that wasn't on their pre-written list. The wartime diet, Patten later reflected, was 'better than I thought it would be . . . Do you think we could have survived all those years if we were producing inedible food?' Although she also once admitted, towards the end of her life: 'People are inclined to make me say I want to go back to the war years. Well, what a load of nonsense. Who wants to go back to six months without a fresh tomato.'

As well as Patten, Lord Woolton had hired Irene Veal, who was only too happy to trot out lines fed to her by the propaganda team. In the preface to her plodding cook book, *Recipes of the 1940s,* with its endless 'Ways with Meat, Ways with Fish, Ways with Potatoes, Ways with Cheese . . .' – ad infinitum – she wrote, 'Never before have the British people been so wisely fed or British women so sensibly interested in cooking. We are acquiring an almost French attitude of mind regarding our food and its preparation . . .'

But on this day, Woolton was presented with a rather more charming little tome, produced by his latest recruit, Doris Grant. Her *'Feeding the Family in War-Time* had an illustration of a bird bringing her hungry nestlings a menu with the words 'Early Worms'; black silhouettes of planes fly above and below there are ships at sea.

The back cover of her book promised to answer questions such as 'Can you make economical, nutritious meals not only palatable but delicious?', 'Do you know how to increase the food value of your rations without added expense?' and the rather stricter: 'Have you learnt how to keep the family up to concert pitch without slackness and lassitude?' Inside she wrote, 'The war has given us all a sense of adventure in cooking. We have had to follow new paths and learn new ways; we have been jolted out of ruts.'

This was just the tone Woolton craved. And he was like-wise delighted as he read on: 'We are eating less meat and sugar, and many of us are surprised to find that we are none the worse for this, but feeling better for it; thanks to the Ministry of Food, we are learning the real value of simple foods like potatoes and carrots ... many a sadly overworked liver must be secretly rejoicing at the rationing of fats and enjoying a much-needed holiday.'

Doris Grant also talked of how 'too much sugar' not only disturbed the balance of the diet but 'spoils the appetite for simple natural foods'. She added: 'Too much meat is harmful' but also warned against the danger of – with the lack of both fresh and dried fruit – filling up 'with too much starch'. She encouraged the eating of wholewheat bread: 'Bread made from white flour should have no place in the diet of those who value their health,' she wrote. She advised on adding the likes of Marmite, wheatgerm and 'Horsfield's Health Porridge' ('a splendid food ... which passes for porridge') to your store cupboard, and suggested sprucing up food with a sprig of parsley or a dusting of paprika. She also made suggestions for substituting food that was hard to come by, proposing soya flour as a replacement for meat, rosehip made into syrup instead of oranges and swede juice for any juice ('the juice can be obtained by grating the swede finely and pressing through muslin').

These were at the more palatable end of food substitutes, with stories abounding of rooks in pies instead of grouse. But as real as it was ubiquitous and loathed, was dried egg. Powdered egg, much of it imported from the United States where the eggs were spray-dried, took up less space, was obviously safer to transport, and needed no refrigeration. British households were allowed a grey packet of dried egg, the supposed equivalent to a dozen eggs, every four weeks.

Recalling life in an English boarding school during the Second World War, Jill Beattie wrote: 'The two words which still make my blood run cold, are DRIED EGG. The very worst breakfast ... was a two inch block of hard scrambled eggs oozing with water which saturated the half slice of so-called toast beneath it – and the TASTE – ugh!'

As for Doris Grant, her recipes include cauliflower soup (boiled with mace and half a leek, then sieved), cabbage puree (with evaporated milk, nutmeg and a shaving of margarine), shredded carrot and sultana salad, nettle tops (boiled for twenty minutes), steamed marrow – browned under the grill with grated cheese – liver casserole simmered with grated carrot, baked corned beef finely chopped with mashed parsnips, and baked apple and raisin pudding. Perhaps Lord Woolton licked his lips as he turned the pages, the lack of any hint of richness permeating the dishes appealing to his naturally austere constitution.

The book, with its sensible instructions, would be a useful addition to his other favourite cookery publication, *Food Facts for the Kitchen Front*. This no-nonsense little tome was filled with the likes of artichokes and potatoes in caper sauce (a dash of milk added to artichoke water and a 'few shavings of cooking fat' completing the dish). There were endless dishes of baked vegetables, of soups and broths (spruced up with 'a dash of milk', 'a piece of dripping', 'a pinch of nutmeg'), of rabbits – baked, boiled, jugged, potted and curried (cut, rolled in flour, fried with apple and spring onions and with a spoonful of curry powder) – and handy packed meals like cold kidney pasties.

Woolton expressed satisfaction about these publications before asking for an update on one of his most major publicity campaigns, which he ran in tandem with the Ministry of Agriculture. Some twelve months previously, Woolton and Minister of Agriculture Robert Hudson had launched the 'Dig for Victory' campaign. This was a countrywide campaign, reinforced on film, posters and radio, to deal with the problem that Britain seriously under-performed as a food-producing nation.

According to Woolton, the country's low level of food security, and its huge reliance of imports, arose from an endemic character trait. 'In the poorest homes people were largely ignorant of anything except their appetites and had no knowledge of food values,' he wrote, adding: 'As a nation, it was broadly true to say that we were indifferent to both our agriculture and our horticulture.'

Most wheat, flour and meat, for example, came from Canada, Australia, Argentina, New Zealand or Denmark. Onions had also been imported from France, which presented huge problems when that country fell to Germany in June 1940. In 1939 Britain produced only 40 per cent of its food (and in the 1930s the only food product that Britain was entirely self-sufficient in was liquid milk). 'It was obvious that to reduce the large figure of imports, we had to use every bit of land to the best advantage,' Woolton said.

So, in addition to directives to farmers to make their fields produce as much food as possible, householders were challenged to not just get their allotments productive but to turn parkland, cricket pitches and golf courses into vegetable patches. Famously, the rose gardens at the front of Buckingham Palace that flanked the Mall were turned over for cabbages, the manicured lawns by the Albert Memorial for carrots, and even the grass lawns that lined the moat around the Tower of London became neat strips of sown vegetables.

To front this campaign on film, the Ministry of Information hired the celebrity gardener of the day, C. H. Middleton, who had appeared on BBC radio throughout the 1930s. He gave advice on everything from composting to harvesting carrots, his message being: 'food is just as important a weapon of war as guns.'

The Dig for Victory campaign was hugely effective; by 1944, the nation was producing some 66 per cent of the food it consumed. Cultivated land rose from 12.9 million acres to 19.4 million and the number of tractors rose from 55,000 to 175,000. It was, the British food historian Colin Spencer has commented, a cultural change that occurred across the country: 'What food rationing did was to force everyone to grow their own vegetables; however small a patch people owned, lawns and flower beds were dug up, soil was dug, fertilized and planted with a year round supply of potatoes, vegetables and salads.'

Much of the work to produce all this veg was done by the 80,000 land girls of the Women's Land Army, who, it later transpired, endured a miserable war. They lived on a diet of bread, butter and potatoes and suffered endless sexual harassment from some of the few male farm workers who hadn't gone to war. The land girls' work was supplemented by German and Italian prisoners of war.

Woolton also wanted to encourage the nation to forage through the countryside. For there, among the hedgerows and in the woods, were fruits, berries and fungi which teams of parents and children – often dressed in Brownie or Cub uniforms – could pick until their heart's content. Walnuts could be pickled, chestnuts made into soup, and nettles used as a substitute for sage and onion. Of course, in reality rural scavenging could be less than romantic. Writer Anne Valery recalled her schoolgirl foraging efforts in her memoir *Talking About The War,* in which she wrote: 'I was one of the harvesters. Every autumn weekend, groups from school fanned out over North Devon, ploughing up hill and down dale, drenched or burnt by the sun, and bitten by every insect known to our biology mistress. Stained like Ancient Britons due to steady sampling, we picked for hours, our backs breaking in the search for the tiny bilberries hidden at ground level, and which the school made into jam.'

The foraging, Lord Woolton was told, would be further encouraged by the latest pamphlet to be produced in co-operation with his ministry. He was shown one such title called *Kitchen Front Recipes and Hints* by Ambrose Heath. The author's name was a pseudonym used by Francis Miller, a writer of countless such books and pamphlets. 'A poached egg on a bed of dandelion or nettle puree covered with cheese sauce is an almost perfect meal,' Woolton read out aloud to the assembled throng. It was a perfect recipe for the war effort, great for those country housewives. But it was not a dish that would go down well with Winston Churchill.

Back in London on 22 May, Woolton had a visitor to his office who wanted to discuss Woolton's plan to ensure everyone in the country was able to get their hands on wholemeal bread. If there was going to be just one type of universally available bread, it would be better for morale if it were the more interesting wholemeal than a relentless supply of the white stuff.

His visitor was the Royal physician Thomas, 1st Baron Horder, one of the country's most respected clinicians and an advisor to Woolton's ministry. The pair went for lunch because, wrote Woolton, 'I am anxious to get him to collect evidence from his professional friends who work in hospitals to the effect that the wholemeal bread is not having a bad effect on people's digestions.'

Woolton was aware of a significant number of people who were wary of wholemeal bread. 'There's a section of the public that is convincing itself that wholemeal bread is doing them harm,' he wrote. 'So much so that people write to tell me that they've never suffered from constipation before, but now they have to eat wholemeal bread they do.' Horder reassured Woolton, 'if wholemeal bread has any effect on this distressing complaint it's the opposite one!'

Rumblings about Woolton's rationing policy continued throughout the summer. There were complaints about tomatoes, potatoes, fish, jam, vegetables, fruit, bread and, of course, eggs. Woolton's attempt at controlling the price of tomatoes had led to them disappearing, critics alleged; they had gone underground. Likewise with fish, price controls – to stop profiteering – seem to have limited the supply. Fixed prices for jam had made it simply too expensive for many and there seemed to be a worrying dearth of new potatoes.

'I am assailed by critics,' he told the *Daily Telegraph* on 9 July. 'I am trying in the national interest, he said' – the reporter describing Woolton as exclaiming and 'throwing up his hands'.

He defended his egg scheme, saying he was trying to bring them into towns and within reach of people who had been finding them either out of reach or too expensive. The plan was simply 'in its birth pangs'. But everywhere he looked there were complaints. '"It's going wrong here" and "it's going wrong there",' he described people telling him, saying: 'I am not disputing that people cannot find something wrong with it, but it is a very big scheme ... and it is necessarily an experiment. No nation-wide scheme could be perfect.'

In July Winston Churchill weighed in after hearing complaints. 'The hen has been part and parcel of the country cottager's life since history began. Townsfolk can eke out their rations by a bought meal. What is the need for this tremendous reduction to one hen per person?' The Cabinet should have been informed, groused Churchill.

Woolton proceeded to defend each policy, then said in some desperation: 'I feel like a navvy [labourer] working in the boiling heat surrounded by lots of little flies, and it takes one all one's time to get them away.' So the profiteers were worms, and his critics flies; and the press continued to pile on the pressure.

'Lord Woolton May Leave', reported the *Manchester Evening News* on 17 July. His name was, the paper said, touted as one who faced the chop in an impending reshuffle. 'The Food Minister has been criticised from many quarters, and in Parliament at the beginning of May public dissatisfaction with the distribution of non-rationing foodstuffs was voiced.' Woolton wrote in his diary that evening: 'My press conference today was confined to eggs, of which I am heartily sick. The press were very critical of the scheme we had put in.'

Two days later, on 19 July, the *Daily Herald* yelled: 'Food Folly!' The press appeared to be turning on him again; this time, publishing an open letter by Labour MP Barbara Ayrton Gould. She attacked Woolton for noticing too late that the country had an issue with malnutrition: 'Did it really take twenty-two months of Total War to bring home to you the evils of malnutrition? I have spent twenty years trying to stop this hideous scandal,' she declared. She went on to attack his egg policy, saying, 'Your egg scheme has involved the nation in a serious and easily avoidable wastage of a vital food.'

Ayrton Gould said she had been investigating Woolton's egg policy and reported that 'the net result of the scheme is to provide the consumer with millions of bad eggs.' She alleged that the country's egg collectors 'who have always collected eggs from all the local farms for immediate dispatch to large towns or sales in local markets were instructed by your ministry to hold the eggs for weeks before dispatching them to your depots. How are they expected to keep those eggs in hot weather? They have no cold storage. Most of them have no stock-in-trade except a light van for collection and distribution.' She added that a collector she knew from the West Country had complained that 'weeks on end in a hot barn will finish them.' Furthermore imported eggs from America and Canada had, she alleged, been 'three months old before they reached the consumer. Didn't your advisers tell you that eggs were perishable, and would not keep good for so many weeks on end?'

Next she assaulted Woolton over potatoes. As with eggs, his scheme was to control prices and distribution. 'Were you as ignorant about the wastage of eggs as apparently you were about the shortage of potatoes?' She claimed that thousands of housewives had queued for up to 'twelve days for potatoes and that many had been turned away empty-handed?'

The Labour MP also didn't buy Woolton's class credentials: 'Perhaps you don't know that in millions of working class homes potatoes are the mainstay of the people's diet, and the lack of them causes serious hardship,' she wrote. 'I should like to know what you think about the malnutrition caused by the action of your ministry in mishandling these two vital foodstuffs.'

A month later – on 9 August – the *Perthshire Advertiser* declared: 'Tears for Woolton'. In a savage piece the paper accused Woolton of poking his nose into the kitchens of the housewife, where 'she has hitherto reigned supreme.' He 'has rushed in, with a host of silk-hatted bureaucrats at his heels; and, with the laudable object of making things easy for everybody, has succeeded in converting order into chaos and efficiency into well-nigh hopeless muddle.' Where there had been, the paper argued, a reasonable supply of eggs in many areas, 'there is now an all-over scarcity; where there was pristine freshness, there is now in too many instances a musty look and a disconcerting smell.' The paper also mentioned 'the soft fruit bungle', which, it said, was 'another example of misbegotten ingenuity'.

Attacks continued, coming from every quarter. Sir Ernest Bevin, writing in the August issue of *Truth* magazine, argued that Woolton's control of pricing had taken away the prospect of profit and as a result 'has upset the balance of the market, if not, indeed, destroyed it'. On 30 August novelist Ursula Bloom, in the *Leader* newspaper, accused Woolton of 'gross mismanagement'. His crimes included creating a bureaucracy in which fruit went putrid ('sacrificed to your little forms, to your blue pencil dockets'), eggs went off and 'market-cornering crooks' went scot-free. 'I stood yesterday in a queue for oranges, doled out one at a time for a family,' she wrote. 'I saw seven different members of one family go twice through that queue, and none of your little forms covers that kind of cheating.'

The next day writer Howard Drayton in the *Sunday Sun* also attacked Woolton's penchant for form-filling. 'Growers can't pick their crops because they haven't received their permits,' he wrote, claiming that as a result, 'much of the plum crop will be lost.' On the same day the *Daily Herald* ran a picture story which, it claimed, 'tells the story of millions of schoolchildren in Britain today who are not being properly fed'. The large headline above the story read: 'This isn't good enough Lord Woolton.'

Yet while Woolton was being publicly lashed, he was getting quite a different press behind the political scenes. On 13 July Alexander Erskine-Hill (a Scottish Unionist Party politician), chairman of the Conservative Party's back-bench 1922 committee – an influential group of MPs who liaised with the Prime Minister – came to see Woolton. 'The Conservative Party is becoming uneasy about the value and strength of Winston as PM,' he told Woolton. 'Things are not going well in the war and we are wondering how long he will last. So I've been tasked to come and speak to you to see whether you have any views about succeeding him.'

Woolton reckoned this was because 'the Party wouldn't mind having me if I would take it on, because they know I don't want to hang on after the war.' However, as he wrote in his diary and told Erskine-Hill: 'I don't want to be Prime Minister.' He didn't, however, say that if offered the role, he wouldn't actually take it on.

By midsummer, chatter about Churchill's future seemed to reach fever pitch. A flurry of MPs came to visit Woolton to sound him out on a job outside the Food Ministry. Kingsley Wood, for example, then Chancellor of the Exchequer, arrived to flatter him on 18 August. 'You've managed the food problem very well indeed,' he said. 'I think you've done your job as Minister for Food and it's time you looked for fresh worlds to conquer. My view is that you should hold very high office in the government.' Then Oliver Stanley, at that point Secretary of State for the Colonies, came to have lunch with Woolton. He was 'full of gossip about the Conservative Party and the fact that it thinks Winston has had his day. They are looking for a new leader.'

This talk of Woolton succeeding Churchill continued well into the following spring and summer of 1943. On 2 April 1943 he made the following small note in his diary: 'Incidentally I was told that the editor of one of the national dailies had asked if I had any political ambition and if I had ever thought of myself as the post-war Prime Minister.' He was clearly puffed up to hear such gossip. But while some were touting his name as a possible successor to Churchill, Woolton realised that there were of course others jostling for the position.

He recalled an occasion in the House of Lords on 1 April 1942 when Lord Beaverbook had put down a motion about the costs of milk distribution. 'There was nothing of note in his [Beaverbrook's] speech but he has adopted a technique of putting down a motion about something or other every week to keep himself before the public,' wrote Woolton, who was less than impressed: 'It's a pathetic effort because nobody takes any notice of him and he has completely worn himself out of public favour. But I think that he has an idea that if ever another PM was needed the public might clamour for him.'

Then on 11 June 1943 he recorded a conversation with the Conservative MP Leslie Pym: 'Somebody had told me a week or two ago that at a meeting of very important people in the political world it had been suggested that, in the event of Winston not holding the Premiership, I was the only member of the present government who could take it on. I told this to Leslie Pym, rather by way of a joke, but to my surprise he didn't laugh, but told me that he himself had heard the same proposal discussed seriously in political circles.'

But for all the talk of Woolton attaining the premiership, he could always rely on the newspapers to bring him back down to earth. On 23 November the *Reynold's News* paper put on its steel-capped boots and took aim: 'Lordly Failure', it declared. The paper wrote how, next to maintaining the nation's food supplies, Woolton's job was to maintain the nation's confidence in the Ministry of Food. 'Lord Woolton is falling down on the job.' The paper cited how in early November Woolton had 'announced that no winter milk shortage was in sight. Then he imposed a token cut of 5 per cent. Next he raised the cut to 15 per cent. Tomorrow, he will limit adults to two pints a week.' *Reynold's News* wasn't happy. 'This monkeying with the people's milk must stop,' it continued. 'The public is prepared to go short, to endure inconvenience, even hardship. What the public is not pre-pared to endure is a continuance of mismanagement in everything Lord Woolton touches.'

Maud, his beloved

Woolton read the article, shrugged his shoulders then had it stuck into his cuttings album. He would discuss it with his wife Maud; she never failed to improve his spirits when he was under attack. The couple, well into late middle-age, were as unified and as besotted as ever. Just a few weeks previously – a weekend night before bedtime in London on 9 October 1942 – Lord Woolton had been relaxing in his apartment. 'It's Saturday and the anniversary of our wedding tomorrow, so we've frivolled,' he wrote. 'Maud and I had lunch together, then to a theatre in the afternoon and dined out afterwards. A very satisfactory day.'

Woolton was never more content than when in the company of Maud and years later, five months after her death on 13 September 1961, he sat down to write a long tribute to her. Across fifty-seven sheets of unlined paper, he told her life story. He expressed his gratitude that she had been by his side through every period of difficulty in his adult life and how he had shared all his thoughts with her, from his worries and concerns to the many official secrets that burdened him. He chose to write those words in the library that she had designed for him at their house, Walberton, in Sussex.

He wrote of her strong religious faith – which he shared – and said that 'somehow she had acquired the secret of living, in tune with the infinity.' He sensed her presence: 'I feel that she is "hereabouts".'

'I loved her so deeply that I am impelled to write of her,' he wrote. 'With her encouragement and constant support and loving care, I have been privileged to occupy a prominent position in the service of my country when its people and its future were imperilled.'

As war had approached, and his political rank had risen, so he realised that he would have to spend at least three days a week in London. The happy days he spent relaxing at their holiday home by Lake Windermere would be severely restricted, and he was concerned that his time with his other half would be similarly lessened. London was also a dangerous place, but, he recorded: 'To my delight Maud decided that whilst she couldn't come all the time she was aiming at doing so. We both knew full well that war was coming and that whatever else happened we were going to be separated a great deal. Both our children were at school or college so we resolved that during term time we would move about together and during holidays Maud would live with the children in the Lakes.'

Lady Woolton was more than a dutiful companion; she developed a nice line in public speaking, filling in for her husband if he was unable to open a British Restaurant or attending a lunch to jolly along some community caterers.

'In all this Maud was not only with me,' he wrote, 'but I constantly talked to her about those very secret things and I know I could do so. Not only with benefit, but with security in this speaking of official secrets of the first magnitude. It was all thrilling – and exhausting!'

Maud was similarly devoted to her Fred, often referring to him with the affectionate 'F'. She was pleased and reassured to once record, in February 1941, that after a lunch with Joseph Cohen, one of the directors of Lewis's, 'a medium came in.' Presumably Cohen's idea of post-lunch entertainment. She was left in the room with Maud. 'It was rather thrilling,' she wrote. 'She began by saying that I was psychic – and my husband was, that we were very much "enwrapped", that we had been together in another life.' The medium went on to say that she could see Woolton, surrounded by important men, one of whom was holding a heraldic shield. Maud posited that this could be 'the coat of arms of Manchester University'. One of the men, said the medium, was Neville Chamberlain. 'A third man wore a frock coat,' recorded Maud, 'had a scroll in his hand and was making a proclamation. I may say that she [the medium] hadn't been told who F was, and thus had no means of knowing. She kept saying that F had a great and responsible job, and that he was very tired. He must rest.'

During the school holidays, Woolton missed his wife and wrote to her often. But he also sent her letters while they were both in London. Theirs was a love that endured over many decades and Woolton penned notes to his wife at a similar rate to the letters sent from his mother to his young self. They are indeed as regular as a modern day email exchange between a devoted couple. When Maud was away, his letters talk of how a speech went down, a broadcast delivered or a tricky meeting handled. And every note started with language that makes very clear his devotion to her.

Finding time between meetings to pen quick missives from his desk at the Ministry of Food he would begin: 'Darling', 'Darlingest' or 'Belovedest'. 'Goodbye darling,' he ended one such note, 'I hope you are resting and sleeping and not worrying about anything but the next meal.' In another: 'Goodbye best of wives: I think of you constantly between speeches. Love to the Woolly one.'

One afternoon he wrote simply: 'to tell you what a gloriously happy time you have given me: you have been so sweet and time doesn't wither nor age decay it,' while on one other occasion he told her: 'You know I really am ridiculously dependent on you.'

13

A Spoonful of Sugar

Better news arrived on 24 October: the 1942 crop of potatoes was a good one. 'I want to get people to eat more potatoes instead of bread,' he wrote. Over the coming months he attempted to get this story into the press. In mid-December his ministry launched a campaign and held fairs across the country that demonstrated the marvels of the potato. In due course, in January 1943, stories appeared in both the *Daily Telegraph* and *The Times* of, as the latter put it on 13 January, the 'Urgent Need to Eat More Potatoes'.

The following spring then handed Woolton a further boost when it was predicted, as the *Observer* reported on May 30, that the 'Harvest Will Be A Record.'

Talking that day to 1,600 land girls at Aylesbury in Buckinghamshire, Woolton announced that 'it appears that we are going to have the prospect of the greatest harvest that we have ever had.' He also thanked the nation's dairy farmers saying: 'You have given us milk in quantities that we scarcely even dared hope to get.'

The bumper harvest of 1943 for British farmers saw a transformation: whereas at the start of the war most of the wheat for bread had been imported, in that year one half of the country's bread grain needs were met by home-grown wheat. The biggest increase in food production came in potatoes, which went up 87 per cent. It rather begged the question of what to do with it all, with Woolton's ministry reckoning the best answer was as a substitute for bread.

According to writer Lizzie Collingham in her book *The Taste of War:* 'The end result was that Britain produced too many potatoes ... Those who benefited were the privileged members of society who had the means to keep a pig, as they were provided with a plentiful and cheap food.'

Woolton finished his triumphant speech in Aylesbury heralding what he long saw as one of his greatest achievements: 'When this war is over we shall have an infant and child population which will not have been damaged by the war.'

Lord Boyd Orr, one of Britain's foremost nutrition expert and post-war head of the United Nations Food and Agriculture Organisation, wrote in his memoirs: 'Lord Woolton produced for the first time in modern history a food plan based on the nutritional needs of the people, with priority in rationing for mothers and children ... the rich got less to eat, which did them no harm, and the poor, so far as the supply would allow, got a diet adequate for health, with free orange juice, cod liver oil, extra milk and other things for mothers and children. This was a great achievement for which Britain is indebted to Lord Woolton.'

But while Woolton was publicly talking of great success, he had a problem in his ministry. In early May of 1943 Woolton was in his office talking with Sir William Rook, Director of Sugar at the Ministry of Food.

The two were having some concerned discussions. Woolton stirred his cup of tea, pausing from puffing on his pipe, and noting to himself how well he had retuned his tastes in recent months. He preferred two teaspoons of sugar in his milky tea, but these days, along with everyone else in the country, he was making do with none. Sometimes Rook, given his job title, would bring in a little sugar as a treat for the minister. But today there was no such luck.

'We are getting uncomfortably short of sugar,' Rook told the minister. 'Our usual supplies have either dried up or the passage by ship has become impossible.'

'Well,' replied Woolton, 'we should find new suppliers. Sugar is such an important commodity, there must be other markets.'

'There is another we haven't used,' said Rook.

'Oh yes?' said Woolton, perking up.

'Yes, Minister. It's a supply in Egypt. But there's a big problem. A big expensive problem. And his name is Pasha Abboud.'

Rook explained: there were considerable quantities of sugar in Egypt, but they were all under the control of Pasha Abboud, an Egyptian who had trained as an engineer on the Clyde. He had taken his engineering skills to Turkey where he'd made a great deal of money before returning to Egypt and building ship-repairing yards in Alexandria. He then started purchasing steamships – most of which were involved in the import and export of sugar – before buying control of the reason they used the ports of Alexandria, the location of the country's largest sugar factory. Such was his fortune that he owned a palace larger than the King's, and, with the right infrastructure at his disposal, he was able to control the price of sugar on the Egyptian market, and now in a time of war and of fragmented supply, all across the world. Indeed, he had become the most powerful global figure in the world of this prized and much-needed commodity.

'So there we have it,' concluded Rook. 'We need sugar, households across the country need it. And the only man we can buy it from wants an extortionate price. So either we pay for it, and destroy the ministry's budgets for other goods, or this nation and her colonies have to learn to live without it. But we all know the dangers of not honouring the ration, of damaging national morale.'

Rook was at a loss. But as he finished talking, he noticed a wry smile come over Woolton's face.

'Don't worry, Sir William,' said Woolton. 'I think I can deal with this problem. Just tell me one thing. Where else in the world is there a reasonable quantity of sugar, regardless of how far away it might be, that we could get our hands on?'

Rook paused then answered: 'Well there's sugar in Queensland, Australia. But it's a considerable distance away and the cost of export to Britain would make it financially unviable.'

'OK,' said Woolton. Then he pressed a button on his telephone and one of his private secretaries came on the line.

'Can you get hold of Lloyd's for me?' he asked. 'Tell them the Ministry of Food wishes to charter a ship for us to take sugar from Queensland, Australia to Egypt.'

Rook looked on astonished as Woolton talked. He put down the receiver and then said to his Director of Sugar. 'Once Lloyd's have agreed, can you let your contacts on the Egyptian sugar market know that there's a new sugar supplier in town?'

'I'm confused, Minister,' said a baffled Rook.

'I'm going to sell sugar in Alexandria. And I'm going to sell it for less than this chap Pasha Abboud charges. So he'll have to compete with me and bring down his prices.'

Rook left the room doubtful to say the least about this high-risk strategy. The ministry would be committing millions of pounds to buying and shipping the sugar from Australia to Egypt with all the transport risks that that entailed. And what did Woolton know about the sugar market?

Woolton was rather more bullish, writing later in his memoirs that Abboud 'knew that he had been trying to make us pay an extortionate price for the things he possessed and I think he reasonably expected to be treated a little roughly.' Which was just as Woolton intended. It was not the first time he had brought his business and commercial chutzpah into the department. But it was not without considerable risk.

While Woolton was still exercising his business acumen, he was supposed to have jettisoned his actual business when he accepted the role of Minister of Food. He had made a great play of it, telling newspapers, fellow politicians and his wife of the financial sacrifices he was making to join the government. In fact, he continued to have occasional meetings with the board of Lewis's, having lunch from time to time with directors and he had several meetings – as recorded in his own diaries – with regards to the potential purchase of the London department store Selfridges. For example, on 27 November 1941, he met with a business contact of his, Ivan Spens, who advised him that Selfridges was 'getting no real management and would like us [Lewis's – the firm Woolton no longer worked for . . .] to put somebody in to take hold of the place, in anticipation of our buying it when the war is over'. Woolton recorded his response: 'I told him we had nobody to spare: but the truth is that I have no intention of letting any of Lewis's people go in to tidy up the place and get it making a profit, so that we put up the purchase price for ourselves.'

This talk of 'us' and 'we' with regards to Lewis's was somewhat at odds with the statement put out by the Ministry of Food as reported in the *Daily Telegraph* on 1 May 1941, when rebutting claims made by a Scottish MP (see page 210) that Lewis's had been selling cooked meat when their rivals had none. The Ministry of Food official had been emphatic that Woolton had 'no connection with Lewis's'.

The following year, on 22 December 1942, a distinguished accountant, Sir William McLintock, met Woolton to discuss the negotiations for the store. Woolton recorded, frustratedly, that: 'In spite of restrictions on supply and trade, and shortage of staff they [Selfridges] are doing very well and it's going to cost us more money than it would have done a year or two back.'

On 6 May 1943 Woolton spent an evening with McLintock at Claridge's. The accountant 'brought with him the proposals for the purchase of Selfridges,' recorded Woolton. 'We spent the evening discussing the details and he has gone away to amend them.' (It was another night when Woolton had to endure eating his eponymous Woolton pie. 'It was so poor that I have had to send McLintock the official recipe in order to convince him that it's really all right.')

Yet, most of the time, Woolton engaged his business brain for the legitimate pursuits of his ministry, albeit in ways that often made his officials squirm. Seeking on one occasion to purchase beef from Argentina, he had a meeting with the Argentinian Ambassador. The price he heard was high, far more than he knew was the market rate, 'a grossly advanced price' as he put it. At the meeting, as he recalled, he 'said some rather hard things about the desire of the Argentinian government to make an excessive profit out of the fact that we were at war'.

His moral pronouncements seemed to have had little effect. The Argentinians stuck to their price. As far as they were concerned Britain needed their meat and had no room to manoeuvre. The British could moralise and talk about principles all they liked but they had no choice but to pay up.

'I accept your decision,' Woolton told the Ambassador. The Argentinian assumed he had won this tussle. Then the minister continued. 'And as we cannot trade I will immediately give instructions that our ships will not call at Argentinian ports.'

British ships were not just passing through Argentinian ports to deliver meat to the UK, they were part of that country's vital import and export business. Furthermore, Argentina's cold storage facilities at the time were full to overflowing; processed food needed chilling and, if British ships could not stop at the ports, the country would lose millions of tons of produce. The Argentinians then backed down; they were now desperate to do the deal. At which point Woolton said he was now revising his terms. The Ambassador assumed the price was going to be reduced further, but instead Woolton told him that he wanted Argentina to raise his price, only by a smaller margin than originally proposed. 'One of us is going to win in this battle and one has to lose, he said. 'I prefer you to win.'

Woolton wanted final recognition of the negotiation to belong to the Ambassador so he could claim to his government that Britain was a reasonable country to deal with; a satisfied supplier meant they would continue to sell to him as a customer. He shook hands with the Argentinian and said: 'So you get the victory: we get the meat.'

Woolton may have brought such negotiations to a fruitful conclusion but not all his staff enjoyed the process – some were horrified at seeing what they regarded as low business tactics being employed among diplomatic circles. Vexed by the traditional command structure in his department, Woolton sometimes felt compelled to circumvent the usual routes to making purchases. His view was that by only ever acting with total propriety, opportunities would be missed. Worried, for example, by rumours that the Germans were negotiating to buy whale oil from the Norwegians (which would be used to make margarine), Woolton hastily made contact with the traders, agreed the first price quoted and then bought the entire stock. According to his memoirs, he then had it transported to Britain and hidden in a secret location, well away from any German spies or foreign agents keen to procure or steal whale oil for their own country's desperate needs.

When a row was looking to brew between his department and the Americans over the sale of a million eggs which had arrived rotten, he intervened. Not wishing to upset the Americans with a complaint, however justified, as he wanted to secure a constant trade before a colleague could discover that the consignment had gone bad, he sent in a secret squad of men. Under cover of darkness they removed the eggs from port and then dropped them down a disused mine in Skelmersdale. 'I wonder if, in years to come, some archaeologists will wonder what sort of people would leave this colossal quantity of eggs in such a small area,' he mused on the incident. 'But by then probably both the eggs – and I hope the smell – will have gone.'

When it came to purchasing essential goods such as wheat, there were the formal channels, the official ways of trading and there was the Woolton way; a way determined by him and without recourse to such tedious things as departmental approval or even paperwork.

On 8 September 1942, for example, Woolton attended a ceremony at Canada House. It was a formal occasion, in which Woolton and his senior staff were ushered through the maple-lined passages of this Greek Revivalist building, with its exterior clad in bold whitish-grey Portland stone. In a room filled with a large number of journalists, with photographers on hand to help record this vital moment, lavish documents concerning trade between Canada and Great Britain were laid out for signature.

The formality was a wheat-buying agreement and the result of months of intense negotiating between the British Government and the Canadian High Commission. A quite beautiful set of papers had been crafted; signatures would seal the occasion, before and after speeches that would talk about the spirit of cooperation between key allies; great nations working together to supply food to the common man or woman. Woolton himself, at the appropriate time, signed his autograph on the document, as photographs were taken. All that was missing was a band of trumpeters to play a robust voluntary to muster the soul and stir up a little fervent patriotism. The pleasantries over, he quickly left the building, a mischievous smile breaking across his face, keen to get back to his office where the actual purchasing of wheat took place, Woolton-style.

That night he made a confession to his diary. 'The sum total of the agreement about which there was all this palaver was 10 million bushels of wheat,' he wrote. 'A few weeks ago I had bought 20 million bushels of wheat, certainly without consultation with anyone except the Treasury and without signing an agreement. The whole thing had been done almost entirely on the telephone – which, after all, is the proper way to buy wheat!'

Woolton's other method in securing wheat was to buy options in wheat markets anonymously. He did it without Treasury consent, buying options in every wheat market in the world before terminating those options on the same day. In that way, without his customers knowing he was acting for the British Government, he got a better deal. Usually he was able to fund the deals with the Ministry of Food budget; but one day he had to involve the Chancellor of the Exchequer, Sir Kingsley Wood.

Woolton had telephoned Wood saying he needed to secure funds – £100 million, to be precise. He made the call saying, 'I've been buying some food,' keenly requesting that the money be made available by three o'clock that afternoon.

'You can't treat me in this manner,' said a startled Chancellor, 'you need to write a paper and go through the official channels.' Woolton replied: 'I will not write a paper about a commercial transaction of this magnitude; it would be impossible to keep it secret and the loss to the Treasury would not be less than 20 million if the markets knew what was happening.'

'Is this the way you normally conduct your business affairs?' asked Wood.

'It is,' replied Woolton. He assured him that he would not have to carry any responsibility for the deal as, noted Woolton: 'I was using him as my banker.' Woolton was having trouble completing the last option and needed extra money from the Treasury, but without the Treasury knowing. So it made sense for him to ask Wood, who ran the department. Woolton felt he could trust the Chancellor having, coincidentally, acted as an advisor to him before the war. Wood agreed and, having successfully secured the money, Woolton then managed to buy all the wheat the country would need for the next six months and at a healthy price of 72 cents a bushel. He went to Wood's office to thank him personally and to apologise for the demands he had put on him that morning.

'You will never live to see wheat at 72 cents again,' he told Wood.

'I suppose you have bought it in the name of the British Government,' said Wood.

'I can assure you,' replied Woolton, 'that if anybody had known it was the British Government that was buying we would have had to pay a much higher price. We bought the wheat under every possible sort of disguise.'

Wood was sanguine. 'Well all that I ask is that you can impose some restraint on your activities. I can see that you are difficult to control. But I might add that you are the only minister who has ever come to me to apologise for saving money.'

Woolton was also at his maverick best when working to import ground-nuts from Nigeria, needed to make margarine. Just as with whale oil, nuts could also be used for spreads. Given the large amount needed, 400,000 tons – as Woolton wrote, 'it takes a lot of ground-nuts to make a ton' – he called on an old friend of his, Lord Swinton. Swinton was Minister Resident in West Africa, or, as Woolton put it, 'Ambassador-at-large in Africa' known to the Nigerians as 'the King of Britain'. 'Will you ask the native chiefs if, on the grounds of patriotism, they will provide us with this large quantity of ground-nuts?' requested Woolton.

Swinton, wrote Woolton, arranged a meeting and flew in to a village in his 'white and glittering plane'. 'I, the King of Britain,' he told the tribal chiefs, 'am disturbed that my country is surrounded by enemies who are trying to starve it and my people are in danger.' He explained how the supply or ground-nuts could alleviate the problem. 'This is more than money can buy,' he continued, 'but not more than your patriotism could afford.' According to Woolton, 'the chiefs went and met other chiefs; they had a pow-wow and then came back to Lord Swinton.'

'Please send a message to the British saying that the people of Nigeria do not want the King's people at home going short of fat for the want of ground-nuts,' they told him. 'The whole affair was conducted with the maximum of solemnity,' recorded Woolton. A promise was given and in due course 400,000 tons of ground-nuts came to Britain.

Meanwhile, Woolton still needed to secure that sugar from Egypt. Word reached Abboud that a certain Lord Woolton was considering entering the Alexandrian sugar market and, to Woolton's amusement, in due course, a telegram came to the Department from the Egyptian saying, in Woolton's words: 'that he would like to come over to interview me, with a view to helping our sugar supplies'.

With a meeting arranged with Abboud, Woolton knew he could call off the Queensland shipment. 'We called the Egyptian bluff,' he wrote. 'To the great relief of the Department I therefore decided not to sell sugar in Egypt.'

Once in London Abboud was brought to see Woolton at his office. He had a Scottish wife, the minister discovered, and, apparently, 'a tender spot in his heart for Britain'. The man who came into Woolton's office that day was expecting a stern-faced, cold minister of the British Government, a tough fight and some hard negotiation. Instead Woolton was at his most relaxed and charming. 'Let me tell you how very glad I am to see you. It really gives me such pleasure to welcome you here,' said a warm and effusive Woolton. 'And let me tell you right now, my dear fellow, that I really know absolutely nothing about sugar and I wouldn't venture for one moment to negotiate with you, such a skilled and successful man.'

Instead, Woolton introduced him to Sir William Rook who would, said Woolton, 'be very glad, and at your convenience, to have some discussions with you'.

Abboud by return expressed pleasant views about Britain saying: 'I have merely the desire that Britain should win the war and I am very affectionate for the people of this country.'

'Well, Mr Abboud, these sentiments are very agreeable for me to hear,' replied Woolton. 'So let me just add that I can't disguise the fact that we need sugar and that, in view of your sentiments, I'm sure you would want us to get it at a price that we can afford to pay.'

The two parted, mutual respect having grown between them, agreeing to meet again in a few days. Two nights later they did meet, this time at a dinner party given by the businessman Lord McGowan. It was a discreet occasion with some dozen government people in attendance. As dinner came to an end, and the port was passed around the table, Brendan Bracken, the Conservative Minister of Information, teased the Egyptian guest about his business methods: 'Well Abboud,' he said, 'I suppose you have come to try to take the skin off Woolton's back.'

Woolton recorded that, at this remark, 'I saw a flush rise to the Egyptian's face; I saw that he was deeply offended, so I hastened to say: "You ought not to have said that. His Excellency [Woolton now addressing him with splendid grandeur] has given me every assurance of his deep affection for this country and his desire to help it."'

At this Abboud go to his feet. 'Lord Woolton,' he said,

'Thank you. Now let me tell you gentlemen. These past few days, I have talked with officials from the Ministry of Food who have made it very clear to me the terms on which they wish to buy sugar from me. So let me tell you my decision. I have come to the view that I will not sell you any sugar.'

There was a gasp of dismay around the table.

'No,' continued Abboud, 'I have decided to *give* you the whole of the sugar you need as my contribution to the war effort.'

There was applause across the room. Abboud had agreed to donate a million tons. Woolton picked up his glass and raised it to him, the two men smiling respectfully at one another.

The next day Abboud and Woolton again met at the Ministry of Food office, this time with Sir William Rook who, noted Woolton, 'was most surprised at this turn in the negotiations'.

Woolton, now fearing he knew this Egyptian rather too well, was concerned that his generosity might be later used to demand some kind of payback. So he told Abboud that His Majesty the King would be very grateful, in actual fact, for a loan of the sugar and that he would either be returned the million tons at the end of the war or the value of the sugar in sterling at the time peace was declared. The Egyptian consented.

'We got the sugar and remained very good friends with Abboud,' wrote Woolton. Some years later Abboud contacted the then former minister, saying how fondly he remembered the deal that they did during the war and whether he would like to spend some time during the cold English winter months with Maud at his palace in Alexandria. Also, would the noble Lord be interested in joining his commercial activities in Egypt on, he wrote, 'financially very advantageous terms'? Abboud had finally met his match and could do with a man like Woolton on his board. Woolton, of course, with immense satisfaction, declined.

14

CHURCHILL, MILK AND JOB OFFERS

By the middle of 1943 Woolton was beginning to feel satisfied with the work of his ministry. 'The food organisation was in reasonable shape,' he wrote modestly in his memoirs. He had the right people operating on the purchasing side, and others in his team never ceased to pile on the pressure when it came to shipping. He had oil tankers cleaned out and used to transport grain and he persuaded liners to share their passenger lists so that food, as he wrote, 'could be squeezed into cabin space'.

The UK supply chain also seemed in good order. Woolton had established emergency warehouses across the country, using the likes of closed church halls and disused cinemas for storage, going so far as appointing Voluntary Food Officers in even the tiniest of villages to keep, under their own secret control, emergency food supplies so that their community could be kept alive in the event of a crisis, either because communications had failed or an invasion launched.

Regular exercises were held to test the strength of these reserves. Woolton was determined to know exactly how the country would cope if supplies were disrupted or halted in the event of roads, power stations or bakeries being bombed. 'It became a constant battle of wits against the enemy,' he later wrote, 'with the harrowing certainty that if we failed the people would go hungry.'

By this stage of the war, Woolton was also proud of the work he had done in hospitals in educating people about the importance of good nutrition. 'Food is so important to health,' he wrote, 'and patients in hospital are probably in a more receptive mood than at any period of their lives.' He felt there was an opportunity to implant the knowledge of what he called 'food values' which, he wrote, 'might do a great deal to reduce subsequent ill-health and the necessity for further hospital treatment'.

But, he added, 'the most satisfactory action we took to safeguard the health of nation was among pregnant women and nursing mothers, where the greatest need existed for teaching food values.'

Woolton's scientific advisors had told him that milk, fruit juices, cod liver oil, halibut oil and eggs were the key foods. So, he declared, 'I grasped the opportunity that lay to my hand. On them rested the future health of the nation.'

But these were not easy foods to get hold of, although Woolton felt, with the data stored in Colwyn Bay, he could at least accurately calculate how much he needed.

He then appealed directly to the United States to send fruit juices for babies. And he imported orange juice in bulk and persuaded Boots, the chemist, to bottle it at cost. It was, he wrote, their 'patriotic service'. Woolton reduced the amount of milk that the general adult population could have, in order that expectant and nursing mothers and children under five could have a whole pint of milk a day. He had been worried about this action and was a little trepidatious when it came to informing one of his scientific advisors, the Royal doctor Lord Horder. But his fears were immediately allayed. 'If you continue with this policy you will reduce the attendance of my consulting rooms by half,' Horder told him. Much of the trouble, the physician explained, was that elderly people suffered because they drank too much milk.

Moreover, Woolton later wrote that 'British-like, everyone was prepared to make sacrifices for children, whether they were their own or other people's.' He wrote in the 1950s of the 'reward . . . [of seeing] the children of the post-war period growing up stronger than any previous generation, and to know that now this scientific care of the feeding of nursing mothers and of children has become a part of our national practice'.

There was, in fact, a joke within the Ministry of Food that such was the zeal of Woolton for feeding prospective mothers that officials could get anything out of him if they could convince him that it was for such ladies, who they called 'the preggies'.

Word reached the front line that the wives and children of serving soldiers were being taken care of. Letters poured in to Woolton. Those wives would often send in pictures of their babies to the minister, in his words, 'bursting with food and good health'. His secretaries would often giggle at such a picture on which so often would be written, 'one of Lord Woolton's babies'.

Woolton was also gratified that the Americans had finally come through with help with the arrangement known as Lend-Lease. This had stalled his deep-seated irritation with America. He had been at his most vociferous once on leaving a meeting with a food producer from the United States who seemed only interested in profit. 'I have an insular prejudice against these itinerant Americans,' he wrote, 'telling us how to run our affairs, especially as I suppose it is true to say that there is nothing in which they have not failed – at any rate in point of time – to fulfil their promises to us. It's quite clear that what is happening is that the Americans are in the doldrums, as they put it, being "caught with their pants down" at Pearl Harbor.'

But Lend-Lease calmed his spirit. It was aid in the form of everything from hardware – such as ships – to oil and food, ending any pretence that the US was neutral. Countries such as France, the United Kingdom and China benefited. Some of the aid could be returned – tanks or warplanes – and some was given in return for US use of Allied army or naval bases. The food tended to be free and anyway – as Lord Woolton noted in his memoirs – 'there was a popular idea that the institution of Lend-Lease solved a large number of our food problems. All that it solved was the problem of paying for them when they came from America, for we no longer had the dollars with which to pay.'

So free food donations did indeed solve that problem. The

first consignment of food under the programme had arrived on 31 May 1941 and Lord Woolton and the US President's personal representative, Averell Harriman, went to the docks to welcome the ships for both their own interest and that of the press. 'It was 4 million eggs, 120,000 pounds of cheese, and 1,000 tons of flour,' he recalled. 'To celebrate, I broke my own regulations – and handed over, for division amongst the unloading staff of 240, a 20 pound cheese.'

He later reflected on the benefit of this arrangement from the United States government, saying that 'without their aid we would ultimately have been reduced to almost iron rations.'

Such were Woolton's successes that by June of 1943 Churchill seemed to have tired of arguing with his Minister of Food and when he disagreed with him would merely make a joke of it. On 29 June Woolton attended a Cabinet meeting to argue for his latest cause: that milk should be pasteurised throughout the country and not just, as was the case, in the capital and in major cities. Woolton had seen statistics that showed that, as he wrote, 'the incidence of germs in raw milk are quite frightening and the public must be protected against germ-infected milk.'

Woolton went to see Churchill before the meeting to brief him in the hope that he might get the rest of the Cabinet to agree, and Churchill asked him to join him in his official car so they could chat on the way to the meeting. 'It was interesting to see the way in which he always had his eye on the public whilst we were talking in his car,' wrote Woolton, 'waving his hat and showing the V sign to the people as we passed. I was very surprised that so great a man should have this sense of public showmanship on a journey he must have taken thousands of times.'

As for the meeting, 'he was,' wrote Woolton, 'in a very good mood in the Cabinet.

'"Have you tasted pasteurised milk, Woolton?" Churchill asked.

'"Prime Minister, 98 per cent of milk in London is pasteurised. I have always attributed your own radiant good health to the fact that you drank pasteurised milk."'

The Cabinet burst into laughter and Churchill looked at Woolton and said: 'I've never tasted the stuff.' He sent for a glass so he could see how it tasted. The milk came and he expressed intense displeasure. 'This whole proposal of yours Woolton is part of a move towards modernism of which I disprove,' he said – and then let Woolton have his way.

As Woolton left the meeting, he reflected on how things had changed. He recalled a letter he had received back in July 1940, when Churchill had written to castigate Woolton on the ration he was implementing. 'The way to lose a war is to try to force the British public into a diet of milk, oatmeal, potatoes etc., washed down on gala occasions with a little lime juice,' he wrote. He had traditional views and was disparaging about anything that was not conventional. 'Almost all the food fadists [sic] I have ever known, nut-eaters and the like, have died young after a long period of senile decay.' And as for the advisors Woolton had on his team, Churchill was frank: 'The British soldier is far more likely to be right than the scientists,' he wrote, before adding: 'All he cares about is beer.'

As autumn approached and the gossip about Churchill's

premiership appeared to diminish, some job offers from outside the political sphere began to arrive at Woolton's door, and then accumulate.

On 25 September 1943 he noted that senior directors at the Bank of England were lobbying the Governor of the Bank for Woolton to be made chairman. Woolton, not averse to this, sent a note to the senior director, Sir Thomas Royden, thanking him. But there were others on the board who would prevent a unanimous vote in his favour, notably Sir Percy Bates with whom he did not appear to get on.

Three days later he was approached to become chairman of the British Red Cross Society, their current incumbent being, Woolton wrote, 'too old and ill to be of any use to them'. He told them he would think about it although he feared it was not a very well-run organisation and 'there may be a job to do there,' suggesting that post-war he wanted a slightly easier number than he'd been given over the past few years.

Two days later he attended a football match at Wembley; in the box were several directors of the Midland Bank. They 'were all very pleasant to me', he wrote. He had heard that his name was in the frame as a possible successor to Reginald McKenna, then chairman, which added another possible job to the pile.

A formal offer, rather than postulated ones, was made on 21 October 1943, for Woolton to become chairman of Martins Bank. Originally a London-based bank which had merged with the Bank of Liverpool in 1918, Martins merged with Barclays in the late 1960s. Woolton knew of them well as they were his retail firm Lewis's bankers. But he now dismissed them, talking of their 'lack of guts' as, at the start of the war, they had refused to confirm that they would stand firm if there was a rush to withdraw money as the conflict began. 'I cannot help remembering the anxiety that Martins and its chairman caused me,' he wrote. Now they were lining him up to be chairman. He was telephoned by Lord Colwyn, from the bank's board, who said he hoped Woolton would become chairman as they were concerned about its future.

Woolton had so many people wooing him he wrote: 'In view of certain other representations that have been made to me I felt I could bear this blushing honour with equanimity.' So he told Colwyn that 'life was too uncertain and I couldn't make any commitments for the time being.'

Next, one can only speculate as to whether employment was discussed at a dinner a few days later with the managing director of Baring Brothers & Co., Arthur Villiers. Woolton's diary records that he and Maud then went to stay for the weekend with Ernest Kleinwort at his family house in Haywards Heath in Sussex. Ernest was the chairman of the family banking firm Kleinwort, Sons & Co. but Woolton does not record whether, over a glass of port after dinner, with Maud and Mrs Benson retired to the drawing room, a nice job was offered at their elegant offices in Fenchurch Street.

Then, on 1 November 1943, Churchill asked Woolton to lunch. 'When I arrived he was dressed in his rompers,' wrote Woolton, 'and obviously not looking well.'

The Prime Minister was not in a joking mood and there was no chit-chat, no back-slapping or teasing, no calling Woolton Goering or asking him how many people he'd flogged that morning. 'With the hors d'oeuvres he went straight into the subject on which he had asked me to lunch,' Woolton wrote.

'I want you to become Minister of Reconstruction,' Churchill said. 'Our focus now at this stage of the war must be what I call WHF: work, homes and food. People need jobs, they need a roof over their head and they must not go hungry.'

Well aware of the enormous challenge that creating and building an entirely new ministry would involve prompted Woolton to ask questions. 'How will this ministry work, Prime Minister? Who will staff it? Where will it be located? How will we resource its budget? What precisely will this Ministry of Reconstruction do?' he demanded, while understanding the principles behind the idea. His questions irritated Churchill who brushed them aside.

'So will you take it, Woolton?' he asked. 'You're the perfect man for the job. That you have amply demonstrated these past few years.'

Churchill, Woolton later wrote, 'seemed to be surprised – and a little grumpy – that I didn't jump at his offer.'

'I will go and think it over,' Woolton said coolly. 'Before I take on such a role I will need to be quite sure that I would have the requisite authority needed to carry the responsibility of running such a ministry.'

'You can join the War Cabinet,' said Churchill. This was a tempting offer, as Woolton had so often been thwarted by discussions in the War Cabinet that he was not privy to. 'That will give you all the authority anyone would need for such a job,' the Prime Minister continued. By this point, Churchill was on to a second generous glass of whisky and, recalled Woolton, 'became easier', the alcohol loosening him a little, putting some colour into his cheeks.

'Woolton, you have a reputation for caring for the well-being of your fellow man and this trait of yours will enable you to get the public confidence that will be necessary as we plan for the future of England, a difficult period of transition between war and peace.' Churchill was getting into his stride; uncomfortable on bureaucratic detail, he was happier on grounds such as human character. He took another long sip from his glass. 'In entrusting this task to you I am paying you a very great compliment,' he added. Such flattery would surely do the trick.

But still Woolton stalled. 'I am conscious of what you say and thank you for it. But I am not going to take on a job unless I am quite sure that I will be able to do it.'

'Well go and ask your wife if she thinks you can do it,' Churchill snapped.

'I should also tell you that I have provisionally made a commitment to be chairman of the Midland Bank,' Woolton added, before their meeting and lunch came to an end.

'Well tell the bank that they can wait,' Churchill insisted, raising his voice somewhat.

Woolton left the meeting pleased that he had managed to elicit compliments from Winston Churchill, get a big job offer and infuriate him all at the same time. Yet he was apprehensive about the role. And he would have to ask Maud.

His conversation with her had, he wrote in his diary, 'most extraordinarily revealing results. Instead of being afraid of the job, as I am, she just said: "Well yes, of course, all the experience you have had in life has been just a preparation for this, hasn't it, and so why should you hesitate.'"

Woolton quickly let Churchill know that he would indeed take on the role, and in the same week he also agreed to become chairman of the Red Cross. Churchill then made a speech at the Mansion House, in which he talked of his new mantra: of work, homes and food; according to Woolton, 'obviously preparing the way for the announcement of my appointment'.

It happened just three days later, on 12 November 1943. 'The papers,' he wrote, 'were full of it.' And, more importantly, 'they were all most flattering to me.' Although he sensed a downside to this: 'The more I read about what I'm to do, the more I'm frightened about it. Obviously people are expecting the new heaven and the new earth. It terrifies me to know that I'm to be the provider of it.'

Meanwhile his desk at the ministry's offices in Portman Court was cleared, and the picture of his wife Maud, his personal books, stationery, pens and diaries all boxed up. His successor, Colonel John Llewellyn, who had been Minister of Aircraft Production, was away in Washington and it would be several days before he returned to London and assumed Woolton's old chair. But he thought it best, having officially left the department, to physically do so.

Offices for the brand new Ministry of Reconstruction were yet to be organised, so Woolton suggested that he decamp somewhere suitable for the time being and had rooms prepared at the Carlton Hotel, which had been partly bombed three years previously and then taken over by the government. Designed in the late 1890s by the architect C. J. Phipps as part of a development that included Her Majesty's Theatre, this grand French Renaissance-style building stood on the corner of Pall Mall and Haymarket (it was demolished in the late 1950s).

Woolton's new office would be at Number Four Richmond Terrace, on the east side of Whitehall, opposite Downing Street. It would enable Woolton to stroll to meetings of the War Cabinet and would also, geographically at least, place him closer to the heart of government.

As he sat in the Carlton Hotel contemplating this new phase in his life, he resolved to try to keep things simple. His last two jobs had involved huge bureaucracies and he was determined that this one would not. Woolton grabbed some smart-looking headed paper, bearing a coat of arms – of lions and shields and a crown – designed for the establishment under which it was stated: 'The Leading and Most Fashionable Hotel and Restaurant in London.' Woolton put two thick lines across those words and wrote instead the distinctly less sexy title: 'Ministry of Reconstruction'. Then he began to build his new department. It would last only as long as the war did and devote itself to post-war planning. Knowing how terrible communication could be between ministries and officials, and how systems of government could be built that seemed only to serve the purpose of stopping anything happening, he took pleasure in noting down how his ministry would bring other departments together.

Whether it was food or jobs, homes or well-being, roads and transport, infrastructure or justice, he would ensure department plans were brought into relation with each other. He would fill gaps and eradicate conflicts. He would employ very few staff and the whole ministry would be located almost within his earshot and certainly not in a far-flung Welsh seaside town. He would be able to walk to work from Whitehall Court and, from time to time, he'd be able to have lunch with Maud.

His early plans formulated that morning of 15 November, he then returned to Portman Square for a final meeting with the staff he had worked with since April 1940, three long years and seven months previously.

There was no actual business, instead senior staff came to say goodbye. It would be his last meeting with Sir Henry French. With the staff assembled, Sir Henry thanked his minister and, recalled Woolton, 'was obviously moved'. This was not expected. In fact Woolton had rather assumed that however successful he might have been, these people would have been secretly rather relieved to see the back of him.

And when the patrician, bold and unswerving Woolton himself started to say a few words he surprised himself as he too came close to tears. 'I found myself becoming quite emotional,' he recalled. He spoke of the honour he had had in working for the ministry, of the enormity of the task they had faced and of the extraordinary loyalty, patience and per-sistence that his staff had shown day in, day out during some of the toughest experiences of their working lives. Yet in the face of terrible odds they had, with him, managed to feed the country. Britain had not starved, it would not now starve and their nation and its allies would now unquestionably succeed in defeating the Third Reich and the corrupt axis of power that propped it up. Woolton would miss his senior staff and the men and women of the ministry.

The meeting broke up and Woolton stood at the door to shake hands with each of them as they walked out. As Woolton said goodbyes and thanks individually to the line of people, he dug as deep as he could to compose himself. 'Many of them were in tears,' he wrote.

As he composed his diary later that night he tried to stop himself from becoming sentimental about the day's events. 'I was sorry to be going,' he wrote, 'I'd had my share of difficulties both with supplies and with staff, but during the past two years things had been working smoothly and I felt I was leaving very good friends behind me.'

He considered how he and Sir Henry French had come to work together so effectively. He recalled how, in due course, he had asked Sir Henry to move his office closer to his and that he had even asked builders to knock a hole in the wall and add a door so the pair could have more constant contact. He had recorded in his diary what he told his senior civil servant after the new door was made: 'Sir Henry, you are welcome at any meeting that I have, whatever is happening.'

Woolton had many reasons to be grateful to Sir Henry. He was a strong administrator, had a great knowledge of food from his long years at the Ministry of Agriculture, and even managed to reach a concordat between Agriculture Minister Robert Hudson and Woolton, which had settled policy between the two ministries for the rest of the war.

The success of the ration owed much to Sir Henry's supervision – that it was fair, efficient and well enforced. His inflexibility had wilted on occasions, such as submitting to Woolton's insistence on hiring businessmen to advise. And his pre-war planning (he was director of the Food (Defence

Plans) department from 1936 to 1939) had enabled the ministry, for all its faults that Woolton tried rectify, to get up-and-running as soon as war had broken out.

Meanwhile Sir Henry's own lack of negotiation skills was ideal as that was Woolton's strong suit, and he learned to focus on administrating while relinquishing the levers of policy to his political boss. While to many people he was unapproachable and vain, this simply amused Woolton who was happy to ignore this aspect of his character. Indeed in later life Woolton enjoyed telling a story of how Sir Henry, in September 1944, made a visit to India. An Indian minister greeted him with the words: 'French, this is the greatest day in the history of India.' Woolton loved the story because Sir Henry often told people about it and appeared to believe it.

Two days later, Woolton had another set of goodbyes to make. He needed to travel to Colwyn Bay for a final time. The train journey, which started at dawn from London, seemed interminable and when he finally arrived in the late afternoon went straight into a series of farewell meetings. The elaborate outfit that was Colwyn Bay never ceased to amaze him and he was rather itching to get going with a simpler organisation. He spent the night in the station hotel exhausted: 'so tired I couldn't sleep,' he wrote.

The next morning he left on the first train which should have got him back to London at 3.30 in the afternoon. But thick fog slowed their progress, outside the air was freezing, while the heating in his carriage was malfunctioning and he spent the long journey 'in intense cold'. Finally the train drew in to London which itself was, he wrote, 'obliterated by fog'. It was, he said, 'a miserable ending to a rather miserable two days.'

Forty-eight hours later he was installed in his new office. Having visited it previously he'd insisted on decorators being employed to give the rooms a fresh lick of paint but it nevertheless had a feeling of gloom about it. 'There's an awful odour of antiquity and decay about the place,' he wrote.

Until Woolton's appointment, the job of reconstruction had been fulfilled by Sir William Jowitt, a grey man in every sense of the word, in his role as Minister without Portfolio. He had been occupying the now refurbished room that Woolton was now sat in. The new minister wondered how on earth anyone could have worked in what had been, Woolton said, 'a dead shade of green'. Given that Woolton was now taking on the role of reconstruction, he was struggling to find out what Jowitt's work had entailed. 'He's a lawyer and not an inspirer,' he noted confidentially. 'I find it difficult to find out what he has been doing. I suspect very little.' Jowitt was still there and had moved to a room next door. Knocking gingerly on the door, recalled Woolton, he 'begged me to give him something to do'.

'I don't think you'll have any difficulty in finding work,' said Woolton, exasperated. He then asked his new assistant to call in for meetings ministers from other departments with whom he would be dealing. There was William, Lord Portal, Minister of Works, 'a good soul but I'm afraid he's not very adaptable', and Harry Willink, Minister for Health. Woolton liked Willink, a Liverpudlian by birth and 'a very pleasant fellow'. Willink had taken over the department from Ernest Brown who, Woolton noted, had taken months to build a couple of cottages for some workmen, so seemed unlikely to manage building housing on a scale that would be needed at the end of the war.

Then there was William Morrison, Minister for Town and Country Planning (the Minister Woolton replaced back in 1940 as Minister for Food). 'His record is not a good one, he has mishandled every office he has held up to now and I can't see him making a spectacular success of this one,' commented Woolton. 'I'm going to have trouble with [his] department. Morrison is afraid of [facing hostile] political reaction and he's weak.

'These are the main people I am to co-ordinate – and they've never been co-ordinated before. I'm afraid my job is going to be a full time one.' Surrounded, in the main, by ineffectual ministers, seemingly insurmountable problems and an expectant British public, Woolton had a giant task ahead of him – but this was familiar territory, of course. The nation was still at war, the city still under attack and the world a precarious and dangerous place.

He recalled a surprising insight into the unbending Sir Henry. In Woolton's eyes, Sir Henry had at first seemed the epitome of a tricky civil servant with whom he would never strike a chord. Managing the relationship seemed almost as insurmountable as feeding an island nation at war. However, a bond that even Sir Henry might have conceded was a 'warm friendship' had developed. Woolton's mind wandered back to an exchange with Sir Henry that took place near the end of his tenure. It occurred at a press conference when an invited guest was digressing, potentially causing problems with timings further down the line.

Sir Henry said: 'You wrote me a note that read, "How you must suffer when you listen to me, wondering when I am going to say the wrong thing: or does custom dull fear?" Lord Woolton, one of these days we shall have to tell each other what we really think of each other. In the meantime I only say that a wife doesn't love her husband because he's either perfect or colourless. My heart has never gone out to any chief, minister or otherwise, as it goes out to you.'

With this implacable civil servant by his side, Woolton had fed and saved Britain. He had given the nation its food, its eggs, and in return it had not descended into chaos and anarchy.

He lit his pipe, blew out a large puff of smoke and then got to work.

15

THE HEALTH OF BRITAIN

Given the successes of his ministry during the Second World War, did what Lord Woolton set out to do – feeding and improving the nutrition of the people of this country – make him, arguably, this country's most successful minister? For Britain, at the end of the war, was not just in good physical shape, it had – and has never been – so healthy. This wasn't just a healthiness that presented itself in the form of slim adults and rosy-cheeked children; child mortality had never been so low, and far fewer mothers died in childbirth. Fewer babies had been stillborn and children were both taller and sturdier. There was also a markedly lower rate of tooth decay. All of which results were achieved with fewer doctors, dentists, nurses and health visitors, most of whom were deployed overseas with the armed forces.

While the rich ate less, the poorer ate more adequately, while rationing restricted sweet snacks for children, who nibbled on carrots rather than chocolate and crisps between meals. As the cook Marguerite Patten wrote, 'For many poor children the school dinners and milk, free cod liver oil and orange juice provided them with a more nutritious diet than they had ever experienced.'

If there was any doubt in the need for decent food for children in the minds of host families or schools, the Board of Education Circular no. 1571, issued on 12 November 1941, stated: 'On the average the energy value of the food required by a healthy child of elementary school age is estimated at about 2,500 calories a day and therefore the midday meal, which for sound reasons is the main meal of the day for nearly all children, should have an energy value of about 1,000 calories. Moreover most of the necessary first class protein and most of the fat must normally be obtained in this meal. As a general guide therefore, a school dinner should be planned to provide per child.'

Minister of Food Lord Woolton saw the war as a fantastic opportunity to target children with healthy meals. In his diary in October 1941, he wrote: 'To preserve the health of the future nation I wanted to secure that every child, in every school, got at least one good hot meal a day, and I saw no other way of securing this than through the schools.'

That same month *The Times* reported him as saying: 'I want to see elementary school children as well fed as children going to Eton and Harrow. I am determined that we shall organise our food front that at the end of the war . . . we shall have preserved, and even improved, the health and physique of the nation.'

With tremendous foresight he wrote that not to do this would imply 'a very heavy cost to the Exchequer'. 'This is a piece of really constructive work,' he added, of his thinking on school meals. 'I hope, though I'm not terribly sanguine about it, that it will remain after the war is over. Anyhow, I'm very pleased at having got it started.'

However, a report on Stoke's school meals in September 1943 found in all schools, except one, the calorie content of the meals was less than a third of daily requirements. In its summary, it said that although some schools were better than others in providing the necessary calories and fat, all the meals lacked the necessary minerals: 'The vitamin A potency was not unsatisfactory but for safety should be increased. The vitamin C content of meals cooked on the same premises as they were eaten was only about half of the desirable standard while those transported contained less than one third of the desirable standard.'

Even in those schools where the meals were cooked on the premises the vitamin C content of vegetables was lower than of domestic cooked vegetables.

'The calorie content of the meal should be improved by increased helpings, especially of potatoes and other vegetables and of puddings. Second helpings should be provided and all the children should be encouraged to ask for them. Full allowances of cheese and of dried skimmed milk should be provided as they will improve the fat, animal protein and calcium content of the diet. They would also increase the variety of the diets. Vitamin A intake should be improved by an increased consumption of cheese, green vegetables and carrots.'

The report went on to suggest improved ways of cooking to preserve vitamin C:

a) Cook in as small volume of water as possible;
b) Do not overcook. The analyses of cabbages suggest that on some days they must have been either cooked or kept hot too long;
c) Wherever possible avoid use of the 'hot plate';
d) Practise serial cooking – that is, cook successive batches of cabbages in the same water.

Factory workers, meanwhile, were fed nutritious food by their canteens and expectant mothers of all classes were given cod liver oil and orange juice. And as the war effort extended employment across the country, many who had been out of work and now had jobs found that they had more money to spend on food.

But, of course, it wasn't to last. Free meals petered out just as subsidised food did via the government-backed British Restaurants. As rationing ended, the 'nanny state' control of what we put into our mouths diminished. The ensuing decades – but particularly the latter two of the twentieth-century – saw a revolution of choice entering the market via supermarkets and restaurants. And with that choice came the freedom to engage in bad habits, often driven by a combination of price and the feeling of being time-poor.

But what of the control that the government, directed by Woolton, had on the food consumption of the nation? The evidence strongly suggests that society had a good mixed diet, which produced great benefits to the nation's health, although what was offered was not without controversy.

Woolton himself had battles with different factions of scientists, although naturally he agreed with the nutritional advice that came out of the scientists approved by his own ministry. One evening in July 1941 Woolton faced a whole barrage of hostile scientists during a dinner at The Café Royal. Having made a brief speech the floor was open and scientist after scientist got to their feet to attack Woolton and his policies. 'They told me of all the things that were wrong with the food of the nation and the way it was being controlled,' he wrote. Woolton listened and then took the lot of them out with one broad swipe.

'You have all joined the great majority of grumblers,' he said. 'But what I entirely fail to see is that you have made any contribution to the well-being of this country.'

Woolton did, however, have a supporter in *The Times*. A leader on 20 August 1941 entitled 'Tokens of Health' reported that: 'Lord Woolton's assertions that there is no sign of malnutrition in this country is fully borne out by such statistical and other evidence as is now available.' It continued: 'It can therefore be said with satisfaction that the health and strength of the nation have not suffered from any privation due to the war.' It was, noted Woolton, 'a very fair and encouraging leader'.

When it came to the issue of meat consumption, Woolton may have had a rather old-fashioned view of vegetarians but he couldn't help himself having a sneaking admiration. 'I sent for the vegetarians in order to ask them how they were living without meat, and without eggs or cheese,' he wrote in February 1941. 'They were a most healthy-looking crowd of people.' It was not a diet for him, however. 'I found vegetarianism to be a flatulent failure,' he said in his memoirs. But, he added, 'it was clear that with many people it produced life and energy of a very high order.'

While Woolton was focused on the local issues of feeding Britain, he also allowed himself to think more ambitiously, writing of his dream to create, globally, a 'general standard of nutrition', arguing in his diary in August 1942 that the 'world is capable of producing so much food that there is no justification, after the war, for any part of it being hungry.' He talked of establishing 'an international food office', pointing out that 'hungry men are dangerous'.

Indeed he began to lobby foreign politicians and diplomats who always appeared thrilled by his idea. He then, in April 1943, lobbied the Chancellor of the Exchequer to create a fund so that the UK could 'build up a stock of food with which we can help to ease the world's food difficulties at the end of the war. We shall have to send so much to the liberated countries that unless we build up enormous reserve stocks now we shall find ourselves in difficulties. It's no use liberating countries and then keeping them in a state of semi-starvation.'

Woolton's other battle was to convince the Cabinet to introduce legislation to make the pasteurisation of milk compulsory. 'The farmers hate it, the doctors approve,' he wrote after a meeting with the National Farmers Union in February 1942. (According to the *British Medical Journal*, between 1912 and 1937 some 65,000 people died of tuberculosis contracted from consuming milk in England and Wales alone.) He was victorious to some extent, as in July 1942 pasteurisation was introduced to the dairies that supplied major city centres. While Woolton was an early advocate, dairy businesses took it under their own discretion to pasteurise milk during the 1950s, although it was not made compulsory until the 1980s, Scotland being the first to introduce legislation in 1983 and then England and Wales in 1989. It was a UN regulatory drive in 1997 that saw the UK-wide spread of the process.

But what lessons can be learned from rationing today? Lord Woolton was happy to see the rewards of controlling what the nation ate but then he had extraordinary powers for extraordinary times. These days any hint at government tampering with our freedom to choose what we put in our mouths can be condemned as the unnecessary actions of 'the nanny state'.

Danny Alexander, a former Liberal Democrat MP and one-time Chief Secretary to the Treasury, had his hands on the reins of power during his time in coalition government, during which he experienced what it was like to affect the lives of millions through the cuts that he delivered to the UK budget. 'There is a strong case for further positive and negative incentives for people to live healthier lifestyles,' he says. 'Not only is that better in the long run for individuals, it also ensure more healthy years of adult life for people to work and contribute, and would reduce one of the fastest growing areas of cost and pressure in the NHS.'

But for him the big question is, of course, what works? 'Tax measures clearly do have an influence on behaviour,' he says, 'but they have to be pretty hefty to make a difference, as tobacco and fuel duties show. And even then, they work in combination with other levers such as health warnings on cigarette packets.' As for a token tax on sugar, Alexander believes that, while that can send a signal if it were set high enough to make its consumption too expensive, it would be 'politically difficult to impose'. He also feels it would be socially regressive because evidence shows that those on lower incomes spend a higher proportion of their income on food. 'A small tax rise on a heated snack from the south of England created a furore in 2012,' he comments, adding: 'think of the row if a government tried to impose a tax that would fall on a lot of foodstuffs.'

It is thus the view of many experts that the most promising route is regulatory. Governments can set reasonable rules for mass produced foods to ensure that they meet what Alexander calls 'socially agreeable nutritional standards'. It is such efforts that have brought down salt levels in many foods, so possibly the same thing could be done for sugars and saturated fats.

But there is one area where governments and authorities can impose control – aside from in prisons – and that's in schools. The 1870 Education Act made elementary education compulsory for all children and the first free school meals started being served in Manchester. This gave an incentive to poor families to send their children to school as they would be able to spend the day studying rather than earning money to pay for a crust of bread. It also meant that children would not be too hungry to study.

In 1906 a further Education Act authorised local councils to serve free school meals to children who were from the poorest families. But recession and the onset and aftermath of war saw such cuts in government expenditure and the diversion of funds to other areas that, by the start of the Second World War, only half of all local authorities (157) were providing free school meals to children.

The work of Lord Woolton and others saw that during the Second World War nutritional standards were set for school meals. (With a minimum of 1,000 calories and 30g of fat for each meal. Interestingly this compares today to a maximum of 530 calories and 20g of fat in primary school standards today.)

The Education Act of 1944 made it compulsory for local education authorities (LEAs) to provide a free meal for children in state schools. Latterly – during the 1970s and 1980s – children started to turn away from school meals and choose instead a packed lunch prepared at home. A 1980 Education Act then removed the legal requirement for LEAs to provide a meal for every pupil and also abolished the minimum nutritional standards.

In 2013, Henry Dimbleby and John Vincent gathered a panel of experts and produced a School Food Plan for government ministers. 'Only one per cent of packed lunches meet the nutritional standards that currently apply to school food.' The country's serious health crisis, they argue, is 'caused by bad diet'. And the problem needs tackling, 'before the costs (both personal and financial) become too heavy to bear'. Their aim is to have children provided with school dinners and to encourage and enable the people with the power to orchestrate this: namely head teachers.

Dimbleby and Vincent recommend that free school meals be extended to all primary school children, starting in the most deprived areas, and that schools and councils fund universal school meals. Dimbleby has noted that as a result of some free meals 'the pupils whose results improved most markedly were the poorest.' He and Vincent believe their plan can 'improve the academic performance of our children and the health of our nation'. But they recognise that 'it requires a cultural change within each school. It means cooking food that is both appetising and nutritious; making the dining hall a welcoming place; keeping queues down; getting the price right; allowing children to eat with their friends; getting them interested in cooking and growing.'

According to Moira Howie, nutritionist for UK supermarket Waitrose, the key difference between our food related behaviour today and during the war years concerns our physical activity. 'The move towards making everything convenient and easy has conspired to make us a sedentary population,' she says. 'So children are driven rather than walk to school, we sit on mowing machines rather than push them, we press a button on a device to change the TV channel rather than get up and down to do it, we use a washing machine rather than clean clothes by hand and, because our houses are warm, we don't naturally engage in physical activities, such as scrubbing the steps, to keep warm.'

Howie further believes that, while the average calorie intake these days is roughly the same as in the 1940s, in gaining those calories we need to do less. We can, for example, buy a fast food burger rather than go out to snare a rabbit. To rectify this, argues Howie, we do not need to engage in anything of 'a massive magnitude'. As she explains: 'A lot of little things make a big difference: taking the stairs rather than the lift at work, walking rather than using a car for short distances, getting a dog so you walk round the block or park regularly . . .'

The facts confronting us now are startling. Today in Britain 69 per cent of men and 58 per cent of women are classified as overweight or obese. According to a report by consultancy firm McKinsey and Company, the side effects of this problem – from diabetes to heart disease – is now a greater burden on the UK's economy than armed violence, war and terrorism. The cost to the National Health Service of the current rate of obesity and overweight conditions could increase to between £10bn and £12bn by 2030 and, needless to say, this is pushing the NHS to breaking point. The overall healthcare and social costs of an increasingly overweight population has been totalled at £47 billion per year.

Cynics would say that government only starts to take an issue like this seriously when the Treasury begins to panic. But there is also a growing clamour for radical action, as evidenced by the UK-based celebrity chef Jamie Oliver who, in the autumn of 2015, called on the government to impose a tax on sugar to help curb the obesity crisis. Oliver's main target is sugary soft drinks, saying: 'I want to see the introduction of a 20p per litre levy on every soft drink containing added sugar – this equates to 7p per 330ml can.' He has claimed that: 'studies show this could have a significant impact on health in the UK, reducing sugary drink consumption by possibly 15 per cent.'

The Times newspaper argued, in a leader column on 22 October 2015, that the government should, 'give serious consideration to a sugar tax', (which indeed the government decided to do in March 2016 when the Chancellor George

Osborne announced a sugar levy to take effect in 2018.

Drinks over 5g of sugar per 100ml will be taxed at 18 pence per litre and those with 8g per 100ml would be hit with a 24 pence tax. It would mean an extra 8 pence on the current price of a standard can of Coca-Cola. While Jamie Oliver heralded it as 'bold and brave' those in the drinks industry said they would challenge the policy, while lawyers said it could be in breach of European Union laws on competitiveness.) The paper also pointed out that 'the impact of obesity is particularly troubling on the young. By the time they leave primary school one in five children is obese.' The figures it quoted were that obesity-related illness is linked to 53,000 premature deaths each year and costs the NHS more than £5 billion annually to treat.

All of which debate makes a look at the state of Britain's health during the Second World War, when the government really did control what the general public consumed, more than prescient.

Epilogue

THE SHOPKEEPERS' STORY

For all that Lord Woolton did, he and his department, indeed the whole government, relied on the diligence and goodwill of the nation's shopkeepers. They were the people who the country's housewives depended upon immediately and to whom everyday frustrations would be vented. Without their patriotic efforts the battle to keep up morale would have failed.

Two stories, recounted over sixty years later, put a spotlight on quite how extraordinary the everyday pursuit of supplying a community with fruit, vegetables or meat was.

Cricklewood

On 3 September 1939 nineteen-year-old Harold Gilbert had just finished his tea when his father switched on the radio to listen to the news. He was tired after a long day's work at the family fruit and vegetable store, S Ginsberg, at 89 Cricklewood Broadway in North London. One of four brothers, he seemed to be the one with the muscles so his metier, in his late teens, consisted of lifting, moving, carrying and positioning large sacks, boxes and cartons of fresh produce. He might heave large sacks of potatoes purchased in Covent Garden onto the family truck, or unload huge crates of bananas back at the shop in Cricklewood. There were two other members of staff and his brothers helped too, but his siblings were never quite as majestically strong as he was. Brothers Asher – two years younger – and Arnold – two years older – might have been equipped for the business mentally, but they couldn't swing a sack of carrots quite like Harold. And Dennis, at just twelve, was more adept at running through the store and pinching a hand-full of cherries, or popping strawberries into his pockets.

So Harold was almost dozing when the news crackled over the radio that a state of war existed between Britain and Germany.

'It wasn't very welcome news,' reflected Harold, in understated dour tones some seventy-seven years later. 'We all wondered what exactly would happen. We were very apprehensive.'

In the days that followed, all three elder brothers attended medicals while it was determined which part of the forces they might join. Arnold was the first to be called up, joining an anti-aircraft regiment, while Asher went into the Navy and spent the next two years in a battle cruiser as part of the Arctic convoys; both brothers would survive the war. Arnold returned home eight days after the Dunkirk evacuation. 'We hadn't heard from him and were all terribly worried. Then one morning he just came into the house with a rifle on his back. I was in the bath and he came in and said hello. But he would never talk about what happened,' said Harold. 'No one could ever get it out of him, not even his children. We discovered that he had been rescued by a boat from the St Helier yacht club, but he obviously wanted to forget the war as he never mentioned anything that happened to anyone for the rest of his life.'

But Harold failed the medical. 'I have very little sight in my right eye,' he said at the age of ninety-five, 'so I stayed and worked with my dad. My little brother Dennis was supposed to be evacuated to the countryside, but he didn't want to go and I don't think my mum would have let him anyway. He just left school and never went back. Mind you he went on to have a very successful career and was the managing director of a public company.'

As for the other staff at the greengrocer they also left, seconded to the local ARP, the air-raid protection unit. That left Harold and his dad, Samuel Ginsberg, known to everyone as Sam. Sam steeled himself with his wife Kitty to survive and get through the war. Not a day would pass when Kitty wouldn't worry about her two boys serving overseas. But at least she still had two at home.

'I had mixed feelings about not going to war,' reflected Harold. 'I had feelings of disappointment, feelings of relief and a feeling of worry that I would spend the rest of the war in the shop. It would mean a lot more work. But although I had a problem with one of my eyes, I was as strong as an ox.'

Sam Ginsberg (the family changed their name to Gilbert in the 1950s), whose father Simon had started the business as an immigrant from Latvia – he had literally begun by buying and selling a few oranges and then steadily building up sales – was fastidious about his produce. 'He would go to the old Covent Garden market very early and his strategy was simply to buy the best,' recalled Harold. 'He got to know growers, particularly from Kent and the Thames Valley, but also traders who imported from overseas.' Sam, dressed always in waistcoat, shirt and tie, would return home from the market with a list of what he'd bought and it would be the job of Harold, in his overall and dark tan trousers, to drive back to market and collect the produce.

In peacetime, stalls at the front of the shop and inside would be piled high with potatoes, cabbages, spring greens, sprouts, cauliflower, peas, runner beans, spinach and rhubarb; there were apples, pears, plums, gooseberries, red and black currants, raspberries, loganberries and strawberries – making S Ginsberg the most colourful store on Cricklewood Broadway. The Ginsbergs knew all of their customers by name and knew their own personal preferences, which fruit and veg each member of their family liked. And any children in tow would always be given an apple or a tangerine. 'It was,' said Harold, 'more like a club than a shop.'

But the onset of war changed all of this, and very quickly. 'There were no more imports of fruit, stocks diminished and so did our income,' said Harold. The display on the street, at the front of the shop – generous piles of fruit and veg adorning the pavement which further enticed you to ponder on the glistening wares of S Ginsberg inside – all went.

'Suddenly we could only depend on English produce, so stocks of fruit fell in particular and inside we only used about half of the shop,' he said. Meanwhile a great number of their customers disappeared. Many went to war, others left London to escape the prospect of bombing. But it never occurred to Sam Ginsberg that he should take his family elsewhere; his business and his home were there in Cricklewood. The atmosphere changed among those customers that stayed too. 'Many people were just very, very worried,' said Harold, 'and you could just see it on their faces; while others managed to take it in their stride.'

Which is what Harold appeared to do. 'I got used to the bombings at night,' he said. 'But you had to be wary of the shrapnel which came down from our own guns shooting at enemy planes. At the start of the war I went to the air raid shelter when the siren went off. But after three nights of that I got fed up and decided to stay home in my bed.'

Harold only slept away the family home on one subsequent occasion, when an unexploded bomb landed in the road just outside the local Windmill pub. 'Our whole street was evacuated to a school for two nights until the army defused the bomb.'

S Ginsberg was never hit, but bombs fell within yards of the shop. 'I went to get the truck one morning to drive to the market and found that it was holding up the roof of our neighbours' house,' he remembered. 'We did get quite a lot of bombs because there was a mainline railway at the back of our shop. But they generally missed. The bakery on our street was bombed, though, and I remember four of their bakers were killed.'

While stocks diminished and business got difficult, when rationing was introduced a hard business got even tougher. 'Rationing affected us a lot, although it was worse for a lot of butchers and bakers, as there were no coupons for fruit and veg,' said Harold. 'My days still started after Dad came back from the market and we'd work until it got dark. That could be seven o'clock in the summer or four in the winter. At dusk there would be no one about.'

So Harold worked day in, day out throughout the conflict and, he said, 'I never had a single day's holiday right through the war. Although I did go to Clacton one Saturday. I'd met a girl at a dance so I went to see her. It was nice but I never saw her again. It wasn't meant to be. I found out she had a boyfriend.'

Of course being in the food business also had its advantages. Harold's family would never be short of fruit or vegetables, although he professed that his family 'only took what we needed. Our aim was to sell everything.' But his father was in a position to ask favours of his suppliers. 'My dad was able to get eggs and poultry from the drivers who brought supplies from the country. If he got a chicken, it would be live, so he'd take it up to the Jewish poultry butcher who would kill it for him. My mother was a born cook and she'd roast the chicken and make lovely soup. She'd also pickle things like onions and would pickle herring. And she'd cook fresh fish if my father got some, although I always hated fish.'

Some of their remaining loyal customers would also ask for a little extra. 'We did our best to please them,' said Harold, 'and my dad might keep something in the back for very old customers – who were mainly all working mums with their husbands away at the war. We would help them if we could – but you couldn't call it the black market; even people at the top were doing it [getting a little extra if they could]. My dad was always very careful and never wanted to have any trouble.'

When the war ended and privations eased, and with a fuller staff and the brothers all home, life started to return to normal at S Ginsberg. Tomatoes arrived, then citrus fruits and grapes. 'I remember the first batch of bananas that came into the market,' said Harold. 'I put them out on display at the front and children stopped and wondered what they were. I had to show them how you peeled one.'

Twyford

On the same day that Harold Gilbert heard the news that his country was at war with Germany, eight-year-old Peter Jennings was also listening to the radio with his family in the village of Twyford in Berkshire.

Peter, born in September 1931, was one of six children and they all lived above the family butcher shop, LJ Jennings. The business was started by his father Leonard Joseph and the premises was adorned with the hanging carcasses of pigs, sheep, chickens and turkeys. The shop was on the red-bricked high street of Twyford, a village typically self-sufficient for the time with an abundance of bakeries, grocers, a bread and cake shop, a sweet shop and three other butchers.

While his parents and eldest brother Norman had seemed concerned at the report of war delivered by a sombre Neville

Chamberlain that day, the news sparked little worry in young Peter. He continued to attend the village school, would play football with his friends in the evening or hang around at the back of the shop. There was a slaughterhouse there, and Peter was always fascinated by the sight of animals being delivered, then butchered and prepared for sale.

'We did our own slaughtering every Monday,' he recalled, 'a bloke would shoot them, and then between noon and ten at night they would be butchered.' So the shop was always closed at that time and, if it was school holidays, Peter would stay and watch as his father positioned haunches of meat on the large wooden block, deftly setting about them with his set of knives. He would saw bones, chop parts with a cleaver, or cut strips with a smaller and very sharp looking blade.

At the age of twelve, Peter moved on to Maidenhead Grammar School where he expected to stay until the age of sixteen. His path to a life as a butcher seemed inevitable, but then events conspired to make this journey rather quicker than he or anyone had anticipated.

Just six months into his new school, in 1943, his father fell ill. It was a sausage machine that did him in. Aged forty-eight, a pressure handle on the device flew off and hit him in the mouth. It seemed fine at first, just a broken tooth and a bruised chin. But a large and sinister black blister then appeared in his mouth. It grew into an abscess which poisoned his blood and three weeks later he died.

'It was a big shock of course,' said Peter. 'I was in the house when he died. My eldest brother Norman, who was seventeen, was training at Colchester for the army and a message was sent calling him back.' Norman was needed to run the business alongside his mother Dorothy who looked after the money side. And while the second eldest son Douglas had died of scarlet fever a few years before the war, the family decided that the shop needed another pair of hands.

So at the tender age of twelve-and-a-half, Peter left school and started work at LJ Jennings. His three younger siblings, sister Moran, brother Robert and youngest sister Anne, were spared the labour. But Peter, dressed by his mother in long apron, white shirt and tie, started work and never returned to school.

'Right after my father died, Norman was still on army service. It wasn't until a few months later that he got out of the army on a class B release [a final discharge]', recalled Peter, 'so for a while I had to manage the shop.'

It was a modestly sized butcher. There was the glass front, then a small room behind the shop, a little office and then the fridge; behind was an alley and the slaughterhouse. Before he joined the shop full-time, Peter had delivered small packages around the village and to houses in the surrounding countryside on the company bicycle. With a large wicker basket secured to the front, the cycle's frame bore a smart sign that advertised 'LJ Jennings Purveyor. Twyford Phone 63'.

Now he was progressing from delivery boy to butcher. He had watched his father working so often that he was a natural when it came to cutting the meat himself. And the idea of doing an adult's job before he even reached his teens didn't faze him: 'I don't suppose it worried me at all as I was so young,' he reflected. So he carved up whole ribs of beef, prepared pork into its different parts for sale and plucked, drew and cleaned chickens. 'I could pluck a chicken in three minutes,' he said some sixty years later, 'and I still can.' He was a good salesman too, chatting with the customers, always spirited and smiling. Sometimes he was too efficient.

'I once sold a couple of customers a rather nice few strips of beef that were sitting at the back. My brother was out and when he came back he said to me: "Where's that beef I left back there?" I said I'd sold it. And he went mad and said, "That was my ration."'

And of course wartime meant a little less hard selling and a little more of simply enabling people to buy the amount that rationing allowed. 'I was always cutting out these coupons,' recalled Peter. 'We then had to keep them and pass them to the local Food Office. They then gave us the amount of meat that we were allowed to sell, according to the exact number of registered customers that we had.'

Peter then used his own ingenuity to eke out that ration for the business and their community. 'I could make eighty pounds of sausages out of eight pounds of sausage meat,' he revealed. His trick was to add in, not pork ends, or any discarded offal or indeed cardboard, but – to the soaked stale bread he got from the bakery opposite – he added luncheon meat. 'I used to make them every Friday ready for Saturday and I thought they tasted fantastic,' said Peter. 'The Food Office came round the village one week and tested and tasted the sausages made by all the butchers. Ours were the only ones in Twyford that passed the test. I've been making delicious sausages ever since.'

Peter and his brother Norman weren't strict when it came to the black market. 'We were always happy and keen to get a bit extra,' he said. 'We were often sold rabbits – which weren't on the ration – by farmers or poachers who came to the back door. I never asked questions; I would just skin them, chop them up and then offer them for sale.'

Peter's youngest brother Bob also showed early entrepreneurial promise. 'He once swapped his school cap for a goat,' said Peter who was more than happy to offer it for sale to his hungry customers. Meanwhile a friend in the village kept pigs at an allotment by Twyford station. 'Every now and then he'd kill one and bring it to us. There was a police station between our butcher and his allotment so he'd have to sneak it past in a van,' recalled Peter. 'One day one of the wheels fell off right outside the station. The police helped fix the van but they never looked inside, thank goodness.

'Another day a lorry from Smithfield pulled up outside. He had four and a quarter sides of beef so I bought them off him and put them in the cellar. If something like that happened then I might say to a customer: "Would you like a bit extra?" We tried to help everybody and if we could get a spare pig then it was very handy. I never thought about getting caught and anyway there weren't that many police about.'

As for his own ration: 'I've always liked every cut of meat and I like vegetables very much. We had roast beef every Sunday – so much so that my mother used to get cross about it. One Sunday she grabbed the beef in a fury and flung it off the table. But I certainly got more than the ration. It's why I've always been fit and healthy.'

Peter's daily routine would start at seven in the morning when his first task was to light the boiler for hot water for the house and shop. Then, after a bowl of porridge, he would open up the butcher and start putting the meat out from the large fridge at the back. He would hang larger pieces up on hooks and place smaller cuts on a marble slab – there were no refrigerated glass cabinets.

'Then I would scrub the benches and cover the floor with a fresh layer of sawdust,' he said. The day would continue with cutting meat and serving customers. Butchery, he felt, was in his veins. 'If I see something in the road I'm after it,' he said. 'It's just my nature.'

With the two brothers serving, their mother Dorothy sat at a desk immaculate in her finest blouse – her hair done, her make up on, her fingers adorned with large glistening rings – and took the money.

After two years of working it occurred to Peter that he ought to be paid. He asked his brother and mother for a weekly wage but they refused – so Peter went on strike. 'I went up the road to a builder's merchants and asked for a job as an electrician.' He returned later to the shop with the news about his new career, at which point they relented and put him on £5 a week.

No bombs fell near LJ Jennings during the war, although Peter recalled hearing the sounds of planes overhead and bombs landing on Reading, some five miles away. Playing football one evening the children saw a plane nose-dive down from the sky. Peter leapt onto his bicycle to the crash site, which happened to be a road bridge nearby. 'I was the first on the scene but there was nothing left of the plane or its occupants.' So he cycled back to the garden at the back of the family shop and resumed his game of football.

Over half a century later Peter could still be found sitting in the same position his mother would have taken in the shop (albeit in a different location – at one point the business had expanded to five shops across the county). He sat at the desk, took the money, did daily deliveries and definitely still took a salary.

The part he had played in the war was just as vital as that of soldiers fighting on the front line. He was one of Lord Woolton's local food heroes; both relied on each other, but did so without being aware of each other's existence.

Postscript

The gravestone of Lord Woolton stands proud in the rustic and grassy cemetery of St Mary's Church, Walberton in West Sussex. Having been born plain Fred Marquis at 163 West Park Street in Ordsall, Salford in Lancashire, on 23 August 1883, he died aged 81 on December 14 1964 as The Right Honourable Frederick James Marquis, First Earl of Woolton at Walberton House, near Arundel. Woolton was given an hereditary earldom in 1956 and the house that demonstrated his ascent up the social ladder would be remembered in the subsidiary title that he took: that of Viscount Walberton.

As newspapers the following day published his obituary, proceedings that afternoon in the House of Lords were altered so that peers could offer their tributes. He was, said the Earl of Longford, 'a many-sided man of far reaching talents and achievements'. The Marquess of Salisbury added that, 'during the war, he never let his fellow countrymen down. He always told them the truth as he understood it, however unpalatable it might be. In this way, I think above all, he gained their trust.'

Collectively the House of Lords sent their sympathy to his surviving son Roger, who inherited the title, and his wife Lady Woolton. This was not of course Maud, for she had died in September 1961. In fact at the age of 79, at noon on Friday 19 October 1962, he married Margaret Thomas, better known as Lyn, the Wooltons' family doctor. Maud had actually died in her arms and out of Woolton's gratitude for her care came affection. Twenty years his junior, she then cared for him as a widower. Woolton installed her in a cottage in the garden, she became his hostess at dinner parties and then he became a little concerned about local gossip. Indeed after their wedding, at the Queen's Chapel at the Savoy in London, he put pen to paper to explain and justify his second marriage. 'What did the village think when they saw my car outside her cottage after I had dined with her?' he wrote.

'I was a lonely old man, in poor health and she twenty years my junior was being very kind to me and there was all there was to it! But was it?' he mused. Woolton had become deeply dependent on her, for her care and for, as he put it, 'the comfort of companionship'.

One sunny afternoon sitting out in the garden at a friend's house, Woolton was feeling a little melancholy. He was there with Lyn and a local friend called Geoffrey. Geoffrey got up to fetch something from the house and when he was out of earshot Woolton said to Lyn: 'I must try to get away from this depression and fear.' Lyn went over to him, put a firm hand on his knee and whispered, 'I will never leave you.'

Back at Walberton, the pair talked. 'Could we go on ignoring the probability of public gossip?' he then reflected, still worrying about his PR and image at that stage of his life. There was one way of dealing with it, of course, but it would break his heart. 'Could we break up this precious friendship?' he said with agony. And so Woolton proposed. He discussed the title she would have to wear and his finances, making the point, as he wrote, 'that it would of course secure her comfort when I died'.

Lyn did not consent at once and was due to go away for a few days with a friend to Wales. 'Think it over,' he said as he waved her off, 'and don't worry, I won't pester you again on the subject.' She did later agree to marry him, or at least gave what he described as 'her reluctant consent' and the couple then waited until after the first anniversary of Maud's death before tying the knot, thus avoiding any accusations of being rather too hasty!

Both Roger and Peggy were very supportive and on the announcement of their forthcoming nuptials the Queen sent a personal telegram. 'I was very surprised at this and very delighted,' he wrote, relieved, no doubt, at not having rocked the establishment with his romantic shenanigans.

On 14 January 1964 he added a final note to the musings on his latest marriage that he had written in October 1962. He wondered if his reader might 'want to know, how it has all turned out,' he wrote, adding: 'I can answer that – as far as I'm concerned. She has made me very happy.'

Woolton liked to have things settled and in order; whether it was family trusts, government departments or his love life. After the Second World War had ended, his desire for stability had focused his mind again on the retail career he had left to join the government. Indeed Churchill's heavy election defeat – which Woolton described as 'shameful' and 'a painful reflection on public gratitude' – meant that he was, as he put it, 'left without occupation'. (His role as Minister of Reconstruction had also been timed to self-destruct the moment peace was declared. And he had tackled the role in reversing Churchill's stated aims for the job; planning for post-war food, homes and jobs.)

But reflecting on a return to Lewis's, he decided that he would better be employed as a less involved chairman of the company (Maud told him: 'You have done all you could do for Lewis's') and that Churchill's defeat in July 1945 had actually galvanised his political instincts. 'I saw that as a consequence the country would be plunged into socialism and much economic disaster.' Lewis's would have to take a back seat while he worked to get what he thought was the sensible party back into power. So he immediately, and for the first time, became a paid-up member of the Conservative Party and joined the Shadow Cabinet.

Churchill now employed Woolton's organisational skills on a matter close to home, he appointed him chairman of the party. This was a perfect task for Woolton because, in his words, 'The organisation of the Conservative Party was the most topsy-like arrangement I had ever come across.'

So he looked at it, dissected and pondered on what to do. He was tempted to venture what he called 'a sound business conclusion and tell the Party that the best thing to do with machinery of this nature was to scrap it and start again'.

But he realised that the organisation was built and run by individuals often working for nothing. So he used a more tender approach and, in working to win the goodwill of members and chairman, build a more effective outfit. From 1946 to 1951 he travelled the country with Maud, both of them making speeches on policy and how a more efficiently run party would have a greater chance at winning the next election. Above all he saw his mission to convince the party, after a heavy defeat, to, as he wrote, 'believe in itself, and in its capacity to convert the electorate to Conservatism'.

The Conservative Party did then win the General Election of 1951 and Woolton was given the added role of Lord President of the Council. It was in this role that he greeted the young Queen – along with Churchill and Attlee – on her return to the UK from Africa following her father George VI's death. He would also play a major role in any Royal succession ceremony.

But then Woolton fell ill and this time not due to his old colonic nemesis. Attending the Conservative Party conference in October 1952 he suffered a perforated appendix and, as he later wrote, was taken to a nursing home where he was attended by '14 doctors and [had] 5 major operations'.

Word reached Churchill that he was dying and with brutal speed he removed Woolton as both chairman of the party and Lord President. Maud heard of this and quickly dispatched a letter of intense anger accusing the Prime Minister of appalling disloyalty to a man who had served his party and country so nobly.

'Churchill had a new experience of having to deal with an infuriated wife who didn't disguise her opinion of him,' wrote Woolton. He reflected that Churchill's actions 'deprived me of any place in the Coronation ceremony'. (King George VI had died on 6 February 1952 and the coronation of Queen Elizabeth II was slated for 2 June 1953)

'I did not die,' wrote Woolton. And Maud's protestations saw him offered the Cabinet post of Chancellor of the Duchy of Lancaster. It was further organised that Woolton was given a role in the subsequent coronation of delivering the Glove to Her Majesty. Not an essential part of the service, it seems that officials conjured up this role as a face-saving gesture. It worked. Woolton sat just behind Prince Philip and travelled just a small distance during the service, presented the Glove to Her Majesty and put it on her hand. The *Manchester Guardian* duly noted that perhaps at future coronations this 'ancient rite will be revived'.

Woolton's restoration to the Cabinet also meant that while weakened from his illness and operation he would be able to retire gracefully from government at a time of his choosing. And this he did some two years later, making a farewell speech as chairman of the party at the Bournemouth conference of 1955.

For his remaining years Woolton continued to serve on various company boards as well as performing his duties as chancellor at Manchester University (one of their halls of residence was renamed Woolton Hall) while spending more time at Walberton where he entertained and set about writing his memoirs.

Now, many years later through the pages of this book,

his diaries, memoirs, notes, letters, essays and private family recollections are brought together the first time to describe and celebrate this monumentally important figure in twentieth-century political and public life.

Paying his own tribute to Woolton the day after he died, post-war Prime Minister Clement (by now Earl) Attlee recalled a conversation he once had about Woolton with an old woman in Devonshire. 'That Lord Woolton,' she said, 'he do sometimes right and sometimes wrong; but we poor folk are beholden to him because he thinks of us.'

Select Bibliography

The Churchill Papers – Churchill College, Cambridge

Hansard (The Official Report) – verbatim reports of proceedings of both the House of Commons and the House of Lords

Food Facts for the Kitchen Front (Collins, 1941)

Papers of Frederick James Marquis, 1st Earl of Woolton (University of Oxford, Department of Special Collections and Western Manuscripts)

Diary of Maud Woolton; 'Really a bit of the life story for her husband Lord Woolton' (Private collection)

Story of Maud Woolton by Lord Woolton – handwritten 1962 (Private collection)

Letters of Lord Woolton and Lady Woolton (Private collection)

Memoirs of The Rt Hon The Earl of Woolton CH, PC, DL, LLD (Cassell, 1959)

The School Food Plan – Henry Dimbleby and John Vincent (July, 2013)

Austerity in Britain; Rationing, Controls and Consumption 1939–1955 – Ina Zweiniger-Bargielowska (Oxford University Press, 2000)

Friends of the People: The Centenary History of Lewis's – Asa Briggs (BT Batsford, 1956)

Nella Last's War: The Second World War Diaries of Housewife, 49 – edited by Richard Broad and Suzie Fleming (Profile Books, 2006)

A Green and Pleasant Land: How England's Gardeners Fought the Second World War – Ursula Buchan (Hutchinson, 2013)

Plenty & Want: A Social History of Food in England from 1815 to the Present Day – John Burnett (Routledge, 1994)

England Eats Out: 1830–Present – John Burnett (Pearson Education, 2004)

The Taste of War; World War Two and the Battle for Food – Lizzie Collingham (Penguin Books, 2012)

Cairo in the War: 1939–45 – Artemis Cooper (Hodder & Stoughton, 2013)

Bitter Ocean: The Battle of the Atlantic, 1939–1945 – David Fairbank White (Simon & Schuster, 2006)

We Are at War – Simon Garfield (Ebury Press, 2005)

Feeding the Enemy in War-Time – Doris Grant (George G Harrap, 1942)

Finest Years; Churchill as Warlord 1940–45 – Max Hastings (Harper Press, 2010)

Rationing in the Second World War: Spuds, Spam and Eating for Victory – Katherine Knight (Tempus Publishing, 2007)

Colwyn Bay Accredited: The Wartime Experience – Cindy Lowe (Bridge Books, 2010)

Wartime Cookbook; Food and Recipes from the Second World War

1939–45 – Anne and Brian Moses (Wayland, 1995)

Colwyn Bay at War; From Old Photographs – Graham Roberts (Amberley Publishing, 2012)

A History of Food in 100 Recipes – William Sitwell (Collins, 2012)

Britain in the Second World War: A Social History – Harold L Smith (Manchester University Press, 1996)

The West End Front: The Wartime Secrets of London's Grand Hotels – Matthew Sweet (Faber & Faber, 2011)

Acknowledgements

Firstly I want to thank Iain MacGregor, Publishing Director for Non Fiction at Simon & Schuster in the UK. He commissioned my first book *A History of Food in 100 Recipes* and now has done it again with this one. The idea for *Eggs or Anarchy* sprang from my research for a chapter for that book so it's only appropriate that Iain does this one! But thank you, Iain. I thought this might be a good yarn, was slightly nervous when you became interested in the idea, unsure as to whether I'd be able to stand the story up. But as I delved deeper and deeper I felt I'd got one hell of a scoop. Whether I was right is up to the reader, but I hope you and they are as excited at what I uncovered as I was! Next my thanks go to Humphrey Price who edited the manuscript with such clarity and wisdom. To Karen Farrington for her researching skills. Also to my wonderful agent Caroline Michel for her constant, enthusiastic support and belief and to her editor at PFD, Tim Binding, who gave me such helpful structural comments after I delivered the first draft. The beginning and ending (the latter which makes me cry even though I wrote it!) owes its success to you. Thanks also to Tess and Emily at PFD and to the proofreading team at Heber, to the ever-joyful Em and her uber-cool posse: Tash and Matilda.

I have a particular thank you to make to Simon Woolton, the third earl and my hero's grandson – son of Roger. Your support for the project, your advice, your insight, kindness, hospitality and the loan of family papers and photographs have been invaluable and one of the most rewarding aspects of this project. Thanks to your cousin Charles Sandeman-Allen also, another grandson of Fred, son of Peggy, who helped correct the first draft and who also gave me great advice – as a history lecturer ('Just get writing,' he said as I was flapping around wondering how to tackle the material) as well as the loan of family letters and sight of his own writings on Fred.

Next I need to give thanks to my hero himself, Fred Woolton. He was so fastidious in keeping newspaper cuttings – both friendly and hostile – that his private albums, lent to me by his grandson Simon, were an extraordinary and useful discovery for me. That he wrote his diaries – which remain unpublished – with such honesty and so often with such punchy and modern-sounding language often left me wide-eyed and quietly fist-pumping as I read them in the hushed confines of the Weston Library – part of the Bodleian – at Oxford University (and thanks to the ever-helpful staff there). And to his wife Maud I must offer thanks for her own diary – bolted shut (Simon gave me permission to break it open) – which not even the family had read and which contained amazing stories and comments about such figures as Churchill and the King and Queen and her own takes on events in Woolton's life. Thanks also to Jonathan Weissler who introduced me to his grandfather Harold Gilbert, and to David Jennings – for responding to a plea by me on Twitter – for introducing me to his father, butcher Peter Jennings.

Then I must thank my colleagues at John Brown Media where I have my day job as editor of *Waitrose Food*. My team on that magazine are the most gifted in the business and I would also like to thank our CEO, Andrew Hirsch, who never fails to encourage my work in the food world when I'm not acting as his private restaurant-booking concierge. Thanks also to our MD, Libby Kay. And also thanks to my colleagues at Waitrose – my most esteemed client – for their friendship and support, particularly to Ollie Rice, Alison Oakervee, Rupert Ellwood and Rupert Thomas. Thanks also to the Plumpton posse: to my wonderful children Alice and Albert, to whom this book is dedicated, and to your quite exceptional mother, my wife Laura. Thanks also to my extraordinary and true friends: Toby and Gaby, Jasper and Vanessa and Alastair.

PICTURE CREDITS

INDEX

Index

Index

Index

and rationing, 73–4
Ministry of Reconstruction (MoR), 301
  and Churchill's offer to FM, 295–7
  FM accepts charge of, 297–8
  FM's role with:
    installed in new office, 302
    meeting other ministers, 302–3
    planning, 298–9
    settling in, 302–3
Ministry of War Transport, 146
Mitford, Nancy, 204
Moreuil, Battle of, 115
Morrison, Herbert, 176
Morrison, William, 5, 39, 45, 303
Munich Agreement, 70

National Farmers' Union, 148–52, 310
National Registration Day, 55, 75
Nazism, and Lewis's, 30
News Chronicle, 53–4
Newspaper Society, 217
newspapers, *see* media; *individual newspaper titles*
Nichols, Beverley, 143
Nigeria, and ground-nuts, 282
1922 Committee, 265
Noel-Baker, Philip, 167
Norway, whale oil from, 278–9

obesity, 315–16
Observer, 271
Odhams Press, 141
Oliver, Jamie, 315–6
Osborne, George, 315–6
Ottawa, 128

Panaghis, 126
Partridge, Frances, 198
pasteurisation, 291–2, 310–11
Patten, Marguerite, 253–4, 306
Pearl Harbor, 290
Pedersen, HEE, 126, 127–8
Perry, Lord, 165
Perthshire Advertiser, 263
Philip, Prince, Duke of Edinburgh, 336
Pichhi, Fortunato, 207
Picture Post, on rationing, 73
Pilgrims Society, 221
Plan Hegira, 97
Pomford, Albert, 29
Pomford, Elizabeth, 26, 29
Portal, Lord, 302
press, *see* media
press barons, 141–2
Priestley, JB, 25–6
Production Executive Committee, 171
profiteering, 172, 175, 181, 188, 210, 217–18
Pym, Leslie, 266

Queen's Hall, 4–5, 44, 47–8
  bombing of, 5
Queen's Messengers, 109–12
  in Coventry, 111
  strategic placing of, 111–2

Rathbone, Eleanor, 210
rationing, 73–83, 117, 119
  and Argentinian beef, 277–8
  and black market, 156, 172, 175–90, 217
    (*see also* black market; Hill, Billy)
    banks asked to help to thwart, 185–6
    and call for death sentence, 189
    enforcers seek to detect, 182
    FM reprimands nation over, 181
    and FM's call for whipping, 251
    FM's leaflets explaining, 181
    and food producers, 183
    near-absence of, in Britain, 175, 176–7
    prosecutions concerning, 180
    punitive measures to prevent, 176, 184, 186, 187–8
  Boyd-Orr praises FM's food plan for, 272–3
  of bread, draft scheme for, 125
  and Chequers, 191–2
  and Churchill, 81, 191–4, 230, 235–7, 292
  continued discontent with, 260–1
  and egg schemes, 158–9, 164, 213, 261–3
    collection and distribution, 262–3
    FM forced to defend, 261
  end of, 308
  exemptions to, 124–5
  fluctuating allowances under, 74
  and FM's wish for more privations, 235–8
  food producers circumvent, 183
  and ground-nuts, 282–3
  growing list of goods hit by, 74
  and hoarders, 152–4
  introduction of, 2, 73–4
  King talks of, 251
  lessons from, 311
  media onslaught on, 262–4
  and milk cuts, 267
    to help mothers and young children, 289
  MoF's new regulations concerning, 191
  and national nutrition, 81
  and official functions, 192–3
  points system of, 230–3
  post-war, 179
  and potato shortage, 261, 263
  press campaigns against, 73
  of soap, 232
  and sugar shortage, 273–5, 283–5

Index

Warner, Jack M, 204
Webb, Maurice, 211–12
weight issues, 315–16
The West End Front (Sweet), 202
wholemeal bread, pros and cons of, 260
Willink, Harry, 302
Wilson, Sir Horace, 33
Winant, John, 173, 221
Women's Land Army, 259, 271–2
Women's Voluntary Service, 111–12
Wood, Sir Kingsley, 52, 69, 265, 281–2
Woolton, 1st Earl of, *see* Marquis, Fred, 1st
    Earl of Woolton
Woolton, Lady (Margaret 'Lyn'), (FM's
    second wife), *see* Marquis, Margaret
    'Lyn', Lady Woolton
Woolton, Lady (Maud), (FM's first wife),
    see Marquis, Maud, Lady Woolton
Woolton Pie, 220–4, 277
Woolton, 2nd Earl of, *see* Marquis, Roger,
    2nd Earl of Woolton
World War One:
  and food policy, 120
  and League of Nations, birth of, 56
  MoF during, 77–8
World War Two:
  and Britain's net ship losses, 122
  food consumption during, 57–8
  Italy enters, 130
  rationing during, 73–83, 117, 119
    and Argentinian beef, 277–8
    and black market, 156, 175–90, 217,
      251 (*see also* black market; Hill,
      Billy)
    Boyd-Orr praises FM's food plan for,
      272–3
    of bread, draft scheme for, 125
    and Chequers, 191–2
    and Churchill, 81, 191–4, 230, 235–7,
      292

    continued discontent with, 260–1
    and egg schemes, 158–9, 164, 213,
      261–3
    end of, 308
    exemptions to, 124–5
    fluctuating allowances under, 74
    and FM's wish for more privations,
      235–8
    food producers circumvent, 183
    and ground-nuts, 282–3
    growing list of goods hit by, 74
    and hoarders, 152–4
    introduction of, 2, 73–4
    King talks of, 251
    lessons from, 311
    media onslaught on, 262–4
    and milk cuts, 267, 289
    MoF's new regulations concerning,
      191
    and national nutrition, 81
    and official functions, 192–3
    points system of, 230–3
    post-war, 179
    and potato shortage, 261, 263
    press campaigns against, 73
    of soap, 232
    and sugar shortage, 273–5, 283–5
  recruitment for, and nation's health,
    56–7
  and refrigerated-meat losses, 122
  and shipping crisis, 118–35
    and Convoy SC 11, 125–30
  start of, 54, 318, 323–4
  U-boat danger during, 56, 75, 114,
    121–2, 130–1
    and Convoy SC 11, 125–30
    in Mediterranean, 130

Zavattoni, Ettore, 207
Zweiniger-Bargielowska, Ina, 181